Best wishes

Andrew

A MUSICAL PRODIGY FROM SOUTH WALES

The Life, Times and Music of
Harry Parr Davies (1914- 1955)

Andrew Everett MA

authorHOUSE®

AuthorHouse™ UK
1663 Liberty Drive
Bloomington, IN 47403 USA
www.authorhouse.co.uk
Phone: 0800 047 8203 (Domestic TFN)
*   +44 1908 723714 (International)*

Published by AuthorHouse 02/21/2020

ISBN: 978-1-7283-9742-9 (sc)
ISBN: 978-1-7283-9743-6 (e)

CONTENTS

INTRODUCTION

Harry Parr-Davies was no more than a name to me until I saw the documentary play about Gracie Fields and realised that the songs *Sing as We Go, Wish Me Luck As You Wave Me Goodbye, Pedro the Fisherman,* and *I Leave My Heart in an English Garden* were all composed by the same man. This set me about discovering more about him. Consulting the internet, I discovered a web-site and even more importantly was given Gabrielle Bell's CD of Harry's music covering the styles and sounds of 30's, 40's and 50's I also gathered as many items of second sheetmusi and two vocal scores. After compiling a family genealogy I now start to collate my material into biographical form so I could explore the man and his music set against the times he lived in.

I consulted local libraries for Groves and Dictionary of National Biography. Giving more personal detail were the archives in Neath and West Glamorgan Libraries. even more usefully I came across accounts of the 2005 Exhibition in Neath about Harry which Edward Beckerleg had mounted with the help of late Bill Hanks. I contacted them both and they were helpful. Sadly Bill died, but Edwardhas provided with copies of material on the boards he had done for the exhibition. Even more importantly, he posted to me CD's of Harry's music covering the styles and sounds of 30's, 40's and 50's. He in addition, sent me a selection of his photographs concerning Harry to use in my book. (see those use in the list below.)

Law's book on *Her Majesty's Life Guards band* gave me further information about his time as a trooper as did the band's archivist at the *Life Guards Museum* at Cumbermere Barracks, Windsor. The census, passenger sailing and newspaper sections of internet genealogical programme *Find My Past* provided me with material not only about Harry, Gracie, but also about the concerts given by the band. Two more resources proved interesting, but less useful. The editions of Gracie's and George Formby's films were interesting in so far as they put their talents on display, despite being often poor in their musical attribution.

Many popularist biographies and autobiographies of George Formby, 'Hutch', the Hulberts and many more that had contact with Harry revealed surprisingly little about him, beyond the detail of a show for which he was providing the music. The 3 biographies of Gracie Fields and her own autobiography were better here because they retail anecdotes of her relationship with him, even if vague about actual dates. Many of the above books contain factual errors concerning incidents, dates, places and people encountered and the reader is rarely given the source of material. Some are mere fabrication against ascertainable facts. This similarly applies to many newspapers cuttings available over the years.

A trawl of local second hand music shops, such internet companies as *Amazon, Abe Books UK* and *The Sheet Music Warehouse,* has resulted in two vocal scores, about 100 items of sheet music and a number of revue programmes. For details of the musicals (8 in all) with which Harry was involved, Ganzl's comprehensive review of British musicals was very useful. Also Harry's contribution to British films (27 in all) reviewed by internet programme from IMDB was invaluable. This has allowed me to compile a list of his compositions, mainly about 230 songs by sorting out what he actually did and did not write for each of 27 film, 9 revues, 8 musicals as well as a few instrumental works and ballet music.

ACKNOWLEDGMENTS

My wife Mary for proof reading

The late Bill Hanks for his information and website

Edward Beckerleg for help with the material from the Davies family archive. He had previously in the possession of Harry's sister Marjorie ('Billie') David. and now in Neath Library. Toni her granddaughter has given permission to use the archived material for instance photographs, letters and anecdotes; for his encouragement and liberal supply of other information, including recorded music from many sources, featuring Harry's music;

West Glamorgan Archives; particularly Harriet Eaton for the text of *The Curfew* and other staff of Neath Library; Neath Antiquarian Society;

staff of Kensington Library;

the widow of Professor Rex Walford (and her posting of a CD of her husband, accompanying Gabrielle Bell, in a selection of Harry's music);

Peter Wilson (Classic CD's of Carlisle);

the archivists of Irish Guards and Life Guards;

George R Laws

AUTHOR'S NOTE

There are some practical difficulties in assessing Harry's complete musical output (mainly c. 260 compositions - mainly songs from all sources). While 2 vocal scores of musicals are readily available second hand, the full orchestral scores of his other musicals were probably not published nor were those for his revues. The BBC TV relays of his musicals and revues do not appear to have survived either. Fortunately various publishers did indeed issue many individual songs as sheet music as well as many individual items he composed and Gracie's and Formby's films have been released as Dvd's.

I found second-hand sheet music and scores together with a variety of available recordings are the best sources on which to make a partial judgement of his achievement. Therefore using what I have able to gather from sheet music, songs records and scores, I have made short comments in the text. I have outlined plots of films and musicals he was involved with as well as giving relevant details in the revues.

INTRODUCTION TO SECOND EDITION

Researching further into Harry's life and background, I have been able to develop several areas not available to me originally. Thesederive from extracts in contemporary newspapers from the archives of internet genealogical facility *FindMyPast*. This has enabled me to add a large amount of further information amounting to about 25000 extra words in 30 refashioned chapters. These cover more closely the 1940-1 Canada tour and the USA tour which followed and have added more details about his unfortunate death.I have clear evidence as well as films, revues and musicals discovered since the fist edition of my first book of 2 musicals, one proposed, the other completed.

In 2019, Sebastian Lassandro issued his comprehensive if discursive 2 volume biography of Gracie. This has provided more useful information and dates which helped me to make further links in his life particularly during 1930's and the 1940-1 Canada/USA tour.

When it was originally published, the first book had errors, omissions as well as clerical mistakes introduced during the publication process. These have been updated and much has been reworded in order to make things clearer. Throughout the whole revised book, references are thus increased because sources needed to be verified. I feel that all this is worth re-publishing as it makes the whole more than a mere biography, more a detailed reference book for not only for Harry's music, but much in the contemporary entertainment scene.

CHAPTER 1

CHILDHOOD (1914-27)

In the all-ready crowded terrace house of 11 Grandison Street, Briton Ferry, a baby born on 24 February 1914 - Harry Parr Davies. His father, David John Davies (born in March 1880 in Rhydyfelin, Pontypridd) was a shoe shop manager and his mother Rosina Parr (born 1882 in Briton Ferry) was a pupil teacher. David John had come to Briton Ferry and lodged with the Parrs. [1] The young Davies family continued to live with Rosina's parents. They had two daughters Glenys Kathleen (born 1908) and Marjorie (nicknamed 'Billie' born 1911). Rosina's parents were from Devon. Henry born in 1844 in Monkleigh, Bideford and Lucy born in 1853 in nearby Buckland Brewer, They had crossed the Bristol Channel to find work in one of the industrial villages dedicated to coal mining, coke production and ironworks to the east of Swansea. Henry had come in 1850's to work in the coke works as a coker while Lucy was a glover.

The household was musical. Both Harry's parents sang; father later became a member and then secretary from 1928 of the *Neath Male Harmonic Society*, a local male voice choir. The family often sang songs at home. Harry (whom the family called *Boy*) had a keen musical ear and began to pick out tunes on the piano, when only 3 or 4 years old.

In August, World War One (WW1)was declared and sometime early in the war, the five members of the Davies family left the Parr's house in Briton Ferry to.move a small way eastwards. Having been refused by the army, David John went to Treherbert up the Rhondda valley from

---

[1]   1901 census

Pontypridd. to work in the offices in Bute Colliery. Owned by *United National Colliery Ltd* based in Cardiff, it employed 120 men.[2] There was possibly a rented house with the job.

The *Rhondda and Swansea Railway* at that time provided a meandering rail line basically carrying coal from the upper Rhondda mines down to Swansea Docks. It ran from Treherbert (its connection with the *Taff Vale Railway* at the side of Bute Colliery) via upper Rhondda to travel down part of the River Neath valley to Swansea Docks. Neath had a connection with this mainline. As the company also carried passengers, it is possible that the family used the railway to go from Neath to Treherbert.

By May 1919, Harry was ready to start school. He became a pupil at *Tynewydd Primary School*, opened in 1863. as a colliery school. set up by the Marquis of Bute, the local colliery owner. There as a five-year old, he played the 1918 popular Tin Pan Alley waltz song, *I'm Forever Blowing Bubbles* on the school piano – a presage of the future, i.e. Harry playing for an audience. Harry kept on with musical activity teaching himself not only to read and write music but compose his own verses with the undoubted encouragement of his parents, sisters and teachers. His sister Billie recalled that he used to rule (presumably in ink) his music out on sheets of paper and hang them out to dry. In the family home, if they wanted him out of the way, they would give him a half-a crown to 'disappear'.

The family now moved back to the Neath area to a terraced house near the town centre at 2 Arthur Street. off Eastland Road. Harry attended the *Gnoll Primary School*, just round the corner from home.

Harry was short-sighted and probably around this time, he was prescribed glasses. In all the photographs of him and in film appearances, he waears glasses. Nevertheless, Harry was self-confident enough in his compositional skills as a 7 year old to send to Princess Mary, the popular Princess Royal, a song/cantata of his own devising on the occasion of here marriage to Viscount Lascelles on 28 February 1922. Typical of her, the effort was graciously acknowledged.

In 1923, (probably September) he transferred to *Neath Intermediate School*, where he continued his general education. While there, he decided that music was to be his career. He not only played the piano, and violin but precociously realised that he had an ability to write melodies. The

---

[2]   1923 *Colliery Year Book and Coal Trades Directory.*

result was he composed a number of songs usually to his own lyrics and later pieces for piano, violin and organ.

Harry was taken up by Seymour Perrott, Borough organist, also organist at *Gnoll Congregationalist Church*. He had been an Associate of the *Royal College of Organists* from 1910. Harry *would take up as much work home for his next lesson in a week as would be sufficient to last an ordinary pupil for a month or six weeks.*[3] Perrott lived just further up Gnoll Road near to Arthur Street across from the communal park, the Victoria Gardens.

Harry despite his other studies and activities decided to consolidate his efforts at composition by trying to get his music published. So he wrote to music publishers, such as Lawrence Wright, one of the main publishers of popular music of the time. Wright had himself composed.500 songs and was active from 1915 until 1941 (using pseudonyms Horatio Nicholls and less often another Everett Linton e.g. in 1926 for the song *I Never see Maggie Alone*). In 1927 he published *Shepherd of the Hills, I Hear You Calling*, and *Among My Souvenirs*, which became both international standards. Harry had read about him:[4]-

Horatio Nicholls
c/o Lawrence Wright Mus. Pub.

Dear Sir,

Please find enclosed MSS of songs I have written. I am only 14 years of age,[5] *and on reading your life story, I decided to write to you. Could you advise me in what way I could make a living for myself at song writing. You will be able to judge by the songs I am sending you whether I shall ever make a 'hit'. I am not very rich, and am at present a pupil at the Neath Intermediate School. What do you advise my next step should be. Would it be possible to gain an interview with You. I know you are the head of the*

---

[3]   Panegyric by Seymour Perrott quoted in obituary articles in *Western Mail* and *South Wales Evening Post*, 15 October 1955

[4]   This letter and all subsequent letters are taken from the original sources, in *Parr-Davies collection*. including awkwardness of phrasing, deletions, mispellings, etc. This applies also to the youthful operetta draft in Appendix 3

[5]   This maybe a white lie or error; he was only 13 years or maybe less, if still at Intermediate School!

Lawrence Wright Music Publishing Company, could you get them to accept one of my song for publication as it is hard to find publishers. To help me get a start in the musical world, I am so anxious to get on. You were in my position once, help me now please. Could you find a competent lyrist (sic) *and make him to write words of a song, and let me set to music, do give me this chance. Hoping that my songs will meet with your approval,*

> *I remain*
> *yrs sincerely*
> *H. Parr-Davies*

P.S/ I know that you are a very busy man, but would it be possible in the near future to join an interview.

He in a few years would actually meet and cooperate with Horatio Nicholls and work on some of his songs.

A similar letter was sent to another well-established publisher:-

Francis Day & Hunter

Dear Sir.

Please find enclosed a few M.SS of songs I have written. I am submitting these to you for your perusal with a view to publication.

I am only 134 years of age and I was wondering whether you hold any auditions, if so I would be glad if you would allow me to be present at the next one you hold.

If you ca If the songs are not up to Publishing standard I would be glad if you would let e know my fault so that I may remedy it.

Could you put me in touch with a competent lyrist, as my greatest difficulty is finding works.

Hoping that my composition will meet with your approval.

> *I remain*
> *yrs sincerely*
> *H. Parr-Davies*

Francis Day and Hunter would also later become a frequent publisher of his songs. Nevertheless, about this he has a foxtrot played at the *Empire Cinema* Neath which opened in 1926,[6] no doubt by resident pianist and music teacher, Gladys Williams.

The Curfew [7]

During his time at the *Intermediate School,* the teachers helping him with the language, structure and music of the piece, he wrote a 3-act operetta *the Curfew.* This was based on a romantic poem, much liked by Queen Victoria, written in 1867 by 16 year old poetess, Rosa Hartwick Thorpe called *The Curfew must not ring tonight.* (see appendix III for transcription of the original text). The story is set at the end of the Civil War. Marie Blanche saves Jack Courtnay her lover from wrongful execution as the murderer of a nobleman. She stops the curfew bell ringing, the signal for his execution to take place. The scenario written in an exercise book, elaborated the poem's structure into 3 acts and developed the plot so as to provide dialogue, interspersed with musical numbers for songs, duets and choruses. This is most likely to be an early draft he provided for his teachers. It would be informative if the finished article and its music could be found.

The model used for the work is akin to Walter Scott's more romantic novels to which mild humour and sentiment are added – as seen in operettas, English musicals and opera semi-seria - i.e. after trails - a happy ending. Set during the trial period of King Charles 1, it is a tour-de-force for one so young., even if he was helped y his teachers.

It scarcely matters too much that it is set at the wrong time of year, for the trial and execution of Charles 1 took place in January 1649, not at the harvest time the operetta celebrates. Charles 1 is the assassin named in the text but imprisoned he could not have done the dirty deed. The motivation behind Gerald de Maur's murder also needs some clarifying. There are

---

[6]   Demolished in 2012

[7]   Some newspaper cuttings refer to Harry writing to 2 operettas. In a newspaper interview with Harry, he only mentions *Curfew.* This does not appear to be an extant copy of the musical score, but *I Hate You* is said to be adapted from *Curfew.* If it is typical, the musical quality must have been high.

other historical anomalies in Act III concerning the priests and Oliver Cromwell. It is possible that the final edition of the work ironed these out.

Its atmosphere is generally convincingly rural. Despite overpunctuation, e.g. a myriad of commas interfere with the enjambement of the verse, some stilted phrasing and repetitive refrains in some songs, the story unfolds clearly and charmingly with interludes for dances to be featured. The dialogue moves the story on and the characterisation is clear for each of the main protagonists. Alert often echoing responses come from the chorus in a Gilbert and Sullivan fashion. The solos are appropriately effective in mood to the situation. Act III after a good start with an *Il trovatore* setting of hero in prison and heroine on stage praying, rather peters out finishing with a series of historical improbabilities and old amorous relationships being revealed. A jolly chorus and a single word 'Finale' hint at general rejoicings for hero and heroine to end the whole work.

As Harry left the *Intermediate School* in May 1927, the operetta must have been given earlier in late 1926 or the first week of April, prior to end of Winter term of 1927.

On 24 May 1927, Harry moved to *Neath Boys Grammar School* (now *Dwr-y-Felin Comprehensive School*). His parents must have had a reasonable standard of living to be able to afford to send Harry to a grammar school as there would be fees to be paid. Many a youth of 14 years old at that time would be expected to help to bring money unto the household by becoming miners or workers at the steel works. This may partly explain Harry's persistent approaches to music publishers. It was his way of supplementing the family's income. Harry used to go to quiet places during his life to work out his music including the restful Victoria Gardens in Neath.

CHAPTER 2

YOUTHFUL
ENTERPRISE (1928-31)

Becoming better known

Harry's reputation began to increase.beyond Neath. and district One
of his compositions, *Memories* a violin solo, was played by Albert Sandler,
the popular light classical violinist and leader of the *Park Lane Hotel
Orchestra.*, who seems to have helped to promote his music. It was then
broadcast, being played by Reginald Foort, the organist of the *Regal
Cinema, Marble Arch* sometime after its opening in November 1928.
(Edward O'Henry organist at the *London's Tussaud Cinema* also played
Harry's music). Another of Harry's songs, *Underneath the Moon in Old
Shanghai*, a title reminiscent of Horatio Nicholls 1925 song *Shanghai*, was
sung by local comedian Seymour Collins and had been published.

With all this success in mind, Harry wrote to one publisher seeking
royalties, which were not very forth coming:-

Empire Music Publishers
319 Oxford St.
London W. C. 2

Dear Sirs/

Re "Underneath the Moon in Old Shanghai"

I believe there are some royalties due to me on account of the publication by you of the above song. They are due (as you state in your memorandum of agreement) on midsummer and Xmas. I should be obliged if you would let me know whether there are royalties due to me at all? If so I would be glad if you would forward them immediately.

yrs sincerely
H. Parr-Davies

Such single-mindedness was remarkable for his age.

Meanwhile his musical development continued. He took part in an Eisteddfod and won first prize for piano. He made so much headway with his music that Seymour Perrott made him assistant organist to Gnoll Road church an achievement for a 14 year old. Harry said that organ playing made him think about popular music. [8]

Perrott then arranged for an interview with Mr J Charles Mclean, secretary to the *Welsh National Council of Music*. On looking over what Harry had written, he was sufficiently impressed to arrange an interview with the Council's director Sir Henry Walford Davies.

Walford Davies a Somerset-born man was an able composer in his own right, chiefly renowned for cello piece *Solemn Melody* and hymn tune to *God be in my head*. He composed much choral chamber and symphonic works, being a supporting part of the 20th century expansion of British music alongside figures like Sir George Dyson. From the beginnings of his Welsh appointment, he worked to promote music throughout Wales, especially with *eisteddfodau*. Harry's father supported him by sending short pieces about his son's music s to the local newspaper, cataloging his current achievements [9]

---

[8]   BBC Radio interview with Harry by Leslie Perowne in 7 February 1940.

[9]   *Western Mail* 17 March 1928

Concerts

Harry now give on to have two local concerts in places of worship in different denominations. On Easter Sunday, the first was held to mark the Rev. Henry Walker's fourth anniversary of coming to the *Bethany English Presbyterian Church*, Bethania Street Glynneath, up river about 11 miles from Neath. A well attended concert conducted by Mr T J Cole was held there in the evening presided over by the Mayor, Councillor William Kindon Owen JP. The participating local artistes accompanied by Miss J Walker and Mr M Davies were:-

> *Madame B Clarke – Neath;*
> *Miss May Davies Contralto – Neath;*
> *Mr A E. Stanaway – Skewen (Swansea);*
> *Mr E E Davies – Port Talbot;*
> *Miss Edna M Morgan (elocutionist) – Glynneath*

Harry played a selection of his own compositions.

This second concert this time at the *English Presbyterian Methodist Chapel* London Road in Neath, where Harry attended at the Sunday School.[10] It was again presided over again by the Mayor It was dedicated entirely to songs with words (with one exception) and all the music composed by Harry. Especially were heard a key selection of excerpts from *Curfew*. The programme was as follows:

ARTISTES

Soprano Miss Mary Parker
Contralto Miss May Davies
Tenor Mr Ro Hocking
Bass Mr J Gwynne
VIOLINIST Master Ken Cole
ORGANIST Mr Phil David
AND THE COMPOSER
PROGRAMME 1 SHILLING

---

[10]   This is the only overtly religious contact that Harry had.

9

Proceeds in aid of the Church Restoration Fund

1 Overture:-	"The Curfew"	H.P.D.
	Harry Parr Davies	
2 Opening Churus :_	"The Curfew"	H.P.D.
	The Choir	
3 Solo"-	"Drifting "	H.P.D.
	Mr J.Gwynne	
4 Solo	"Home"	H.P.D.
	(Words by Judge Parry)	
	Miss Mary Parker	
5 Violin Solo:-	"La Rêve d"Amour"	H.P.D.
	Master Ken Cole	
6 Solo"_	"Tho' skies were blue"	H.P.D.
	Mr Roy Hocking	
7 Solo	"Cottage of dreams come true"	H.P.D.
	Miss May Davies	
8 Organ solo"-	"Melodie"	H.P.D.
	Mr P David	
9 Duet:-	'Serenade (The Curfew)"	H.P.D.:
	Mr J Gwynne and Miss M Davies	
	INTERVAL	
1 Pianoforte Solo:-	"Legends"	H.P.D.
	Harry Parr Davies	
2 Opening Chorus :-	"Priest's Chorus" (The Curfew)	H.P.D.
	The Choir	
3 Solo:_	'Harbour Lights"	H.P.D.
	Mr Roy Hocking	
4 Violin Solo:-	"Nocturne"	H.P.D.
	Master Ken Cole	
5 duet:-	"Dearie" (The Curfew)	H.P.D.

	Miss Mary Parker and	
	Mr Roy Hocking	
6 Solo:-	Wandering"	H.P.D.
	Mr J Gwynne	
7 Solo:-	"The Shades of Night" (The Curfew)	H.P.D.
	Miss May Davies	
8 Solo:_	"Love Finds A Way" (The Curfew)	H.P.D.
	Miss Mary Parker	
9 Solo and Chorus :_	"Prayer" (The Curfew)	H.P.D.
	Miss Mary Parker and Choir	
	DOXOLOGY	

He even wrote a march for organ *Tesgar* in honour of the Methodist minister's son Tesgar Humphreys. It is a typical Welsh marching hymn tune like *Llanfair* or *Cwm Rhondda* with a distinct bass line

Walford Davies having heard Harry's music and music-making at school now started pushing Harry towards the Classics and a career as a serious musician. At this time, further musical education relied heavily on the Viennese school of masters - Mozart, Haydn, Beethoven. The expressive features of Italian and French opera while popular and given to many provincial audiences by touring companies like the Carl Rosa were regarded with some disdain by the British musical establishment. Opera was still heavily under the reforming influence of Wagner.

Davies sent Harry a weighty package of what he deemed appropriate music for Harry to examine. He advised him to emulate the style of the 'greats'. Well meaning, Davies promised to review what he produced after such study. He was beginning to groom Harry for Oxford or Cambridge. At first, Harry acquiesced.

Shortly after completing *The Curfew*, Harry was in London escorted by his aunt, (most) likely Gertrude May Protheroe, the younger of his mother's two sisters who lived in Briton Ferry) for an organ exam[11]. This would be to sit the Certificate of the *Royal College of Organists* (RCOG) in its then Kensington premises. Perrott no doubt advised Harry to work for it. (Perrott

---

[11]   BBC Radio interview with Harry interviewed by Leslie Perowne in 1939.

himself gained his Associate RCOG as a 19 yearly in 1910[12] and gained his Fellowship in July 29).[13] Harry did not proceed to a Diploma, meeting his subscription to the RCOG lapse in 1934.

While in London, Harry became acquainted with successful national pantomime impresario Julian Wylie. Hearing his music, he suggested Harry write a song for a new musical in its pre-production. Harry responded with a song, *Peter the Pup is Twenty-one To-day.* Unfortunately the production never happened. Harry responded with other songs as six of them were eventually published.

After many more discussions, he eventually came to a conscious decision not to follow a more academic path. This was quite a remarkable and risky thing for a teenager to do, especially in the 1920's and in the provinces. He seemingly knew his own strengths and limitations, wanting to continue with lighter more lyrical works. His models at this stage were Eric Coates and Edward German, composers familiar from radio, concert hall and stage. They both provided light music of quality, admired by their contemporaries.

Eric Coates wrote popular marches, orchestral pieces and songs throughout his professional life from 1909 until 1957, including *By a Sleepy Lagoon, the Dam Busters March, Knightsbridge* – all still familiar through use by radio, film and TV as theme tunes. Mainly put into orchestral form as suites *(3 Elizabeths)* or fantasy pieces *(The Three Bears)* His songs are likewise charming miniatures *(Bird songs at Eventide* and *Green Hills of Somerset.* He used clearly outlined melodies in a well-ordered orchestral or pianistic dressing. [14] This is probably his legacy to Harry, who applied the principle to the 200 songs he wrote. Interestingly Coates did not come round to using his melodic gifts for stage works. For this, Harry had Edward German as a model. [15]

Edward German composed a wide range of works, orchestral pieces, songs, choral and chamber works as well as a lot of incidental music

---

[12]   *The Rhondda Reader,* 10 August 1910

[13]   Personal communication of RCOG archivist for Perrott and Harry

[14]   Self, Geoffrey, 1986, *In Town Tonight,- a centenary study of the life and music of Eric Coates,* Thames Publishing

[15]   *The New Groves Dictionary of Music and Musicians,* 2001, 2nd Edition, Oxford University Press – Eric Coates and Edward German

for plays and 6 operettas of charm, *Merrie England* and *Tom Jones* and others. He uses broad expansive melodies that are finely and appropriately orchestrated. His vocal music lies well in the voice of the character and style being portrayed. [16] Harry's *Curfew* is certainly in a similar strain to German's operettas wordwise. Later especially in *Dear Miss Phoebe*, the musical model throughout is very reminiscent of German's style.

Performances of his music, its publication throughout his childhood and youth, his musical activity in Neath area, his efforts to promote beyond Neath his own music, his career and finances, his tuition by experts, all were a sound preparation for the future. He was learning how to organise and work at his future career as composer and pianist. All he needed was a catalyst. He had carefully prepared the ground.

---

[16]   Self, Geoffrey, 1986, In Town Tonight,- a centenary study of the life and music of Eric Coates, Thames Publishing

13

CHAPTER 3

MEETING GRACIE (1931)

Harry following on from his earlier forays into the entertainment world decided to try and meet with the increasingly well known and popular Gracie Fields. She preferred the spontaneity of live audiences as a comedienne/singer. She built up her reputation by hard work in learning timing, rapport with audiences, comic routines and well as words and music in a wide repertoire of singing styles. She toured the country and from 1924 starred in revues, organised by her theatrical agent, her husband Archie Pitts, from whom she was estranged domestically. The Parr family could well have seen her on these provincial tours for instance in *Mr Tower of London*.

Sally in Our Alley

The British film industry was just moving out of the earlier 'silent' era. So the time was ripe for Gracie to start a film career. Her first film was with the *Associated Talking Picture*s (ATP) in a part documentary drama - part musical comedy film set in World War One, *Sally in Our Alley*. Directed by the experienced Maurice Elvey, Basil Dean was its producer with the veteran conductor- composer-arranger Ernest Irving responsible for the music. Archie Pitt with his music hall and stage experience wrote some of the scenes.

The film allowed Gracie to import into the film the song, which became her signature tune *Sally*. Released on 17 July 1931, it was very successful nationally. Indeed Harry is likely to have seen it when it was at the Empire Cinema, Neath during 1931. The world behind making films - all became part of Harry's world up to World War Two (WW2) and beyond.

14

Walk This Way

After the success of *Sally*, Archie Pitt continued to build up Gracie's career by showcasing her talents in a revue called *Walk This Way*. This had the usual preview tour, starting on 27 July at the *Opera House, Blackpool*. It then moved on to *Palace Theatre, Manchester;* by 21 September it was given at *Theatre Royal, Nottingham*, 12 October at *Grand Theatre Leeds* and *30 November at Southsea*. It finally opened in London on 17 December at the *Winter Gardens Theatre,*[17] *Drury Lane* in 17 December, closing after a total of 149 performances on 23 March 1932.

Revues

Originally revues in Britain had been developed by the French actor impresario André Charlot. He put over 30 from 1917 between 1935. His great rival was Charles B Cochrane who put on 150 popular stage productions, including revues. Between them they gave a wide variety of actors, singers, comedians, variety acts and playwrights their opportunities to show off their talents.

Revues themselves were in some ways an up-market cross between contrasting musical hall acts and some of the more loosely structured musical comedies and operettas. Usually in two acts, each act featured an average of 6 or 7 individual sections. The material would be built around a company of popular performers, whether comedians, singers, dancers or acrobats. The sketches themselves could be sentimental, satirical, whimsical, musical or a mixture of them all and could include acrobatics or a ballet sequence. Sometime the entire musical score would be provided by a specific composer, but more often, it was done by a number of composers each writing items appropriate to the sketches etc. The resulting music was usually assembled and arranged by the musical director, who conducted the resident orchestras as well.

Walk This Way was a typical example. Built around Gracie as singer, comedienne and character actor (e.g. as a Pearly Queen). It included Irene Pitts, Gracie's step-daughter and Gracie herself in the characteristic *The*

---

[17]   Now called the *New Theatre*

Doll and The Golliwog. Gracie's brother Tommy provided the comedy and singing (he had a pleasant evenly toned baritone voice) and her brother-in-law Douglas (Dougie) Wakefield was another comic character actor. Added to this were different music hall friends and colleagues, many of whom appeared again in her 1930's films. This review was in fact the last in which she appeared. Henceforth, concert and films were her choice of performing venue.

Meeting Gracie

In 1931, Harry was on his Christmas holidays from school. *I was smitten with the idea that I had written just the song for Gracie Fields.... I raised the wind (from his sisters?) to buy a half-day ticket to London.* He would have come to know about Gracie as a major performer of the time. At his parent's home, he is likely to have heard her broadcasts, from the BBC from 10 January 1928, listened to gramophone records of her singing after their first cutting from 3 April 1928, even traveled with them to Cardiff saw her in two productions - on 29 November 1930 in *Archie Pitt's Road Show* and in October 1931 *Walk This Way.* [18]

He told his parents about what he wanted to do. He wanted, to make money to go to University.[19] There was a direct train to Paddington, after he joined the train from Swansea. He made his way to Theatreland. Wylie for whom he had written a song earlier was sufficiently impressed to have a word with Gracie. So it is likely Harry was half expected by her. [20]He recounted it five years later with typical Welsh exuberance:-

---

[18]   Lassandro, Sebastiano, *Pride of Our Alley*, 2019, BearManor Media vol 1, p., 97, 99, 165 and 181 respectively,

[19]   *Liverpool Echo*, 7 March 1932

[20]   There is a plethora of accounts available about this key encounter in the lives of Harry and Gracie. Many have different details and internal contradictions. The basis for the author's account is the *Parr-Davies Collection* and an undated (c. 1937) unsourced newspaper interview entitled *I "Gatecrashed" Miss Fields* given by Harry. Much of it has the ring of authenticity. Nevertheless he gives his age at this interview as a year too young and so it doesn't fit the school record from *Dwr-y-felin* School. Other interviews given by Harry both written and spoken also differ from this rather fuller account but are often just summaries of the meeting and its effects plus some journalistic variations.

Probably a school boy was a new phenomenon in the experience of the hardboiled guardian of the stage door, but he had pity on my youth and shyness.

'What do you want?' he demanded.'I've written a song that I want to play to Miss Fields'. That speech was meant to be my passport to the great actress and since I had anticipated no opposition, I had prepare no argument to follow it.

The stage-door keeper was not at that disadvantage. He had polished his technique of resistance in the hard school of experience. I am prepared to swear that he swelled to twice his size, making the door literally impassable.

I might write and ask for an appointment with her manager. Or I might send the song by post. Or possibly he might relieve me of it himself and let his wastepaper basket save Miss Fields and her manager a lot of bother. Or I might take myself off to the devil. There were plenty of alternative to my seeing Miss Fields.

Gracie was in her dressing room. *Our debate had achieved a 'fortissimo' when the unmistakable voice of Miss Fields came down the passage soaring over our row.*

"What's going on down there?" she asked.

"Another of these song writers. A kid this time", he answered, but I will swear that his form here began to shrink for I could see past him into the passage.

"A kid? Let's see what he's got" Came the command.

It was victory after all, for my enemy became the conductor to the rooms of the great Gracie Fields. .... I was shown in .... by the grace of one chance in a million there was a piano in it. ..... a piano is never part of a dressing room furniture. This was the stage piano, shoved into this room out of the way, because there was no room for it on stage.[21]

A tall, lanky lad of seventeen, with glasses, because he was short-sighted, was looking half-scared as he edged his way into her dressing-room.[22]

"What have you got there, Lad?"

---

[21] *I "Gatecrashed" Gracie Fields*.- unsourced and undated newspaper interview with Harry, c1937 after tours of South Africa and USA, in the Parr-Davies Collection.

[22] Fields, Gracie, 1960, *Sing as We Go, The Autobiography of Gracie Fields*, Frederick Mulle, p.106

"A song I think you will like." I answered. "It is called "I Hate You"". Suddenly the title seemed to me undiplomatic, but Miss Fields burst out laughing, opened the piano and invited me to sit down.

I spread out my song and began to play.

"You're a grand player, lad, but what about the words? Go on, sing up!"

Now I cannot sing and at sixteen my voice was a wretched croak. I did my miserable best.

"Not much of a singer, are you, lad?" observed my heroine but I thought she was taken with tune, and she herself began to sing the words, singing them with interest too.

"I like this", she said, "and I shall use it my next film." She kept her promise.

She sent me along to see her manager.

Having heard him play, she then discussed it with her husband / manager Archie Pitt and his live-in mistress Annie Lipman, (she conducted the orchestra sometimes), [23] They were all impressed. It was arranged to engage him at once, as her composer He returned home, *I was afraid to go to sleep that night lest I wake up and find it was a dream. It was not until a formal contract came along that my parent could believe that I had fallen in with a group of London leg-pullers.* [24]

He came back probably in February 1932with his parents' consent to London to sign the contract drawn up by Bert Aza, Gracie's agent (Archie's brother) for his compositions. He was scarcely able to believe his good fortune. He and his parents realised *'I had not been conned by some of the big London leg pullers.*[25] He had an enjoyable fortnight [26] with Gracie and her husband Archie. Getting a job like as a 17-year old was an opportunity not to be missed in a period of high unemployment.

Despite Gracie's keenness to have *I Hate You* introduced as a number into *Walk This Way*,[27] it didn't happen. Harry commented *I should have had to conduct the Winter Garden Orchestra for some time on that particular scene.* It was put instead in her next film. He was asked to do a new ballad

23   *Liverpool Echo 7* March 1932
24   *I "Gatecrashed" Gracie Fields*
25   Lassandro, Sebastiano, *Pride of Our Alley*, 2019, BearManor Media vol 1, p.183
26   This would tally with absences he had from school.
27   *Western Mail*, 16 February 1932

for *Walk This Way. They were very eager to keep me in London, but I was intent upon sitting for my matriculation at the County school in July.* [28] He still had therefore some lingering ideas of going to University, seeing his composing as a lucrative sideline.

.He was again in London to meet with Gracie for the weekend 5-6 March 1932 to discuss more of his songs as they would provide with money to go to University. [29] *One night, as Harry stood in the wings with me before I went on I said "That piano looks proper lonely out there Harry, why don't you go and sit at it?" He had never been on a stage before and was terrified. But I got him at the piano that night* [30] [31]

Oddly, Grace did not do any more revues after this one closed on 22 April 32. She continued her preference for live appearances during concerts as before, travelling up and down the land. At that time she had three musical directors, who provided orchestral backing.when she needed it. First of all there was violinist/conductor Lou Ross (Louis Rosenbloom) from 1927, Harry Green from 1929 and William Pethers as well as Annie Lipman on occasions. Harry learned to fit in with them depending on the format to be presented was band or piano. Some scheme was worked out between him and where necessary the conductors (and their orchestras) as to which part of Gracie's performance it was most effective for him to accompany her. Often, he played the more flexible parts of her programme, while the orchestra accompanied her for more extended or more serious pieces. Genererally therefore unless there is a specific record or programme, it is difficult to state what Harry actually did at any specific concert.

---

[28]   Undated (c. February/ March) 1932 interview in *South Wales Daily Post*

[29]   *Liverpool Echo* 7 March 1932

[30]   Fields, Gracie, 1960, *Sing as We Go, The Autobiography of Gracie Fields,* Frederick Mulle, p.107

[31]   Not professionally, but he had more experience in performing than Gracie realised! He was obviously more nervous by being put in the spotlight.

CHAPTER 4

HARRY THE
SONG-MAKER

Publishers

Very likely through the agency of Bert Aza and resultant musical link-
ups of various film companies with publishing houses Harry's music came
to be known to a number of well-known publishers of light music other than
Lawrence Wright. These were:

- the venerable publishing firm **Chappell**, originally set up in Bond
  Street in 1818, but by this time having New York offices. It did
  much of publishing Harry's music;
- **Francis Day and Hunter**
- **Keith Prowse**, another popular London musical firm started in
  1878 and later **Sterling Music Publishing Company Ltd** of
  Sydney for the Australian market who published some of his songs
  for Gracie's film in the 1930's.

Sun Music Publishing Company Limited.

Sometime in 1934, [32] probably on the advice of some of his friends
and associates, Harry had been involved in setting up (probably through

---

[32]   The year of the earliest song I have found so far *Believe It Beloved*, is in 1934.
The latest date is 1951.

investing) his own publishing company, the **Sun Music Publishing Company Limited.** [33] In its heyday, it regularly published new songs each year. They sometimes published his music, e.g. the score and sheet music of *Dear Miss Phoebe*. Some publications were 'hits', others less so as would be expected. Whoever the company's publishers/ editors were, they from time to time showed themselves shrewd enough to pick successful songs for publication over a period of 20 years. In 1937 it was *Boo-Hoo;* in 1941 *Let me Love You To-night;* in 1947, *Chi baba, chi baba,* The two big hits were in 1949 *Lavender Blue* and in 1951 *Too Young.* No doubt this gave Harry yet another source of income.

Besides songs for films and then revues and complete musicals, Harry wrote a lot of one-off songs, seemingly for specific people to sing, but others possibly just to satisfy his creative urge.

Harry must have found the backstage atmosphere of bustle and intrigue bewildering after the relatively orderly days of school and home in Neath. Nevertheless, he became involved with Gracie's professional and domestic life.

His personality traits

He carried out his accompanying Gracie despite having some personality difficulties away from the keyboard. He lacked much subtlety. According to Gracie, he could feel 'that road (rode?) out', (possibly meaning flat or weary). He was somewhat obsessive about his bowel functions. The indications are that he suffered from some kind of obsessional disorder bordering on autism. Once started on a project, he found it difficult to 'switch off', even for food. Having set himself goals, he could be irritable about incidental things, like the poor pianos he had to play on during their Canadian tour.

At other times, he was kindly, funny, very reliable, truthful and importantly always there. Gracie recalled *We became friends. He was as Welsh as they come, and temperamental and would often pick a row just to make himself feel better. But we had a brother-sister affection for each other and he became part of the family, who accepted him as much I did.* [34] In many ways, Harry's function

---

[33]   It lasted many years and was taken over in 1970's by *Sony/ATV/EMI Publishing.*

[34]   Fields, Gracie, 1960, *Sing as We Go, The Autobiography of Gracie Fields,* Frederick Mulle, p.107

was as a provider and enabler of those around him. He didn't particularly like the being the focus of attention himself, but enjoyed helping others.[35] His developing role as song-writer and accompanist to Gracie brought him further in to the 'show business' limelight. Gracie and he spent a lot of time together over the succeeding years until her operation and the outbreak of war.

Once Harry became established as her accompanist, touring Britain with Gracie, allowed him to move in the same circles as she did, both professionally and domestically. He met many of Gracie's family in particular Tommy her brother, who had appeared with her on stage (with his accordion-playing partner Nick Rossini) her brother-in-law Douglas (Duggie) Wakefield.

His songs

What type of songs did Harry compose?

Those which reflected mainly contemporary models and which while diverse proved a workable structure for music aimed at performers on the concert platform, (mainly Gracie), films, (first of all Gracie of course, then George Formby and many others). Later he diversified into stage revues and musicals for the popular light music market.

Where did he compose them?

He remarked in one newspaper that he preferred to do this at home. His sister said he used to walk round Victoria Park Neath. Later after they moved to Swansea, he used the Gower peninsula as his place of solitude for working out his songs. What is notable throughout his output is a facility not only for composing and harmonising melodies, but welded them to the words he is setting. He was influenced by British folk song, Welsh hymnody, British musicals, popular revues, music-hall ballads, Viennese style operettas, Eric Coates, Edward German, Gilbert and Sullivan. British revues at the time and musicals were dominated by Noel Coward, Vivian Ellis, Ivor Novello (another Welsh composer originally with a Davies surname!) Noel Gay and Horatio Nichols. Added to the foregoing was American *Tin-Pan Alley*, contemporary crazes, like the Charleston, jazz, swing and Latin American dances.

---

[35]   Bill Hanks, 2005, *The Sweetest Song in the World*, p.9, billhanks.co.uk

In addition American musicals and its film scene, familiar on both sides of the Atlantic showcased the multiple talents of George Gershwin, Jerome Kern, Irving Berlin, Cole Porter, Richard Rodgers.(responding so fruitfully to lyrics from Lorenz Hart) and ex-patriots from Hungary like Siegmund Romberg and Emmerich Kalman, Rudolf Friml from Czechoslovakia and many others. The reflection of these voices, their harmonic progressions and harmonies can be heard at different times in his music.

Song Structures

One of the best features of Harry's songs is their clearly crafted structure. There were 3 main types:-

a basic **song** - short introduction, a melody (often repeated twice) with a middle contrasting section then a repeat of first with as a coda a final chord or flourish.

More frequently used is the second, especially in his earlier days the American **Tin-Pan Alley model** with its three distinct sections - introduction, (4 bars), verse often a slower part about a problem or situation (16 bars) and then a refrain (32 bars), usually repeated and give na more up-beat solution to the ideas in the verse. Harry's use of this model is not at all rigid. It was used more as a flexible base in response to the lyrics and something to fall back on.

.Lastly he used the older **strophic model** for songs, if they were in style either of a folk song or a music-hall narrative song. They have still an introduction-verse-refrain structure. However, the verses are more numerous to cover their narrative content with the refrain being relegated to becoming the same tail piece after each verse. Therefore it lasted longer than the Tin Pan Alley model. Somewhere in the song, an interlude may be included for some speech-over or an instrumental break e.g. George Formby's ukulele.

His process of composition

Harry uses the common major keys (or relative minor), especially B flat, C, D, E flat, F and G. Remote keys using 5 or 6 flat or sharps would put amateur (and some professional players) off. He does use G flat major (5 flats) in his later musicals. The vocal range of his published songs is normally about an octave and a half. There are two likely reasons for this. Many artistes had a limited vocal range (apart from Gracie and Patricia Burke). Secondly, the songs published were meant for an 'amateur' audience to buy and so had to be besides being melodious both playable and singable. Similarly he uses 4/4 or common time for much of his music from marches through to dance music like the charleston, the quickstep, the foxtrot, swing numbers,Latin American and for more traditional styles like music hall ballads and romantic or whimsical songs. Some numbers are deceptive. Although *Sing as we Go* feels like a 2/4 quick march, with triplets in each beat gives it a great lift when sung. He did the same in contemporary *Joe the Jolly Marine*. Alternatively, he uses waltz time for more nostalgic or sentimental moments or even mock–continental numbers.

All this occurs because he is being particularly good at fitting melodies to lyrics in a natural way. He makes key words in the verse fall at the appropriate accent in the music, sometimes dropping this in pitch to an unexpected note rather than a more conventional interval He thus avoids triteness and is particularly effective in more romantic or whimsical features such as mimicking music hall and nursery rhyme models where the lyrics seem to ask for it.

His harmony is essentially diatonic. He gives support to the voice by playing by the melodic line usually in the treble with suitable harmonies and rhythm. At the end of many phrases where the voice is sustaining a note, he often places short counter melodic phrases under the voice. Occasionally he does use dissonance, e.g. in passing phrases or at the end of introductions where it resolves when the voices enter.

He stated in a newspaper interview that he liked Debussy, Delius and Wagner. Their influence is more apparent in the shifting, often chromatic harmonies he uses in chords under the melody to create uncertainty of mood. (He played Debussy's *Clair de Lune* as a popular concert solo).

Adjusting to the performer

The vocal range and cadences within the song are normally carefully tuned to the artist featuring them and are partly dependant on the rhythm and/or mood of the verse. Gracie was often given phrases which explore her middle and upper register. She also often add ed to this on her own initiative finishing a song with an upper cadence or flourish from the basic tune ending on a top A, B or C. Other artists had to transpose such apparently simple tuneful songs as *Sing as We Go* in order to sing them comfortably.

For George Formby, whose voice was obviously more limited in range and timbre than Gracie's, Harry keeps the melody simple and clear tuned to his vocal range but providing passages for him to do his famous ukulele improvisations. The songs themselves have many felicitous touches in harmony and melodic counter-phrases. He did the same for other singers as time went on.

Orchestration

Where it comes to orchestrating his music, there is no clear evidence how or even if he did this. His prior training with Parrott and Walford Davies are likely to have provided him some elements of how to do this exacting task. Nevertheless he followed contemporary practice and left arranging the orchestration and how the piece would be finally heard to the musical director of whatever film, play, revue or musical he was involved at the time. The arranger would add orchestral colours to the harmonised melodies Harry provided, extend or curtail the structure as appropriate, sometimes eliminate the introduction, put in bridge pieces or ritornellos as needed. The resultant work had significant differences in detail when published as sheet music or in scores from what is heard in films or sound recordings.

In practice, conductor/arrangers were an essential contributor to the feeling of film, but were rather kept in the background, often unnamed They were hard working, qualified musicians of experience in both stage and film work but not in the public eye as the stars were. Nor were they acknowledged usually by the 'serious' music fraternity. For most of the films with which Harry was involved during the 1930's, Ernest Irving was *Associated Talking Picture*'s (ATP) main residential conductor/arranger. Others like Bretton Byrd, Charles Williams and later Debroys Somers performed this task for some of Harry's revues and musicals. A case in point, there is a MSS version in Neath Library of the first page of the overture to *Lisbon Story* – presumably Harry's thoughts about it. The printed score is quite different.

Lyricists

From early childhood as has been already noted, Harry wrote his own words to his music, a habit of a lifetime. He had some facility in versifying and wedding word and music easily. His early songs for inserting Gracie's film were therefore all his own. Harry's word setting is exemplary, clearly based not only on the varying metre of the lyric, itself based on speech patterns of the English language, sometimes quite colloquial in their diction but with appropriate emphases. This results in a coherent feel to the song.

Besides his own lyrics, he set a quantity of verse by other people. This was sometimes for a single song, sometimes for a single project such as a film or revue. However from about 1936, he began to work with specific writers. These would become his main source of lyrics, although not totally exclusively. While all are fit for purpose, like his own verse, they lack the adroitness of Cole Porter, Lorenz Hart and Irving Berlin or Noel Coward.

In succession, the main providers of lyrics for Harry (apart from himself) were:

> **Eddie Pola.** From 1935 to 1940 he provided a few workmanlike lyrics for solo songs.

> **Roma Beaumont** From 1936-44 she was a singer in some of Ivor Novello's shows providing some pleasant if slightly sentimental lyrics.

> **Roma Campbell-Hunter** From 1938 to 1940, she provided a number of lyrics. She can turn out quite attractive slightly whimsical items.

> **Phil Park** From 1939 to 1945, he was a consistent partner of Harry's for films, revues and individual numbers.

Although he can sometimes provide ideas for Harry to respond to, his verse can be rather predictable in meter and conventional in sentiment, (as seen so often in his many translations of operettas by Johann Strauss, Lehar and Offenbach for amateur performances).

Barbara Gordon and Basil Thomas From 1942 to 1950's they continued to provide Harry with variety of ideas and metres but sadly also wrote the rather dismal lyrics for *The Knight was Bold*.

Harold Purcell From 1943 to 1950. Harry and he collaborated regularly. He provided Harry with a consistent quality of words to set. His diction and metre are similar to that used by Christopher Hassall for Ivor Novello's musicals, namely romantic, mildly witty and above all fluent. Harry responded quite consistently to what Purcell provided for him.

Christopher Hassall From 1950-55, this accomplished BBC broadcaster provided the lyrics for *Dear Miss Phoebe* and some later songs. They were working on new material with him up to the time of Harry's death.

In addition, there were a number of one-off collaborations through the years. (see Appendix A Alphabetical List of Musical Compositions and Appendix B Chronological list of Musical Compositions)

To some extent, by reading between the musical and lyrical lines, an attempt to understand Harry's emotional responses to the external events in his life can be made. The topics of many of his songs reveal his concerns. Love is the most frequent, whether expectant of fulfilment or a partly idealised statement of feeling, frequently nostalgic, mentioning sleeplessness and dreams as in *Counting Sheep* and *Lying Awake and Dreaming* but they are never erotic. Once working more independently of Gracie, many of his songs take on a more underlying nostalgia, including songs and pieces about Capri.

27

Many numbers, especially in the early days sing about seeing sunshine in things. This allowed him to accentuate the bubbly side of Gracie's personality with whistling songs like *Just a Happy Little Tune*. Other songs were frankly sentimental, e.g. the one written jointly for their mothers, *Mary Rose*. Harry provides it with a nostalgia with an almost Donizettian turn of phrase. Linked with these, weather references include the hackneyed rainbow, blue birds and rain followed by better weather, trite over worked symbols of lovers and their plight.

Places figure less in his songs. There are songs e.g. with an Irish flavour (*Valley of Dreams*), a Scottish flavour (*Glen Echo*) a London scene and one or two titles with an Italian provenance including *My Capri Serenade* and *Anna from Anacapresi*. He provides Gracie with more developed numbers as in his effective, but mild spoof Viennese waltz, *Do You Remember My First Love Song*, with its upward extension to A.

There is no evidence Harry spoke Welsh, nor did he have a distinct south Walian accent. His recorded voice (like his sister 'Billie') shows a clearly articulated voice, mostly BBC Kensington in sound, except occasionally a slight Gallic lilt detectable in a few words. Despite its fine tradition of choral and instrumental Welsh music was not a directly significant contributory influence on his output. Even in *Jenny Jones*, the music published tends to remains more West End than *Cymru*. For the time being his developing role as song-writer and accompanist to Gracie carried him with her further into 'show business'.

CHAPTER 5

STARTING TO ACCOMPANY GRACIE (1932)

The Fields network

Harry witnessed Gracie's rather restless personal arrangements as she drifted from Archie Pitt into the arms of artist John Flanagan and later on to Monty Banks He on the other hand, encountered and benefitted from the close family networks around her as a kind of substitute for his own in Neath. It was the beginning of a close working friendship with her until the 1940s.

This situation was primarily Gracie at the centre of a hub; with her younger sisters Betty and Edith (Edie) and well as Edie's husband/character actor Douglas (Duggie) Wakefield. Other members of Gracie's entourage were her husband Archie Pitt (Archibald Selinger) who remained her manager until 1939 despite their marital separation in 1932; his mistress Annie Lipman; Bert Aza, Archie's brother who was their theatrical agent and Irene Pitt, Archie's daughter by his first marriage. She had married Lou Ross (Louis Rosenbloom), a violinist, conductor and another of Gracie's musical director/conductors until 1938, especially at the London Palladium. Lastly Gracie had close friendship with John Flanagan an Irish painter to whom she was introduced in 1929. She had an ongoing relationship with him during the next few years until summer 1935 when John ended it, feeling crushed by Gracie's whirlwind lifestyle.

A summer trial period

Harry was offered and took up a summer vocation trial period as Gracie's accompanist and began his introduction into Gracie's network. She appeared mostly for a week (usually Monday/Tuesday to Saturday including a midweek and Saturday matinee in a number of variety shows in in the British Isles). The show was built from number of different variety acts as they were available., some touring like her, others using local talent. She usually was the top of the bill, with a performance of her songs and comedy routines lasting about half to three quarters of an hour. Many shows were in the *Moss Empire Group (*M) of theatres, which Newcastle born George Black manager of *London Palladium* had taken over in 1932 and no doubt were arranged by Bert Aza. The association with Black would benefit Harry the composer when at the end of the decade, he wrote music for a number of Black's revues, during the war years. This lasted until Black's death in 1945.

From now onwards (July 1932) until his call up in August 1941, Harry's contribution to Gracie's concert tours can only be surmised, unless there is a specific reference in a programme or newspaper article, nevertheless Harry became a staple of her act being always there for her, it reduced the need for a touring orchestra and she could rely on his accompanying her with his extraordinary pianistic ability

Gracie's initial tour with a week in each place was:

July

25 - Finsbury Park Empire [36]
29 - Grand Theatre, Blackpool; [37]

August

8 - Empire, Kingston;
15 - Hippodrome, Birmingham; [38]
27- Liverpool Empire (M) [39]

---

[36] *The Stage* 28 July 1932
[37] *Yorkshire Post and Leeds Intelligencer,* 30 July 1932
[38] *Birmingham Daily Gazette*, 13 August 1932
[39] *Liverpool Echo*, 26 August 1932

Gracie crossed over to Ireland to appear from 1 September at Dublin's Theatre Royal. He may have gone with her to Dublin. When she began her autumn tour, Harry stayed on accompanying her and accustoming himself more and more to the varied idiosyncrasies in Gracie's performances.

Harry's increasing skill as Gracie's accompanist

She came to find that how exceptional he was. She had habits which could infuriate any accompanist of hers, suddenly changing key in the middle of a numbered mischievous aims to raise a laugh by trying put him off, such as often demonstrating her early acrobatic prowess by doing cartwheels during her stage appearances. [40] It did not bother Harry, he never once failed her. Her comment to the audience was typical. *This is the little lad that mucks around on the piano.*[41] He learnt to play her repertoire of an estimated 150 songs of many different types from memory. He preferred not to sight-read music as he was short-sighted.[42] During a number, Harry would soon realise what trick she was going to do. A sign from her or bit of repartee would provide him with a clue to the change ahead. His prodigious memory added to an enviable ability to transpose rapidly helped him to cope with any expressive or comedic halts, witty wisecracks (and the subsequent audience laughter) plus any further physical tricks which Gracie felt inclined to make.His therefore was a unique supporting if underestimated talent to say the least!

Furthermore, he was able to help her become subtler musically, putting it in his own whimsical way. *You're nervous, Gracie, you're singing too loud. Your mother may like it, I don't!* [43] Thus Harry became a help for her singing style. He penned for her diverse performance styles suitable solo songs for her concerts in addition to those he wrote for her films.

---

[40] Lassandro, Sebastiano, *Pride of Our Alley*, 2019, BearManor Media v 1. p;. 194-197 dates here given do not always tally with those in contemporary newspapers.

[41] Undated (c 1940) BBC broadcast Introduction to a programme about Gracie by conductor Louis Levy

[42] Rex Walford 2004, *Harry Parr Davies*, Oxford Dictionary of National Biography, p. 369

[43] Muriel Burgess with Tommy Keen, 1980, *Gracie Fields*, W H Allen, p.83

Notwithstanding, Harry as part of Gracie's professional entourage began to develop his career. The sound quality of gramophone recordings had improved through the development of the electrical over the earlier acoustic of the 1920's. Harry was therefore recorded on the piano accompanying Gracie as well as either playing solo or being as part of an orchestral backing.They both in addition made a number of BBC broadcasts together for both national and local radio stations over the next years. All this meant that he spent much of the 1930's around her. Getting such a job was for a 18-year old at that time an opportunity not to be missed in a period of high unemployment. He did not go therefore in practice go to either Oxford or Cambridge University.

The Autumn Tour

Gracie started her next tour spending a week (or more) each time

September

26 - Hippodrome Manchester [44]

October

3 - Theatre Royal, Chatham;
10 - (2 weeks) at the London Palladium (M); with 2 different casts;[45]
13 - 2.30 pm - a matinee - Metropolitan Charity show for St Mary's Hospital; [46]
24 - Hippodrome, Southend; [47]

November

at Hippodrome Theatres, in Portsmouth, Newcastle (? Empire) and Stratford Empire Palace of Varieties (M), Hippodrome, Brighton (M);

---

[44]   *The Stage*, 29 September 1932
[45]   *The Era* 12 October 1932
[46]   *Kensington Post* 7 October 1932
[47]   *The Era* 26 October 1932

Christmas time

Gracie was at the Empire, Leeds (M) then Empress, Brixton on Boxing Day. For Harry this was to some extent a baptism of fire, making him hone his talent to Gracie's requirements. Furthermore once Harry became established as her accompanist, he began to move in the same circles as she did, both professionally and domestically. He met many in the Gracie family network, for instance Tommy her brother, who had appeared with her on stage (plus his accordion-playing partner Nick Rossini) and her brother-in-law Douglas (Duggie) Wakefield.

Harry's ability as a pianist is heard in recordings e.g. in a selection made from *This Week of Grace* He reveals a firm but light and agile touch. He uses his melodies as a basis for jazz-style or more lyrical variations making the whole flow graciously long through shifts of mood and tempo, very much in the Albert Sandler tradition. By contrast, his contemporary 'Hutch' show a much heavier and plodding percussive style dedicated solely to accompanying himself.

Extra tuition

Harry spent time with the noted and expert talents of Herbert Farjeon and Harold Craxton. as his tutors[48] Farjeon was a key figure in contemporary London theatre. He was an able lyricist, theatre critic specialising in Elizabethan drama and a revue theatre manager. He was an invaluable source to approach for help in orientating Harry to an entertainment career.

Craxton was a noted pianist, accompanist and composer. He became Professor at the *Royal Academy of Music* from 1919 to 1961 and taught piano at *Matthay's Pianoforte School* on Wimpole Street from 1919 to 1940. Earlier, he himself had been a pupil there. From him Harry would learn how to accompany better and appear as soloist. It was all part of Harry's making progress in his career and slowly becoming independent from Gracie.

---

[48]   BBC Radio interview with Harry done by Leslie Perowne on 7 February 1940

Looking on the Bright Side

This, the next ATP film for Gracie was shot at Ealing Studios and released in September 1932. It had Graham Cutts as very able director and Basil Dean as co-director, screen writer (the story line was his own idea) and producer. Musical arrangements for this score were made by conductor/pianist Carol Gibbons.

The plot is simple, possibly an idealised even prophetic reflection of Gracie's her relationship with Harry. Gracie and Laurie (Richard Dollman) are cast as lovers, who have joined to form a duo, in which she sings and he writes the songs. When Laurie gets a taste of fame, he runs off with a glamorous actress but he returns to her again for the sake of the act. Harry's song *I Hate You* was indeed used in the film, where it is given two hearings, the second by Gracie. Its expressively plaintive tune in a bluesy style has strange bitter but evocative words. Its intensity make it the best musical number in the film, despite it not being acknowledged in the film list of attributions.

CHAPTER 6

MUSIC FOR GRACIE (1933)

As well as composing for Gracie's next film, there was her New Year's tour of venues as before:

January

1 - Hackney Empire (M);
9 - Shepherd's Bush Empire;[49]
15 - Empire Palace Theatre, Edinburgh () - (M);[50]
22 - Empire Nottingham;
30 - Hippodrome or Empire, Birmingham 9 M);[51]

February

(early February -a concert at Queen's Hospital, Birmingham
13 pm - Metropolitan, Edgeware Road

As part of publicity stunt for a recording of *Looking on the Bright Side*, Gracie, Jenny and Harry visited the HMV recording studies at Hayes

49   *West London Observer* 6 January 1933
50   *The Stage* 12 January 1933
51   *Birmingham Daily Gazette*, 26 January 1933

Middlesex,. Gracie sang the title song and the crowd joined in, and Jenny was pushed forward and she collided with Harry. The management were sent for to restore order. This was followed by a 'Lancashire'meal at 12-45 at the Trocadero Hotel, Piccadilly.

The tour continued :-

20 London Palladium ;[52];

27- Rochdale for a week fund raising for charity (making £1 117.

14s). It was broadcast by the *BBC Northern Regional programme* at 7.20 pm; gracie singing *How Deep the Ocean, The Rochdale Hunt, Song of the Bells,Sally.* then *Toselli's Serenade*; and probably a selection from her film, *Looking on the Bright Side.*

March

6 - Plymouth Palace;

13 - Victoria Palace for a week; featuring the songs *How Deep is the Ocean* and *Say it isn't so;*[53]

20 - Wimbledon Theatre for a week; [54]

April

4- Holborn Empire (M)[55] for a week;[56]

23- Finsbury Park Empire for a week

June,

19 Empire Finsbury Park for a week [57]

---

[52]   *The Era*, 22 February 1933

[53]   *The Stage* 16 March 1933

[54]   *The Stage* 23 March 1933

[55]   Lassandro, Sebastiano, *Pride of Our Alley*, 2019, BearManor Media vol 1, 198-201

[56]   *The Stage* 26 April 1933

[57]   *The Stage* 15 June 1933

British Film Industry and Gracie

Many British films were made at Ealing Studios and Harry was to provide increasingly songs for the more musical of them. The relatively new 'talkie' medium *recruited from music hall, variety, musical comedy and the radio. The majority of those from the halls shared roots with and maintained the allegiance of their predominantly working class following.* [58] They had still remained popular in London and often toured provincial theatres throughout Britain, despite the increasingly well-made 'silent' films. They continued to be popular during the 1930's, getting another boost at the beginning of World War Two (WW2).a period which would provide Harry with new vehicles for his talents.

Gracie's films, after her first *Sally in Our Alley* in 1931, began to include members of her family regularly in her films, Indeed around Gracie had developed an extended network, dealing with performances on stage, screen radio and concert hall as well as marital matters.

The range of other talent included was wide. with character actors, speciality acts, experienced artists of all ages as well as rising young players like Kenneth More and Muriel Pavlov.

These films had loosely worked out plots devised to provide more or less convincing reasons for set solos, comedy sketches, slapstick routines balletic and acrobatic routines, previously seen in revues. Sets were often quite stagey.

On the other hand, there are often subplots and background especially in the earlier films, of social justice being played out. Indeed, in two of Priestley's scripts (*Sing As We Go* and *The Show Goes On*) despite the buffoonery, a message of social equality emerges. To make it seem more authentic, actual documentary footage is used in both. Gracie here uses comic means to obtain social justice. For some reason, in many of her films. Gracie seldom 'gets' her leading man (especially handsome suave John Loder).

Orchestrally those film scores made in Ealing Studios were well served. The *London Philharmonic Orchestra*, recently and opportunely founded in 1932 by Sir Thomas Beecham, was the studio's resident orchestra. Later

---

[58]   Robert Murphy (editor), 2009, 3rd Edition, *the British Cinema Book*, p. 107 - Richard Dacre, *Traditions of British Comedy*

others like the *Queen's Hall Light Orchestra* or noted brass bands like *Bess o' th' Barns* were also used. They played the soundtracks, usually conducted by Ernest Irving, Brendan Byrd or Charles Williams - all experienced composer/arrangers in their own right. While they provided playing of quality, only gradually did the actual quality of sound in the films improve. Similarly, the integration of studio set and the addition of more documentary footage became smoother.

Harry's next film venture for Gracie showed he had learned what was effective for Gracie's personality and for the range of her remarkably even soprano voice. She often embellished songs with her own brand of decoration leading to a climactic finish. Harry must have seen *Sally in Our Alley* which would have presented him with a paradigm for his own songs for her.

There was a 15 minute broadcast of Harry's music from BBC West Region at 6.15 on 5 May, probably including *I Hate You.*[59] However preparing four songs for the Gracie's next film could well have been the reason for not appearing on 9 May at a concert at the *Public Hall, Briton Ferry.* in aid of the *Briton Ferry Nursing Association.* [60]

This Week of Grace

This new film was released in London on 27 July 1933. at the Prince Edward Theatre, on 10 September at the Plaza Theatre and on 14 September 1933 at the *London Trade Show* before going on general release in 16 October.[61] It was made in *Twickenham Studios*, directed by Maurice Elvey after a dispute with *Radio Pictures* (RKO). (The title strongly echoes that of Noel Coward's successful play *This Year of Grace).* With a fee of £20,000, Gracie features in a film intended to show some equality between the social classes. It has good sets and costumes. Thomas Percival Montague Mackay was the conductor and music arranger. The songs were published by Francis, Day and Hunter.

---

[59]   *Hartlepool Northern Daily Mail* and other newspapers 5 May 1933
[60]   *Western Mail* 10 May 1933
[61]   Lassandro, Sebastiano, *Pride of Our Alley*, 2019, BearManor Media vol 1, p 208-

The story unfolds about Mr and Mrs Milroy (Frank Pettingell and Minnie Raynor) a well-matched pair cinematically and their two children Joe (Duggie Wakefield) and Grace (Gracie). Father and son run a garage in a haphazard way and rely to some extent on Gracie' wages.

Grace loses her job in a factory when she is late. She gets a job eventually after meeting the eccentric Duchess of Swinford (Nina Boucicault) in the park. Grace is to be housekeeper at the Duchess's home, nearby Swinford Castle. She wants Gracie to sort out a group of scroungers, who are reducing the family estate to poverty. with the situation is complicated by her family coming to live.

Initially kept at a distance by the other staff, the house librarian (John Stewart) helps Grace to become more socially adept. The result is she soon captivates them through her personality and hard work and falls in love with the Duchess' nephew, Viscount Clive Swinford (Harry Kendall). He not only rejects his current girlfriend for Gracie, but proposes to her. Later she wrongly believes that he has married her thinking she was rich. She leaves him at the altar to go and take a job back home on the stage working in the chorus line. Eventually the misunderstandings are cleared up and the couple make up. Harry provided 5 well-crafted songs each showing up different aspects for Gracie's vocal art:-

A Melody at Dawn with words jointly by Gracie and Harry. This has a pastoral wistful feel being a more meditative song that the others in the score. The first verse has many open air references, the second is more about dreams. The refrain mingles these sentiments to an underlying tango rhythm until the final chord. - a delightful number.

Happy Ending with words also by Harry has a Tin Pan Alley structure. The 2 verses denote the present state, The refrain an effective expression of hope for the future.

Mary Rose has words jointly by both Gracie and Harry. The structure is like that of *Happy Ending* but instead is a slow waltz. The 2 verses have slow lilting phrases slowing for the refrain. This has an early romantic somewhat

Italian feeling. This makes the tribute to both Harry's and Gracie's mothers a wistfully charming song.

My Lucky Day has words again jointly by Gracie and Harry. He however modifies the usual Tin Pan Alley structure with 2 verses and a refrain. This contrast makes the song sound glad and feeling alive at the present.

Lastly *When Cupid Calls* has words by Harry. This is a pleasant perky rather girlish number, with in the usual structure, which Gracie vocalised appropriately.

For the film, orchestrations were done by the experienced conductors/arrangers Thomas Percival and Montague Mackey The variety, effectiveness and freshness of Harry's songs went some ways to making them popular enough for him to it to make a piano selection of them as his first record to be released by *Edison Bell Winner Records Company,* who specialised in recording middle-of-the-road pieces from the popular to light classical. [62]

Harry had acquired a place for himself (this address is on a draft of *Just a Catchy Little Tune* for the next film.) 168b Sutherland Avenue, Maida Vale W 9. – a convenient pied-à-terre for Central London. This was a basement flat in a brick built terrace. He would buy a mews flat in the area during the war.

Once filming was over, there was a further round of concerts:-

July

3 Garrick Theatre, Southport for a week [63]
17 Pavilion Bournemouth for a week [64]
24 Palladium London for 2 weeks [65]

---

[62]   *Nottingham Evening Post,* 18 December 1933
[63]   *Lancashire Evening Post,* 4 July 1933
[64]   *Bournemouth Graphic,* 21 July 1933
[65]   *The Stage,* 27 July 1933

August

7 Opera House, Scarborough for a week [66]

14 Grand Blackpool for a week [67]

28 Garrick, Southport for a week

September

4, His Majesty's Theatre, Aberdeen for a week [68]

11 Empire, Liverpool for a week[69]

18 Opera House, Belfast for a week, featuring songs *Reflections on the Water, I Can't Remember* and *Heaven Protect an Honest Girls* (latest film)[70]

October

1 Hippodrome, Brighton for a week [71]

15 Kings Theatre,Edinburgh for a week[72]

22 Alhambra Bradford for a week [73]

The Theatrical Ladies Guild

Gracie used the money she had accrued from her hard work to buy houses. The *Theatrical Ladies Guild* which started up in 1891 as an association looking after theatre folk was looking for a place to be made available for children of those in entertainment in the widest sense when their parents could not look after them, because of their commitments at home or abroad., children of actors, singers, dancers, travelling circus people and so on. In response to an approach from the Guild's secretary

[66]   *The Stage*, 17 August 1933

[67]   *The Stage* 10 August 1933

[68]   *Aberdeen Press and Journal*, 5 September 1933

[69]   *Liverpool Echo*, 4 September 1933

[70]   *The Stage*, 21 September 1933

[71]   *Mid Sussex Times*, 3 October 1933

[72]   *Southern Reporter* 16 October 1933

[73]   *Leeds Mercury*, 17 October 1933

Lottie Albert in 1933, Gracie donated the house to the *Guild*. The official opening ceremony sometime in 1933 was attended an assortment of guests - American character actor, Charles Coburn, witty Liverpool comedian Rob Wilton, comic singer/pianist Norman Long., comic actor, Charles Austin, charity promoter, Sir Harry Preston and Labour politician, John Henry Thomas among others. Gracie continued to finance it, although she left the Guild the responsibility of running it. [74] She often visited it and mingled with the children, even doing a Christmas concert with Harry as an unnamed Santa Claus. On 7 December as Chairwoman and entertainer Gracie attended *The Variety Artists Ladies Guild Annual* Dinner and Ball raised £1500 Harry is not mentioned, but probably accompanied her as there is no mention of an orchestra.[75]

---

[74] *The Official Gracie Fields website* graciefields.org
[75] *the Stage* 7 December 1933

CHAPTER 7

HARRY SETTLES IN (1934)

Where Harry lived

Gracie bought 2 houses in Peacehaven near Brighton Sussex for her parents. in c.1924 They liked the second one better at 29 Telscombe Way because it had a sea view. With characteristic impulsive generosity, she made the first one she had purchased 'Telford' 17 Dorothy Avenue North into the *Gracie Fields Children's Home and Orphanage. Regarding Harry* she remarked later *we had a brother and sister affection for each other and he became part of the family, who accepted him as much as I did*[76] This meant that that he had a number of places to stay. If he was working with Gracie, e.g. on new songs, he could be with her at Hampstead or at her parents' house in Sussex or in Capri. Otherwise, he would be in Neath (or later in Swansea) enjoying time with his own family.

Harry around this time, had become part of Gracie's entourage mixing with Archie, Annie Lipman, Bert Aza and John Flanagan. Gracie's attitude to relationships whether, marital or performance-related is odd. She had lived in with Archie and Annie only moving out later. Her relationship with Irish painter John Flanagan looked to be more than platonic. She seemed almost motherly to Archie's daughter Irene and sisterly to Harry. Harry himself is not recorded as having any recorded amorous relationships.

---

[76] Fields, Gracie, 1960, *Sing as We Go, The Autobiography of Gracie Fields,* Frederick Mulle, p. 109

He left his basement flat in Maida Vale and moved wherever Gracie was. She had earlier acquired a villa *Il Postino* on Capri, which she developed as *La Canzone del Mare (Song of the Sea)* in 1932.[77] Harry often accompanied her to Capri, especially to prepare the words and music for songs for their next film. He had taken up smoking, a habit he was to continue for the rest of his life, as many photos show. This would affect his health in later life. She acquired 'Greentrees', 19 Finchley Road, Hampstead a larger house which she refurbished as her latest London house in 1935 and from 1934 Harry stayed a room there and stayed frequently.[78] Harry had some obsessional traits, for instance absorbed in playing the piano most of the day, he would complain that he didn't get any breakfast, despite Mary Barrett and Gracie's mother continuing leaving him trays.[79]

They continued to spend time together over the succeeding years until her operation, her re-marriage and the outbreak of war and his call-up caused them to be apart. He needed the time and space not only to work at learning new repertory for Gracie but to compose new music for her films or concerts as well as making up different songs just to please himself. His other place of quiet was to go back home to Neath.

Harry later recalled how he was involved with Gracie's songs ending up on screen, *When making a film she concentrates on the sound part first of all usually doing as most of the big recording jobs on Sundays. The song is then 'played back' on to the floor, where Miss Fields, with the camera focussed on her, supplies the visual part of the number. Together we map out the routine of a number about three weeks before the actual recording. It is difficult work, as the final arrangements take days to complete, and often the music needs additions even after the last days of 'shooting.* [80]

It is likely Harry was somewhat in love with Gracie, even if it was on a platonic level. Many of his solo songs are concerned about gaining or being in love or nostalgia for unobtainable lost love. Gracie intent on her

---

77

78 This is the address e.g. on 'banknote' Christmas card of 1937 and on 30 November 1938 boat passenger list

79 *Sing as We Go, The Autobiography of Gracie Fields, 1960,* Frederick Muller p. 108

80 Unsourced undated (c. 1936) USA newspaper interview vide supra

own marital and relationship problems possibly did not (or did not want) to recognise that he had romantic feelings for her. Their relationship though close for many years, remained professional and very friendly.

Gracie was filming her next film *Love Life And Laughter.* This ATP film filmed during December 1933 and New Year 1934 and completed on 9 February for release in March 1934 is similar to Sigmund Romberg's *Student Prince* and Franz Lehar's *Die Csarewitch* namely the love of prince and commoner denied. It was a vehicle for Gracie, but Harry did not provide any music for it. Working either in Hampstead or at home in Neath. Harry in the meantime had published 3 more songs

Croon to Me recorded by Leslie (Hutch) Hutchinson - a routine sentimental song which falls easily in Hutch's range, another song *The Night You Sang 'O Sole Mio'.* [81]

Finally there was a little gem possibly written at Harold Craxton's suggestion for Walter Widdop the distinguished operatic tenor called, *Tree Top Lullaby.* It is possible that Harry's love of Wagner lead him to go and hear Widdop at Covent Garden as Siegmund (in 1932 *Die Walküre*) or as Tristan (in 1933 *Tristan und Isolde*). Widdop sang in oratorios and concerts, for which he may have wanted a suitably quiet song as a contrast to more weighty items. In a simple format reminiscent of Arthur Butterworth's *Shepherd's Cradle Song* and of other English composers in a pastoral mode, Harry's song s charming almost artless and particularly good at exploiting the *mezza voce* middle register of the tenor voice.

He also roved some of the works for a charming song *Blue Bird Of Happiness.*On 5 May from 6-30 to 6-45 pm there was a short broadcast of his music on gramophone records from *BBC Western Regional* programme. [82]

---

[81]   no sheet music copy found as yet.

[82]   *Staffordshire Sentinel*, 5 May 1934

Capri

In May Harry travelled to Capri (probably for the first time) with Gracie and J B Priestley to work on her next film i.e. the words and music of his songs.[83] He told in a later interview how they worked together *Before making a film Miss Fields and I usually manage to escape to Canzone del Mare (Song of the Sea), her beautiful villa in Capri.... I 'fiddle about' at the piano for a couple of hours, after breakfast, developing ideas and carrying out experiments. When I get a good theme I ask Miss Field's opinion. If she likes it I go ahead and work it out. Together we discuss ideas for lyrics and possible situations for the numbers.... She is most particular that her audience shall understand every single word she sings .... and .... avoid distortion of diction.* [84] [85] Gracie's hoped her relationship with John Flanagan (also at Capri) would move from close companionship to marriage but at this time the idea floundered. She remained friendly with him however in the years ahead.

Sing As We Go

This was directed by Basil Dean and filmed during 26 May for 3 weeks and was released in September 1934. It is a lively, entertaining comedy with a message of uplift, shot mainly in a quasi-documentary way in Blackpool using local people in the location shots. It was fortunate in a number of ways. Its screen play was written by John Boynton (JB) Priestley, who is particularly remembered for his 'reality–orientated' novels *The Good Companions* (1929) and *Angel Pavement* (1930). Its scenario editor was Australian-born Gordon Wellesley, who had just started to write for British films and would spend the next 30 years writing for both British cinema and TV. The film reinforced the growing popularity of Gracie as a film star.

The whole film works as a happy mixture of humour and sentimentality and also gives a social portrait of not only the hardship but the stoic humour

[83] Lassandro, Sebastiano, *Pride of Our Alley*, 2019, BearManor Media vol 1, 222

[84] *Song Writing for Gracie Fields*, unsourced undated (c.1936) USA newspaper interview with Harry in Parr-Davies Collection

[85] There s a draft by Gracie for the song which Harry developed in the above collection.

of working class life in 1934. The main storyline is about Gracie Platts (Gracie), a Lancashire mill-girl working at Rochdale's *Grey Beck Cotton Mill*, living at home in a house full of broken clocks with Uncle Murgatroyd and shrewish Aunt Alice. She also loves her boss at the factory (John Loder) but from afar. Gracie loses her job caused by a strike. *Even t'clocks are on strike,* she comments sardonically. Undeterred, wearing shorts and bearing pots and pans, she cycles to Blackpool to find a job, asking a policeman (Stanley Holloway) the way and dithers, nearly colliding with a tram. Arriving among the holiday crowds at Blackpool, she has a go at a variety of jobs, chambermaid, fortune teller, song demonstrator, magician's assistant, toffee seller, contestant in a beauty competition, even a human spider chased around site and falling into the *Tower Circus* water tank at part of its finale of the *Circus*. All these situations show her going through a repertory of comic and romantic 'turns' and songs.

The strike ends, her boss goes off with the winner of a beauty contest (Dorothy Hyson). Whereupon Gracie leads the mill-girls back into the now reopened Grey Beck Mill with the marching song *Sing As We Go*, accompanied by the brass band *Besses o' the Barn* from Bury. The film also had a sterling supporting cast including 13 year old Muriel Pavlow.

Harry's title song was the final spur to ensure the film's popularity. It remains one the songs by which he is still remembered and foreshadowed his future success as a composer. Reworked for Gracie Fields from earlier song *Peter the Pup* he had written, it is basically a quick march akin to a schottische with a bugle call which Gracie vocalised in the repeat. The new words for the tune were apparently written on the back of an envelope while he and a salesman friend of his were travelling and stopped in a shoe shop in Hyde. [86] Gracie liked it and Basil Dean agreed to have it as the film's title song. [87] The conductor arranger for this and most of the films with Harry's music during the 1930's was resident musician Ernest Irving. The title song in particular was a cheery song for the difficult days of the Depression and Irving orchestrates *Sing as We Go* in number of guises until it becomes almost a *leitmotif* expressing Gracie's determination to succeed. The other two songs Harry wrote for the film were:-

---

[86]   Lassandro, Sebastiano, *Pride of Our Alley*, 2019, BearManor Media vol 1, 226. Whyere were they travelling to and who was the salesman friend.

[87]   Lassandro, Sebastiano, *Pride of Our Alley*, 2019, BearManor Media vol 1, 223.

Just a Catchy Little Tune is well suited to Gracie's jaunty music hall style, which include phrases to show her whistling ability. She sings it in *Blackpool Tower Theatre* and Harry lengthens the usual *Tin Pan Alley* structure to make the song an effective and effervescent song of happiness.

If all the World were Mine, alternatively is more meditative and longing in the vein and structure of a song like *Happy Ending* in *This Week of Grace*. It provides a contrast to the other 2 songs.

Once her filming was completed, Gracie was almost immediately on another UK tour :"

June

June 22 Regal Cinema Southampton;

23- a week at Empire Finsbury Park Empire (M); singing *Play, Fiddle, Play, Stormy, Weather, I Can't Remember, Playing with Fire Mother's Wedding Group* and *Heaven Will Protect an Honest Girl*;[88]

July

3 - Garrick Theatre, Southport for a week;[89]

9 - *Clifton Hall Garden Party* Holgate Nottingham;

12 -Pavilion Bournemouth for a week;[90]

17 Gracie was at at West Pier Brighton for a week in revival of 'comedy melodrama *the Streets of London.* [91]

---

[88]   *The Stage* 22 June 1934

[89]   *Lancashire Evening Post*, 30 June 1934

[90]   *Bournemouth Graphic*, 14 July 1934

[91]   *Mid Sussex Times*, 18 July 1934

Harry is not likely to have been needed for the next few weeks, so he possibly went home to his parents for a break Gracie after that had a week off again in Capri:-

She continued:

July /August

26 Grand Blackpool for 4weeks finishing on 25 August.[92]

August/September

26 for 2weeks - London Palladium (M)[93]

September

10 - Bournemouth Pavilion;,[94]

17 another 2 weeks at London Palladium [95] For the first time Harry is mentioned in a newspaper article, although not by name, but as having 'her own pianist' during this run at Palladium.

October

3 - Brighton Hippodrome

9 a concert at *British Legion Annual Carnival* in Preston.

10 - Holborn Empire this whole show very enterprisingly was issued by HMV as a 3-record album the next day (11)

16 - Edinburgh Empire Palace (M)

23 - Bradford Alhambra(M)[96]

---

[92]   *The Stage*,13 July,2 and 3 August 1934,

[93]   *The Stage*,6 September 1934,

[94]   *Western Gazette, 31 August 1934*

[95]   `*The Stage*, 13 September 1934;

[96]   Lassandro, Sebastiano, *Pride of Our Alley*, 2019, BearManor Media vol 1, 208-13

November

During November Gracie travelled to s in Capri, returning to England at Folkestone on 26 November to do a charity week

December

3 Rochdale. Gracie left Rochdale for London on the Saturday 8 December to appear next day at London Palladium.

10 - Palace Manchester

Thus ended a busy year. the next one was to prove even more wide-ranging.

CHAPTER 8

MONTY BANKS AND GEORGE FORMBY (1935)

Harry's relationship with publisher Lawrence Wright was cemented when he gave Harry £1000 cheque in advance for £1000 for songs to be published. They provided between them words and music for Gracie next film *Look up and Laugh*.[97] There were further tours in venues lasting a week with Gracie :

January

    7 - Metropolitan Theatre, London
    14 - Hippodrome, Birmingham
    21 - Empire Stratford`
    28 - Empress, Brixton
    30 March 1936 Harry and Gracie broadcast on *BBC Regional Programme* (441 at 10 pm with the *BBC Variety Orchestra* under Lou Ross, Gracie sang with Harry at piano.[98]

---

[97]   *Liverpool Echo* 7 March 1935
[98]   *Radio Times* Issue 652 29 March - 4 April 1952

Monty Banks

A new man had entered into Gracie's life, Mario Bianchi (his name anglicised as Monty Banks). He had had a long acting career in American silent films. When the 'talkies' came in, he moved into directing. He was a mildly exuberant personality. The meeting with Gracie was brought about through Bert Aza, her agent, who had business with him and brought him to Greentrees. [99] This meeting would mark a new departure in the film-making business for both Gracie and for Harry. Gracie moved on to work with Monty as film director displacing Basil Dean, who turned to other stars. Monty became involved with the British films even often appearing in cameo roles in them. Harry initially found his very Italian greeting of hugs and kisses a bit overwhelming, but was accepted aspart of Gracie's entourage. As for Harry, Monty was another person who came to know him and use his talents in Gracie's films.and for other people which both Basil Dean and Monty promoted. Domestically, things for Harry continued as before, with Monty increasingly replacing John Flanagan as her romantic partner. Harry as before was a kind of half brother to and half *chaperon* for Gracie.

Another enterprise which Gracie and Harry became involved was the BBC outside broadcast from *Radio North Manchester* of the Anzac Day concert (25 April) from *Queen Mary's Hospital for Disabled ex-Service Men* at Roehampton. This was the 99th concert since its foundation.

Move to Swansea

Harry came home for a dinner given on 13 July in his father's honour as singer and honorary secretary of the *Neath Male Philharmonic Society* at the *Cambrian Hotel,* Neath. The Society's President, Herbert Waring presented them with a combination bureau-book-case and hall chair. He thanked David John for his work as secretary to the society over the last 9 years, especially his arranging for the recent visit of Paul Robeson to sing at a recent concert. He wished them well in their new home in Swansea. Harry's father responded that he would always take an interest in the Society.

---

[99] *Sing as We Go, The Autobiography of Gracie Fields,* 1960, Frederick Muller p. 91

Under the conductorship of a Madame Wynne Richard-Thomas, LRAM, a musical programme was given, including popular songs by Harry. [100]

Harry's mother and father moved from Neath to 9 Lôn Cadog, Cwmgwyn, Swansea. It was a larger dwelling in a more up-market setting, when compared to the terrace house in Neath. It had double bay windows, small gardens front and back, set in a more spacious street lay-out. Being above Swansea Bay it had clear views towards Mumbles Head and the Islands. Glennys was now working at the *Midland Bank* on Windsor Street in Swansea. 'Billie' worked at *Lloyds Bank* on Wind Street, where she met her future husband. 28 year old Geoffrey David, whom she married in Autumn 1936 and they lived at nearby Lôn Draenen, Sketty, Swansea,

Look Up and Laugh

This next ATP film was directed by Monty Banks. It had a script with a social message with again written by J B Priestley and his Australian-born scenario coordinator Gordon Wellesley. A vehicle for Gracie, it is less socially perceptive or believably realistic than Priestley's earlier film script. Its sets are more studio bound with the effect of the whole being more like a stage farce especially in the long 'demolition' scene in the department store. It provided supporting roles for members of the cast who had came from silent and talking film and the stage or were new talent like Kenneth More.

Grace Pearson (Gracie) returns to Plumborough for a holiday after touring in a revue - *Mind Those Legs*. There is trouble at the old market where her father is a stallholder in the old market and she learns this is to close completely and be torn down. She therefore embarks on a battle to save it from intended closure by Belfer a rich tycoon (played by long established silent film and talkies character actor Alfred Drayton. He gains the agreement of the bumbling mayor (Rob Wilton) and his cronies on the local council. They are opening a more modern emporium in its place. A young emerging actress Vivien Leigh plays Belfer's daughter. (She got a fee of £300 for this bit part).[101] Grace's brother Sydney (her brother Tommy

---

[100]   *South Wales Evening Post*, 17 June 1935

[101]   Darwin Porter and Ray Moreley, 2011, *Damn You, Scarlett O'Hara – The Private Lives of Vivien Leigh and Laurence Olivier*, Blood Moon Productions, p. 192/3

Fields) and friend Joe Chirk (brother in law Douglas 'Duggie' Wakefield In true farcical style, they and race set about making Belfer the tycoon totally uncomfortable in the opening of his new store.

She helps children wreck the displays in his store and then attacks the owner in a social context in a special 'prima donna' scene. Having locked an Italian singer due to appear as a guest for the opening in a closet, Grace takes her place and presents the kind of comedy in which she excelled. Harry has a cameo role, appearing in morning suit and tie as the accompanist to Gracie (together with a clarinettist). She sends up operatic foibles using Violetta's double arias at the end of Act I of Verdi's La Traviata, *Ah! Fors è Lui* with its cabaletta *Sempre Libera* as a basis. Singing a text in garbled Italian and French (e.g 'amour' for 'amor') she sings it more or less straight, but the cabaletta in reality a fast waltz, she musically garbles interjecting all kinds of warbling, but ending up with a clear high C. What a pity she did not record it straight! Harry as her accompanist supports her not only by his musical accompaniment, but with facial expressions and comedy timing.

She suffers a setback when Grace's brother falls for the tycoon's daughter, who has been talked round. The store is blown up by a convenient gas leak, leaving the market to continue as it was founded originally by Royal Charter (cf *Passport to Pimlico*). All ends well though Gracie is faded out rather than having a sung exit. So she has been successful. The songs by Harry were:

> There is a bright-and-breezy song to a quickstep tempo, *Look Up and Laugh*. After slower verses (2 of them) there is a refrain of up-lifting good humour Gracie supplied Harry with the verses, which are partly used. It shows clearly how they interacted to arrive at the completed song, [102]
>
> *Anna from Annacapresi* (Horatio Nichols again provided some of the lyrics) is a 5 verse nonsense waltz song about nationalities which Gracie, Tommy her brother and Duggie her brother-in-law take up. Each one has a verse about a person from a different country, Gracie has a verse for the

---

[102] H Parr-Davies collection.

Italian of the title, Tommy and Duggie, verses about the Spanish Alfonso, the Swiss Hiwitch and the Welsh Tony from Tonypandy with Gracie ending with Russian Olga. After the introduction, each verse has a comic rigmarole revealing the character assumed with the voices come together in a concerted number before the next verse. It is a well-crafted 'music hall' number for a group of seasoned entertainers.

Lastly frankly sentimental but optimistic, *Love is Everywhere* is a simply expressed song of the joy of being in love, the refrain being particularly haunting. Again these three songs showed his versatility in reflecting situations in the film.

There was a trade show preview of the film on the evening of the 27 June at the Capital, Cinema Cardiff. Gracie attended of course with her co-star Jack Milford as well as Harry who had been written a song for George Formby's new film *No Limit).* Betty Davies, Formby's leading lady in the film, her lyricist Eric Spear and comic actor Harry Tate who had appeared in both Gracie's and George's films that year attended as well [103]The film went on release on 4 August 1935.

After working on 4 films for Gracie, Harry during 1935, embarked on working with another film star, the Northern comedian, George Formby. Monty was the director of the first 2 films. Harry would go on to give George both sentimental and comic songs in 5 films from 1935-44. George's humour was more slapstick, his musical style more robustly comic, but like Gracie, it derived from the music hall. His singing while less accomplished in tonal quality than Gracie's but was very witty and accurate. He usually topped his songs off with an interlude of virtuoso performance on the banjolele. Harry's contribution to George's repertoire was small but fitted George's requirements whether comic or sentimental very ably.

---

[103]   *Western Mail* 28 June 1935

August

4 - London Palladium (for 3 weeks)
25 - Brighton

September

1 - Palace Manchester.

Gracie in 1934 h ad bought a large studio flat, - 28 Mallord Street Chelsea which painter Augustus John had built for himself. At 6 October, at 8 .m., Gracie, accompanied by Harry, were heard in a broadcast live to Australia and New Zealand specially set up by General Post Office, They were introduced by Basil Dean and heard in perfect reception by 65 stations there. [104]

No Limit

Monty moved to work on to George Formby films with Harry writing some of the songs. George came to enjoy Harry's company and they spent time in the pub. Possibly Beryl, George's uxorious wife thought him a suitable companion for George [105] curbing George's tenancy to ogle the ladies.

The story line of the film released on 28 October. concerns a chimney sweep from Wigan George Shuttleworth (George) who dreams of winning the Isle of Man TT Race. With money 'borrowed' from his grandfather Shuttleworth (character actor Edward Rigby), George builds the "Shuttleworth Snap" motorcycle after failing to join the *Rainbow Motor-Cycle* team. He not only succeeds in winning the race but getting the girl Florrie Dibney (Florence Desmond) as well.

---

[104] Lassandro, Sebastiano, *Pride of Our Alley*, 2019, BearManor Media vol 1, p. 275
[105] Bret, David, 1995, *The Real Gracie Fields*, J R Books Ltd p.76-7 He includes offensive personal comments about Harry said to have been made by Monty and Beryl Formby. They may be possibly be true but typical of Brett in citing nosource for such scurrility.

Of the 4 songs in the film.Harry wrote one *Your Way is My Way*. This is a charmingly naive love song for George and cFlorence Desmond. The ever present Ernest Irving served as the film's its musical director and arranger.

Away from film, Harry wrote other songs to different authors and in different styles, again possibly for consumption by USA as well as British markets. The title *Bring Back the Girl in the Old-fashioned Gown* sounds like a nostalgic reprise of 1919 hit song *My Sweet Little Alice Blue Gown* and *Carnival in Spain* similar to any Latin American number of the time.

> The oddest piece of music that Harry wrote for Gracie was *'Erbert 'Enery 'Epplethwaite*. This is basically a comic verse monologue about a Lancashire lad wanting to be a crooner. The verses are underpinned with sustained chords in the orchestra as Gracie declaims in the same way as Stanley Holloway did with his popular of the time monologues about *Sam* and *Albert*.

> *Joe the Jolly Marine* is similar in feel and structure to *Sing as We Go* in its infectious '3 naval step' rhythm - a quick march tempo. In keeping with its theme, its prevailing mood is akin to *There's Something about a Soldier* song in the 1934 cartoon short *Betty Boop*.

> *Blue Bird of Happiness* is unique in Harry's output, in that he provided the lyrics (not the music) with experienced lyricist Edward Hayman for a haunting tune tenor by Hungarian ex-patriot classical composer Sandor Haymati. This was for Jewish cantor/operatic for Jan Peerce who made it his signature tune. Harry was possibly fulfilling reciprocal part of his contact, by providing further lyrics for the song for the British part of the market just as his songs were published in USA. Peerce's version for RCA Victor is a singular charmless version being much too operatically full voiced and further spoiled by a central sentimental *parlando* section to it. Others recorded it - Shirley Temple, Gracie herself, Jimmy Durante. Jo Stafford

and Gordon Mc Rae recorded it giving it a due gentleness and calm appropriate to the music, which no others reach. Gracie finally closed her relationship with John Flanagan the artist, but not before he had done a fine an oil painting of Harry for his 21st birthday.[106]

On Top of the World

From October 21 Gracie was busy filming her next film *Queen of Hearts,* for which she had contracted with 20th Century Fox. Harry wrote the words and music for 2 songs featured in it. (for details see below in chapter 9).

With Gracie involved with this, her sister Betty her sister now took over the lead role over in a film originally intended as a vehicle for Gracie. It was entitled *On Top of the World* from the lesser known *City Film Cooperation* at *Shepperton Studios.Betty* also possessed a soprano voice, lighter in texture than *Gracie*. The film was.similar in its social message to many of Gracie's other films.,being about a working class girl whose dog wins the races, which she uses to provide a soup kitchen for the local needy and intervenes between angry management and the work force,. Harry provided the title song. The film's musical director was Eric Spear.

---

[106] It is now hangs in Neath Library

CHAPTER 9

SOUTH AFRICA 1935-6

After this, Gracie, Tommy Fields, his comedy partner Nino Rossini, Monty and Harry all sailed on Thursday 21 November for Cape Town for a 4-month South African tour aboard the Union Castle line steamer, *Windsor Castle*.[107] This meant that again though Gracie and her family and friends, Harry was able to widen his experience of the world.

While on board ship, Gracie accompanied by Harry gave a concert. Once they had disembarked in Cape Town on 20 December, Gracie was given a lively street parade reception. Her first concert there was with an orchestra, but it was only for half-an-hour. For many other concerts, Harry played for her. She said about him that the tour would never have been such a success without the brilliance of her pianist. While she here praised Harry's abilities, but she also recalled how touchy he could be. A Mr White a South African of Welsh origin was a conductor in Cape Town. He and Harry both got into their heads that the other was mimicking his Welsh accent with very intense non-verbal results. This incident showed how touchy Harry could be and how easy it was for Gracie and Harry to fall out. [108]

The tour took them on to Johannesburg and surrounding towns like Benoni, Orange Free State. Notwithstanding the busy schedule, they had found itme for sightseeing. They went off on 7 January and visited East Geduld Gold Mine near Benoni, (also producing platinum and silver) a diamond mine

---

[107] *Sunderland Echo and Shipping Gazette*, 20 November 1935
[108] *Sing as We Go, The Autobiography of Gracie Fields*, 1960, Frederick Muller
      p. 106

and a snake farm [109] with aquarium, aviaries museum and tea-rooms. The tour was so wildly successful that they extended their stay by a further 6 weeks. They moved on to Pretoria in the Transvaal (now called Gauteng) appearing at the *Vaudette Theatre*, Pritchard Street. giving 3 shows. there.

They moved a long way south east to start on 7 February for a fortnight at the *Theatre Royal* Durban; then on 21 February at the Grand Theatre Pietermaritzburg,(now KwaZulu Natal) for a week, before returning to Cape Town. for a week [110].At the final concert, Gracie sang Harry's song, *You've Got to Smile When You Say Goodbye.* prior to boarding the SS *Stirling Castle* on 13 March.

. They gave a typical variety concert on board on the Cabin Class Deck. Harry gets two spots, first as the 'warm-up' act but now in his own right and then as accompanist to Gracie as 'top-of-the bill':-

1. *Harry at the piano played a selection*
2. *Doreen – xylophone*
3. *Jack Daly – the Irish Entertainer [a pleasant baritone who specialised in Irish songs]*
4. *Raymond Smith –Ventriloquist*
5. *Tommy Fields and Nich Rossini – A Kouple of Komics Call out of Prize Winners*
6. *Impressions – Disa Bolton*
7. *Payne and Holland - in Burlesque Episode*
8. *Freddie Phyllis and Anne – the latest in Rhythm. [modern dance act]*
9. *GRACIE FIELDS*

Radio Broadcasts

Arriving home on 30 March, Gracie and Harry did a short broadcast for BBC National, 10-10.20 pm with BBC Variety Orchestra, conducted by Lou Ross with Harry at the piano [111]

---

[109] Possibly the *National Zoological Gardens* of Pretoria dating from 1898. It today houses all mentioned above.

[110] Lassandro, Sebastiano, *Pride of Our Alley*, 2019, BearManor Media vol 1, p. 286-90

[111] *The Scotsman*, 30 March and others

On 24 May, Gracie,as President of *the Variety Artists Ladies Guild and Orphanage* with Harry accompanying her in her typical songs, including the comic *I've Never Cried So Much in All my Life'.* headed a variety concert at the Phoenix Hotel with acts from comedians like Norman Evans, singers and pianist, accordionists and auction on the Guild's behalf.

The next day 25 May they broadcast to Australia, this time from the BBC. These broadcasts had started in 1932. Even before she went to the southern hemisphere later Grace was known and appreciated there. Broadcasting from BBC was an important way of communicating to the Empire what was happening in UK.

Keep Your Seats Please

This was the second ATP film which Monty directed as a vehicle for George Formby. It was released 1 August 1936. George Withers (George Formby) is set to inherit jewels from his Aunt Georgina (May Whitty). Deceived by unscrupulous lawyer, (Alastair Sims in good form), whom he seeks to help. It transpires that they are hidden in 1 of 6 antique chairs, but which one? Before he can get to the auction, they are sold off separately and so he has to find them.

> Harry wrote one song, *Binkie's Lullaby* for the little girl Binkie, who appears in the film (although possibly not used) to lyrics by Arthur Wilson. Again the music was conducted and arranged by Ernest Irving.[112]

Queen of Hearts

This film was yet another ATP film, released on 5 October 1936. Basil Dean was Director and Monty Banks as producer. Its script was by Clifford Grey and HF Maltby. The cast apart from Gracie included Monty (in cameo as passerby), her sister Edith Fields, John Loder (as Derek Cooper) and stage-singing actress Enid Stamp-Taylor (Yvonne).

---

[112] A copy of this was donated by Harry's two sisters and registered in 1966 under the third series of the US Catalog of Copyright ~Entries

Harry in a cameo role as street busker and unemployed miner in an outdoor café in London has a hand written notice 'Wife and Three Kids to Support'. Grace Perkins (Gracie Fields) an ordinary working class seamstress is mistaken for a rich patron of the art by a show's producer. When she's asked to back a new show she plays along with the charade, hoping that she can become the production's leading lady. She auditions and finds herself in the show, where instead of singing she dances the apache dance with dancer Carl Balliol.

When the show finally opens in the final scene set in Venice, she emerges from a gondola and starts to sing a spoof Viennese operetta waltz song with words by Harry, *Do You Remember My First Love Song?* a slow waltz admirably suited to Gracie's range and style. She fully meets the challenges in the song which stretches through 2 octaves.

Another song featured earlier in the picture, *Why did I have to Meet You* is reminiscent of *I Hate You* in its characteristic slightly sour nostalgic mood. The lyrics are by Clifford Gray who provided some of the other lyrics used in the film. It is a sophisticated number, its melody and its harmonies giving an unsettling feeling with a middle section, termed an interlude recalling the past. In the recording of the song, Gracie having repeated the first section with vocal tracery leaves the tune in the air with a high climactic G. These two numbers reveal more ambitious and less conventional musical planning from Harry They are also more demanding on the singer, vocally and emotionally.

Harry wrote a new Christmas number *The Angel* (or *Fairy*) *on the Christmas Tree*.possibly intended for a Gracie Christmas concert or just the popular Christmas sheet music market. It had slightly odd covertly sexist lyrics by Roma Campbell-Hunter, masquerading as a child's song.

Girls want to be angels in USA (or in UK fairies) on the Christmas tree, while boys are just happy with presents they receive. The message of the lyrics without taking them too seriously is a slightly esoteric one about the superiority of female over male aspirations. It has a *Treetop Lullaby* structure, and a lightly scored introduction. It still occurs occasionally in Christmas popular song anthologies.

Harry also received the unheard-of advance cheque of £1000 from Horatio Nicholl to write songs for his publishing firm in the future - a reward indeed for his original persistence! Harry had set occasionally some lyrics by other writers but had not yet found a consistent co-worker. Roma provided him lyrics for some of his songs from this time on, either as single items or for British revues.

On 4 December Gracie,as President of *the Variety Artists Ladies Guild and Orphanage* presented another event, a Dinner and dance at the Savoy Hotel for the Guild with Harry accompanying her.in My *first Love Song, I Never Cried So Much in All My Life,* and the inevitable *Sally* It was attended by a number of colleagues, artistes and family An auction raised £200.

CHAPTER 10

USA TOUR (1937)

St Moritz

Gracie, her parents Fred and Jenny and Harry went off to ski resort St Moritz for a winter holiday. at the end of January. They were photographed wrapped up warmly in a sleigh outside a clinic. The hoard outside the clinic announces a Doctor Naegeli, doctor and gynaecologist with an X-ray facility in his clinic. Was this merely an uncanny prognostication of things to come for Gracie, or had she come for a private consultation?

There was a request for Gracie to open a new cinema in Gateshead, the *Black's Regal ob* High Street and she responded by going there after the brief St Moritz holiday to open it on 5 February. Albert Black was the promoter of this chain of cinemas. He was the brother of George an impresario for whom. Harry would work regularly before and during WW2.[113]

Using the media

By 1937 Harry's reputation both as pianist and as a songwriter for Gracie's and George Formby's light comedy musical films was well established. His songs were sung increasingly not only in films, but in concerts, broadcasts and on records. Gracie herself from 1932 sang and recorded his songs as did many other artistes. Although Harry had departed UK for United States of America, the *BBC Western Programme* broadcast

---

[113]   *Evening Chronicle* as dated

64

on 17 March 1937 for instance was a selection of Harry's music, namely *Sing as We Go*, possibly *Binkie's Lullaby* from *Keep Your Seats Please* and some of songs he had done for *This Week of Grace*, arranged by Leonard Morris and Garfield Philipps and played by *Garfield Philipps Quintet*. [114]

The Show Goes On

This ATP film released in 24 March 1937 was the last film for Gracie directed by Basil Dean. It included some autobiographical material drawn from Gracie's life, i.e. a rag–to-riches formula. Sally Lee's (Gracie) mother (Amy Veness) is willing to promote her aspirations as a performer (as Jenny Stansfield did) and father (and Edmund Rigby)., who doesn't agree with this -(they are both mature former silent movie veterans. Sally works at the mill and loves mill workman the film's interiors are better than some of the stats interiors. Mack McDonald the leading man (John Stuart). Plucked from the mill by a composer Martin Fraser (another silent film stalwart Owen Nares) who needs a voice capable of performing his songs she learns vocal technique enough to sing his songs and comes to love him also. She becomes increasingly successful using more popular material and then gains stardom. Fraser leaves for convalescence in California, as he suffers from TB. It is ultimately a poor vehicle for Gracie, whose talents essentially rely on personal contact with her audience, rather than showcased in lavish productions.

The film's opening musical ditty *We're All Good Pals Together.* (lyrics by Haines and Harper, who'd provided the words and music to so many of George Formby's songs) is typical jolly audience participation material appropriate for end of pantomime camaraderie.

Gracie sings *Smile When You Say Goodbye* toward the end of the film from the deck of the *Queen* Mary to men on a group ship sailing east. This is one of Harry's most enduring songs set to his own words. He is said to have composed words and music in 30 mins. [115] It anticipates similar songs of his during the war years. With the familiar Tin Pan Alley structure, it is

---

[114]   *Sunderland Daily Echo and Shipping Gazette*,27 February 1937
[115]   Red Letter Days, *The Gracie I Know* c. Mid-September 1955 interview with Harry,

a slow foxtrot, which after introduction, questions in the verse, the refrain gives an answer in the title.

Other songs Harry wrote for film were, *A Song In My Heart,*. a slow waltz of charm, when sung as a solo with feeling by Gracie. It is transmuted as the film's finale into a Viennese waltz, with very sub Busby Berkeley routines of poor quality and imagination by Andreas Malandrinos moving down and around a ritual staircase.This does no credit to Gracie, as her dance routine is poorly choreographed nor does her singing convince set against a (MGM-style) chorus.

My Love For You, (lyrics by Eddie Pola), is like the above a restrained vehicle fo Gracie to show how she can project more serious vocalisation. The title song *The Show Goes On* (lyrics by Harry) is a jolly sea-side chorus again written for duo Flanagan and Allan, very much a quick march, the verse sings of welcome and camaraderie and the refrain has lots of lively oom-pah sound accompaniment making it a pleasantly rowdy number. Haines and Harper provide Harry not only with a standard version of their lyrics, but give 3 alternatives -in Cockney, Dude and Scotch (sic).
Ernest Irving as usual arranged the film score.

Before its actual release, Harry had already sailed on 5 March 1937 from Southampton to New York on *Queen Mary* (the London address on the ship's manifest is 31 Finchley Road). [116] He wrote home in a spirit of naive and rather adolescent wonder the next day with letter headed paper:-

Cunard White Star
R.M.S. Queen Mary
Wed. 6. (March)

Dear All,

Thanks for cards. Gracie received hers also and sends her thanks. We set off this afternoon at 2 p.m. It is a wonderful ship. You should see my room. I even have an electric fire in it, also my own bathroom and lav. It really is marvellous. It's like an enormous hotel.

---

[116]   David Bret, 2010, *The Real Gracie Fields The Authorised Biography*, JR Books Ltd. p. 67

We set out back on April 15ᵗʰ from Hollywood. So we shall get back in London ten days later. No more news, Love Boy.

Once they have travelled down to California they got off the train at Pasadena, the station before Los Angeles to avoid the media. A photo shows them getting into the cab, with Gracie signing autographs, Harry looking on. The cab would take them on to the *Beverly Wilshire Hotel*, Beverly Hills. Harry writes home again in a state of wonderment:

Monday March 11

Dear Glenys,

We arrived here at noon after a very tiring three days in the train[117]. This is really a wonderful place. I went to Twentieth Century Fox studios this afternoon. They have a wonderful place.

We have a flat in this hotel, which is the hotel in California. Marlene Dietrich has only just moved out of this flat & underneath us we have Clark Gable. Also Myrnna Loy is statin on third floor. We are on the 7ᵗʰ floor. It is a lovely flat with drawing room, dining room, kitchen, hall etc. We are looking right over Hollywood.

I think I shall be lucky and get a song in the first film. Of course, the competition is terrific. She is going to do a few broadcasts. The first will be with Eddie Cantor. She is going to sing "Smile when you say goodbye" & she is going to make it in this country her signature tune, like Sally in England. Chappells of New York have bought the rights from Lawrence Wright & are putting it out in this country very soon. I fixed it before I left New York. I shall get very little money out of it because naturally Lawrence

---

[117] The train was the *Atcheson, Topeka and Santa Fe Railroad*'s express *The Super Chief*, which ran from Chicago to Los Angeles in 39 hours 49 minutes. Nicknamed *The Train of the Stars*, it was a diesel powered streamlined all-Pullman sleeper with dining room and a bar/lounge. To make a connection with New York, the party are likely to have travelled on the luxury sleeper steam hauled expresses run by *New York Central - 20ᵗʰ Century Limited* (or that of its rival *Pennsylvania Railroad - Broadway Limited*). Each took at this time 16 hours and 30 minutes for the journey. Total travel time therefore was 56 hours 15 minutes as a minimum, without adding station transfer time in Chicago.

Wright purchased the American rights. Still I shall get Performing rights. Apart from that if it is a hit, it will do me good. The studio [118] are giving G. a big lunch tomorrow and the next day a big party to meet all the stars. No more news, Boy

P.S. Has Daddy started his new job yet?

If you can write to this address up until April 15th we stay here for the complete tour.

The lunch mentioned above must have been painful for Gracie as she had had a total clearance of her teeth and had new dentures put in immediately. The fare was roast beef, Yorkshire pudding and roast potatoes!

By the next Sunday, Harry is savouring the different personalities he has met and their gossip, looking how Gracie comes over, as well as having some musical and financial ambitions himself:-

Sunday (22nd) -[Monday in UK]

Dear All,

Just another note. We went to Charlie Chaplin's to dinner. He was marvellous. I got on very well with him. He is very musical. He is the most charming person I have ever met. So cultured and a perfect host. Paulette Godard was there.[119] She was delightful. Also Constance Collier. She is the woman out here. She is English society & coaches the stars. – She coached Norma Shearer for Romeo and Juliet & Garbo for Christina. We are going to her house to dinner tomorrow night. King Vidor a big director was there also. Gracie sang and they were charmed. Then Chaplin did some funny songs. They were marvellous. Do you remember the tune in "Modern Times"? well I happened to say I liked it and he was thrilled so he told me if I wanted to write a song on it I could do as I liked. So I shall trun it into a popular song. It is a great publicity angle. Tell Daddy he can put it in

---

[118]   Presumably 20th Century Fox
[119]   Charlie's third wife from 1936 to 42

the Post if he likes that I am writing a song with Charlie Chaplin. [120]We are going out with them again on Thursday.

Last night we went to a dinner given to G. by the Lancashire people of California and after we went to the Clover Club. [121] Robert Montgomery, Miriam Hopkins,[122] Binnie Barnes,[123] etc. Gracie is quite a society success out here. They go for the English here. Tonight we have been to the Trocacadero [124] where all the big people dine. And when I was dancing with her, I could see all the people discussing her. She looks exceptionally smart and her teeth have made a tremendous difference. Gracie Allen and Burns (you know Burns and Allen) have invited us to dinner next Tuesday. Gracie has the reputation of being a terrific snob because she wouldn't go out to all the parties she had been asked to. She couldn't because was having her teeth out. She only goes out with the people. Chaplin is considered it out here. Miriam Hopkins told Binnie Barnes that she thought G. was 'too society' to both with then and very catty because G. wouldn't lunch with her. After all if she accepted every invitation she'd go daft. We are broadcasting next Sunday with Eddie Cantor.

I shall be very sorry to leave here.
I must buy a camera and take some snaps.
No more news
Boy

The proposed broadcast on *Eddie Cantor Texaco Show* on 29th did not happen. Eddie Cantor invited Gracie Monty and Harry to dinner to prime her about the show. He in a rather bumptious way tried to tell Gracie how she needed to remodel her act change to fit in what he perceived was the way things were done in USA. This progressively unnerved Gracie so much, her mind went blank. *Harry jumped up "what'll you sing, Grace?* She could only thing of *Sally.* She sang it far too loudly because she was nervous.

---

[120] The request reported in some newspapers by Chaplin for Harry to write for Hollywood could have been made at this time

[121] On *Sunset Boulevard*, i.e.at 8477 Sunset Strip a noted and notorious gambling casino and night club, raided eventually by police and closed in 1938.

[122] Versatile American actress

[123] English supporting actress, domiciled at this time in USA

[124] Another fashionable night club on the Strip

Harry was thudding away at the accompaniment, his eyes and mouth screwed up in an agonised expression. Despite Monty and Harry continuing to smooth things over, they left. Gracie didn't do the radio broadcast.

Harry also met Shirley Temple and *the late George Gershwin, who, after playing his own dance numbers specially composed for the next Fred Astaire film,* [125] *invited his judgement.* The trio spent Christmas and New Year at a ranch near Palm Springs, Florida tasting barbecue food and enjoying the parties held.[126]

They returned to Britain no doubt for the Coronation of King George VI which was to take place on 12 May. Shortly after this they made an appearance in an early telecast variety programme called 'Star', televised from Alexandra Palace on 22 May 1937. They appeared with BBC Television Orchestra conducted by its founder (in 1936) the violinist composer Hyam Greenbaum. It showed Gracie and Harry willing to respond to the new technology, undergoing the preparation and by facing the cameras and equipment of TV in 1937.

As they commonly did throughout the years, Harry's family came to see what ever he was involved with. For instance Rosina Harry's mother came to London during the third week in July. Mother and son went to see Gracie's latest film *The Show Goes On* (and hear the latest 6 songs from Harry in it of course). Rosina also saw him accompanying Gracie in a mixed variety show at the Palladium on 19 July. [127]

Harry went mid-August to Capri to work with Gracie on her next film, *We're Going to be Rich,* prior to the filming starting in September [128]

---

[125]   RKO's *Shall We Dance?*

[126]   Fields, Gracie, 1960, *Sing as We Go, The Autobiography of Gracie Fields,* Frederick Mulle, p.116-8

[127]   *The Era,* 22 July 1937

[128]   *South Wales News,* 27 July /*Western Mail* 12 November 1937

CHAPTER 11

A BUSY 15 MONTHS (1937-1938)

His return from the United States saw the beginning of a busy 15 months of composition from this time onward until Christmas 1938 as well as his accompanying Gracie. Harry was steadily emerging as an pianist/composer in on his own behalf.

In late September, Gracie recorded a number of songs on 3 new gramophone records (for Rex Label), with Harry accompanying her at the piano. They included some of Harry's songs - the 6 songs from *The Show Goes On* and other numbers, *I Never Cried SO Much in All My Life* and *In a Little Lancashire Town.*[129]

On Sunday 11 November, Gracie as President of *the Variety Artists Ladies Guild and Orphanage* presented another event - a Dinner and Dance at the Savoy Hotel for the Guild with Harry accompanying her in the usual solo spot as she sang *Little Old Lady, The Organ,the Monkey and me, Walter,* followed by *Sally* as usual. It was attended by a number of colleagues, artistes and family The usual auction followed. The proceedings carried on until the early hours of the next morning.

That very evening, 12 November, Gracie appeared in the *Royal Command Performance* in the presence of recently crowned King George VI and Queen Elizabeth accompanied by Prince George and Princess Marina, Duke and Duchess of Kent at the *Palladium*, where £6342 was

---

[129] *Littlehampton Gazette*, 24 September 1937

raised *the Variety Artists Benevolent Fund and Institution*. Comedians Norman Evans and George Formby the Crazy Gang, as well as the Boy Scouts Gang show and the racy Max Miller and female counterparts Cicely Courtneidge and Florence Desmond, doing impressions of the famous. Lou Ross conducted the orchestra, Gracie came next on the bill with Harry at the piano in *Little Old Lady, The Organ, the Monkey and me, I Never Cried So Much in All My Life,* then a variant of *The man I Love* followed by *Sally* as usual The whole was rounded off by Will Fyfe, the Scottish comedian and the drummers and papers of the *Scots Guards, The Royal Scots Fusiliers* and the *Cameronians*.

There was another BBC broadcast by them both on 17 November This was closely followed (it is likely that Harry attended this also) on Friday 25 November, with *A Glamorous Night* (shades of Ivor Novello) at the *8th Annual Film Ball* at the *Albert Hall* in aid of the *Associated British Social Sports Club*.

Towards the end of the year, he penned another Christmas number, *Let's have an Old-fashioned Christmas*. His ability to give a personal message in a humorous and original twist was shown when he sent his friends an imitation banknote as a Christmas card. Its address was still Gracie's house at *Green Trees*.

Harry crossed again the Atlantic to New York at the end of 1937 - this time by plane with Gracie, Monty Banks and Mary Barrett, her companion/secretary. They travelled to Palm Springs and Hollywood. There he bought himself a loud sports jacket and a pair of pale green trousers. He said, *Movietone City I love it.* [130] They returned in January, for Gracie to receive the CBE for her charity work and services to entertainment. It was presented to her by King George VI in February 1938 at Buckingham Palace; the distinguished concert pianist Harriet Cohen was another recipient of royal honour

Derby reception

Fresh from the above honours, Gracie went to Derby, on Saturday 12 February where she received a rapturous reception from the station to her

---

[130]   Muriel Burgess with Tommy Keen, 1980, *Gracie Fields*, W H Allen, p.84

hotel. She had come to perform 2 concerts, one at the *Grand Theatre*, the other at the central Hall, both in aid of the *Derby Royal Infirmary*. With Harry at the piano as well as providing some repartee with Gracie, she performed favourites - *Rochdale Hounds, Walter, Walter Lead Me to the Altar, Little old Lady, Sally* and capped it with her quasi-operatic comedy version of Toselli's *Serenade.* [131]

For a short holiday, she, Monty and Harry left for USA on 3 March for New York, Arriving there on 9 March and stayed for a couple of weeks. They met Charlie Chaplin and Paulette Goddard once again but this time on board ship. Once disembarked on 24 March, they were welcomed by Fred and Jenny Fields

---

[131]   *Derby Daily Telegraph* 14 February 1938.

CHAPTER 12

MORE FILM
MUSIC (1938)

In 1938 besides his usual accompaniment of Gracie on stage, on records and in broadcasts, Harry went on to write 15 songs for different films.

I See Ice

This was the next ATP film featuring George Formby and Harry wrote 2 songs for it. Its well-worn plot has a naïve fellow outwitting criminals, more sophisticated than him. This theme went on to be recycled with variations for him and for later British comedians like Norman Wisdom and Morecambe and Wise as vehicles for their essentially music hall humour on the big screen. George Formby in this film, directed by Anthony Kimmins released on 10 February 1938, is in the guise of a inept 'prop' manager for an ice-ballet company.

This provides some background spectacle as well as love interest through Kay Walsh. George somehow invents a camera concealed in a bow-tie. Unwittingly he snaps crooks in suspicious circumstances. He has to do something to prevent them and gets caught up various comic adventures. Harry wrote two songs for the film: *Noughts and Crosses* and *In My Little Snapshot Album*.

Noughts and Crosses is a slow swing number which Harry employs for George in slightly skittish romantically bashful mood, while he plays the actual game on the restaurant table cloth to woo Kay Walsh. Starting with a bouncy figure, Harry sets Roma Campbell-Hunters verse with phases of apology, which rise in pitch as he assets himself. The refrain starts with a jerky rhythm to give it a quirky swinging feeling to the lyrics concerning George's self-depreciation. This is followed by a smoother tune about the game, but finishing the insistent rhythms of the introduction. Unusually the refrain while musically the same repeats with a new set of words of similar sentiments to the first. In the recording George consistently sings 'Oughts' instead of 'Noughts' ! Nevertheless in this music, mood voice and patter come together with great deal of charm.

The situation is the same for *In My Little Snapshot Album* with the heroine sitting beside George in the film and reacting as best she can, the verse has a number of *double-entendres*.[132] It is in fact a classic music hall ballad in a very quick march tempo with a short refrain to the words of the title, at the end of each of four verses, explaining how he came to get a camera and the effects of using it!. In the film and recording, there is a ukelele episode. It makes a neat song well tailored for George's talents.

Another song *Mother! Mother! What a Naughty Boy am I* was published in 1938, but was not included in this film. Provided with the lyrics by George's usual lyricists (Harper and Haines),it reads like an alternative to *Mother What'll I do now*, written by George Formby and Fred E

---

[132] Bret, David, 1999, *George Formby*, Robson Books Ltd. p 71 The song had verses by Haines and Harper. Bret without referring to any source comments that Harry had offered it to Gracie, she said it would be better for George as it was too rude for her!

Cliffe in the prison scene of the film. Using some of the refrain and an introduction in march time, the refrain has *Mother* repeated 8 times before it gets going. Harry ends it with a perfunctory phrase, repeated a tone higher. It continues on for a further 3 verses. The whole is a suggestive patter song for George to perform in his own inimitable fashion. It could well have fallen foul of the Lord Chamberlain and *British Board of Censors* and so was replaced by the other song.

Meanwhile Harry had been both involved with Gracie's next film *We're Going To Be Rich*. Gracie and he did some more concerts.

On 18 April they were in a variety show at Chiswick. Travelling from London by train, they gave a couple of evening concerts.

On 25 April at the *Hippodrome Coventry*, starting with *Little Old Lady, Sally*, a selection from recently released *Snow White and the Seven Dwarfs* and *Ave Maria* (?Bach-Gounod or Schubert) in Latin, some other songs and *Sing as We Go*.[133]

Harry was now engaged in writing song for 5 films released between July and the end of September.

We're Going To Be Rich

Gracie's films were by now regarded as popular money-spinners at least in Britain. In this new picture, backed by American dollars from 20th *Century Fox*, she made a bid for more universal appeal, the production company aimed at something different. It reflected in some ways the time Gracie and Harry had spent on tour in South Africa and the visit to the Johannesburg gold mine the previous year. Two British born actors, now Hollywood stalwarts, Victor McLaglen and Brian Donlevy were Gracie's male counterparts and the young Coral Browne completed the quartet.

Directed this time by Monty Banks, the musical arrangements or the film was given to experienced conductor/arranger Irishman Bretton Byrd. It was set in Victorian times with suitable costumes to match the

---

[133]   *Coventry Evening Telegraph*, 26 April 1938

two settings - Australia and South Africa. Kitty Dobson, the *Lancashire Lark* (Gracie) is a singer well loved by Australian settlers. She is married to ne'er-do-well Dobby (Victor McLaglen). He is too fond of alcohol. She is giving a final performance before returning to England. She sings the attractive waltz song *The Sweetest Song in the World*.

> This song has a gentle theme in the verses (2 of them) putting nostalgic statements, ending in mild triumph. The refrain is confident in its expression of love, making a charmingly sentimental song, very suited to Gracie's softer style.

Dobby tricks her into going to South Africa. He has bought half-shares in a loss-making Gold mine there. Once there, after a brawl, Dobby lands in gaol with Monty in a cameo as another prisoner. She decides to make money by singing to the 'trekkers' in a saloon, owned by fiery-tempered Yankee Gordon (Brian Dunleavy). She has to fight him off. His erstwhile ex- saloon singer/lover Pearl (Coral Browne) retaliates by trying to make up to Dobby. He dumps him in a horse trough, but Gracie tells him that they are finished. Gordon and Dobby fight. Dobby loses the contest, and Pearl floors Gordon with a frying pan! Gordon now acts as a marital peacemaker and Kitty and Dobby make it up. It was out on general release from 7 May.

Its success encouraged 20th Century Fox to make a further offer of a £20000 contract for 4 more films. Harry only contributed 2 songs to this film.

> The *Trek Song* arranged from 2 Afrikaans tunes *Vat jou goed en trek Fereira*, and *Sarie Marais*. Harry starts with a music-box-like sound to introduce it. In the first song he supports the tune with a accented drone-like beat. Immediately the smoother second tune follows with 2 strong march-like beats to accompany it. The first tune is repeated and a coda using the music box sound again. The version Gracie recorded has the verses, which Harry writes in English sung by a male voice chorus, while Gracie sings

the original words in very passable Afrikaans. It makes a very attractive number in either format.

The Sweetest Song in All the World is another pleasantly nostalgic item using a waltz song format for Gracie. with a clear structure as a Victorian musical hall; did it reflecting Harry's feelings? The verse recalls the lovers' past meeting, the chorus considers yesterday and today in nostalgically lyrics phrases. the second verse looks back from projected future parting. There was a third more comic song *Oh You Naughty, Naughty man.*

Keep Smiling

This was the next 20th Century Fox with Gracie (as Gracie Grey), directed by Monty Banks, released in 12 August 1938. The cast included the wire haired terrier Asta, Tommy Fields (as one of 3 Bolas), comedian M'sieu Eddie Gray (Silvo), Roger Livesey (Bert Wattle) and Nino Rossini (another of 3 Bolas). Basically it is a revue, cast as a series of turns in a road movie. After the company are cheated out of money by an ex-manager, a group of performers club together to buy a bus and travel around the country doing shows. Again Harry contributed 2 songs set to his own texts:

Giddy Up is a charming pantomime-like character song about the old horse Susan as the company go home from the fair. Harry sets it at a steady plod, the verse telling about the old horse 'Susan', the refrain encouraging her to take the company home.

Swing Your Way to Happiness is a moderate quickstep to classic *Tin Pan Alley* formula. Harry provides a cheery upbeat number to his own words. The refrain incorporates many jazz intervals and harmonies to give it an underlying feeling of tension which is eventually resolved - a very satisfying genre piece.

On 23 August a more social occasion took place. Gracie was asked to a beauty contest held in the afternoon at the *Royal Ordnance Factory*[134] sports and gala ground at Euxton, west of Chorley. Sir John Jackson, Deputy Lord Lieutenant of Lancashire was one of the judges. In the evening there was an at home reception held at *Prospect House* Whin Lane, Wheelton near Chorley to celebrate Sir John's 70th birthday. Besides Sir John, Lady Jackson and their daughter Pat, there were a number of guests including Gracie Harry and the *Cafe Colette* Orchestra, a small spa-style orchestra conducted by Walford Hayden (his wife had been invited too). Sadly, Sir John died a month later. [135]

Other work as an alternative outlet to stage and film work for Gracie and Harry were radio broadcasts from the commercial radio station, Radio Luxembourg, the then sole radio broadcast alternative to be heard in Britain to the BBC from 1933. Harry wrote one of his most effectively nostalgic songs (verses jointly written with long time publisher friend, 'Horatio Nicholls' and Roma Beaumont-Campbell) *London is Saying Good Night*. It was used when the station was shutting *down*.

At Radio Luxembourg

---

[134]   Where the 'bouncing' bomb would later be made.

[135]   Lancashire `*Evening Post*, 22 August 1938

Basically a fox-trot, marked 'slowly', it begins with high pitched chords in the accompaniment suggesting London bells. The refrain resembles a lullaby, as night descends on the city and it awaits the dawn. Harry uses enhancing short chromatic figures in the accompaniment. The whole makes it one of Harry's most satisfying songs.

Again as earlier with *On Top of the World*, Gracie was contracted to *20th Century Fox*. This meant that she was not available for *Lassie from Lancashire* or *Penny Paradise*. There had to be the female lead as a substitute for Gracie. It is possible that Harry wrote the songs in both films originally for Gracie but then adapted them to make them lie naturally within the voice of the new leads. They were both charming singer/actresses and sounded and looked like Gracie, but without the soprano extension or more extrovert comic persona.

Lassie from Lancashire

The scenario of *Lassie from Lancashire* was about a typical good hearted girl in the usual Northern social setting. John Paddy Carstairs (later the director of Norman Wisdom comedy films) promoted a light musical film for the *British National Productions*. Dance band leader and studio musical director Ronnie Munro arranged the music. It featured as the new lead the pretty and charming 28 year old singer dancer Marjorie Browne. The screenplay was written by Ernest Dudley in collaboration with Doris Montgomery from her original story.Jenny (Marjorie Browne), a struggling young actress joins her Dad (Mark Daly) when he moves into his sister's boarding house (Elsie Wagstaffe), who tries to work the pair to death. Jenny however begins to fall in love with Tom (Hal Thompson), a struggling songwriter. The two become close but their romance is nearly ended when the star in a local pantomime jealously plots to destroy their love. Jenny and Tom overcome the star's attempts to part them. They dream of a positive future after being offered a theatre contract in London's West End. Like Gracie, Marjorie was a Lancashire girl and had played a number of singing and comic roles on stage and in films. Harry supplied 2 songs to his own words which lie well in the mid-voice.

> *For the First time in My Life I'm in Love* is a romantic lilting waltz. *Good Night, Little Sweetheart* is a gentle lover's farewell song - even a kind of lullaby. The verse describes sunset and the refrain provide a smoothly soothing ending. Appropriately enough it was given its first performance at the Plaza Cinema, Chorley on 5 September in the presence Marjorie Browne. The local press were in favour. [136]

It's in the Air

At the same time, Harry wrote the title song for an ATP film usually thought to be the best and funniest of Formby's films, directed by Anthony Kimmins. Released in 6 September in London it was given a general release on 27 February 1939. Intended as a morale booster.for the nation which felt that war was going to happen despite Neville Chamberlain's return from Munich on 30 September with his message *Peace for our time*. This is partly captured in this film, where George Brown (George Formby), rejected by the *Home Guard* wants to join the *Royal Air Force* (RAF). A friend of his conveniently leaves behind some very important documents, which allows George to realise his dream of joining up. He puts on a RAF uniform and delivers the documents, mistaken for a dispatch driver from head office (HQ). He sings a mocking song about the Sergeant Major (SM) (Julian Mitchell), who retaliates by making George the butt of his jokes. This means he stays at the air base.

George falls in love with the SM's daughter Peggy (Polly Ward). When SM realises who George actually is, he threatens to report him. On the annual inspection day, George attempts to flee ending up inside a plane. With the inspector looking on, George's solo air plane display is memorable as he is the only passenger in a pilotless plane as it does 'loop-the-loop'. George manages to land the plane and is as a result accepted as a flyer by

---

[136] The Lancashire `*Evening Post*, 6 September 1938

the RAF. The SM actually insists he should be commended as he wants to cover the mistakes that have been made.

> Harry wrote one number, *It's in the Air,* which George sings it to Peggy. The verse conveys George's anticipation of change via a brisk quick march in the refrain. It is a deft combination of march and romance with room for George's banjolele solo on the refrain's repeat. The words and music of this were by Harry. The song was later adopted by RAF military bands and other forces as a WW2 battle song.

Penny Paradise

In her autobiography, Betty Driver remembers the ATP film *Penny Paradise* as the last Basil Dean made for Ealing Studios because his time would soon be taken up with the organisation of ENSA and more during the war years. Released on 24 September and written by Thomas Browne, Walter Needham and Thomas Thompson, it was directed by another co-writer Carol Reed, later famous for his film, *The Third Man*. Having launched the screen careers of both Gracie Fields and George Formby, Dean wanted to create one more 'stars'. He chose Betty Driver an eighteen year old, offering her a 5-year film deal. Looking like a young Gracie, she had a pleasant voice and warm personality and had already appeared as in music-hall singer and London revues.[137]

The film another typical scenario intended for Gracie opens with some action shots of Liverpool harbour. It is about a Liverpool tugboat skipper, Joe Higgins (Edmund Gwenn), who had top billing in this film, later becoming famous in films as Lassie the dog's master). He thinks he has won the football pools. He gives his job up and starts to celebrate his win by throwing a party for family and friends in the local pub. Some of these hope to get hold of a share of the winnings. He pays particular attention to a widow Clegg (Maire O'Neill) whom he fancies. His daughter Betty (Betty Driver) is propositioned by a rogue who thinks there is a chance of some money. The party stops altogether, when Pat

---

[137] Betty went on to become the long term favourite barmaid Betty Turpin in TV series *Coronation Street*

(Jimmy O'Dea), Higgins' Irish first mate on the tugboat has to admit that he forgot to post the winning coupon. Betty sorts out the problems of the elusive fortune and her own romantic mistakes at the same time. It closes with Higgins coming out even better than he hoped. His former employer offers him the captaincy of the best tugboat on the Mersey, a job he had always hoped to have.

While O'Dea's song is clearly provided for comic effect, Betty gets 3 songs by Harry to his own lyrics *Learn How to Sing a Love Song.* a slow romantic number and *Stick Out Your Chin* a light hearted brisk number and *You Can't Have Your Cake.* all for Betty. Ernest Irving and Gideon Fagan shared the music arranging for the film.

From 8 November there was another week at the *Empire Holborn* and on 10 November, Harry and Gracie with orchestral backing recorded Adam's well-loved song *The Holy City* and the *Biggest Aspidistra in the World* for Regal Zonophone.

On 13 November at the fund raising Annual Ball for the *Variety Artists Guild and Orphanage.* The next morning (14 November) Gracie with secretary Mary and Harry flew to Rotterdam, Holland doing 2 shows there as promotion for opening at the Grand Cinema of *We're Going to be Rich.*

On 15, they performed at the *Royal Variety Command Performance* on behalf of the Variety Artists *Benevolent Fund and Institution* at the *Palladium.* The artists included Max Miller, Florence Desmond, George Formby, Norman Evans. Will Fyffe was top of the bill after Harry had accompanied Gracie when she sang *Little Old Lady, The Organ The Monkey and Me* and *I Never Cried So Much in All My Life.* [138]

Other songs Harry wrote around this time were *The Sweetest Girl in the World* and one which had some popularity at the time, and *The Sweetest Sweetheart of All*, with words by Welsh-Greek musician songwriter. Jimmy Messini who proceeded to record it. It was then featured by duo Herman and Constance on a broadcast from *Central Pier Blackpool* and also played by Joe Kirkham and his band. Reminiscent in sentiment but less beguiling than the earlier *Mary Rose* this song comments about ageing motherhood. The tune is repeated in a second verse recalling the love for the old lady.

---

[138] *The Stage*, 18 November 1937

Off to USA again

After attending the *9ᵗʰ Annual Film Ball* at the *Royal Albert Hall* on 18 November. Next day, Gracie and Harry went down to Southampton to board the French luxury liner SS *Normandie* for New York to make appearances in USA as well as some time out over the Christmas period.[139] Marlene Dietrich was also on board. On arrival, they travelling on down to California, Harry is in the background likely accompanying Gracie as necessary

15 December received a golf badge from *Santa Monica Police Department*

17 December - a concert for the *Lancashire Society of California*, featuring the inevitable *She's a Lassie from Lancashire* and *The Holy City* (Gracie told the audience that Rochdale was my *Holy City*).

18 December at a party at the Trocadero hosted by Darryl Zanuck

After an undated appearance on the *Eddie Cantor Show*, (now previous misunderstandings with him ironed out) Gracie and Harry retired to the *Coachella Ranch*, near Palm Springs California for Christmas.

---

[139] Lassandro, Sebastiano, *Pride of Our Alley*, 2019, BearManor Media vol 1,9 354-362

CHAPTER 13

MUCH CHANGE (1939)

1939 was a not a year of unmitigated happiness for Gracie. Indeed it would bring major changes to the world as well.It also marked a busy time for Harry. now beginning to widen further his musical scope. Grace, Harry and Monty returned from California, travelling by train to New York, embarking on the French Line t luxury cabin cruiser *SS Champlain and* arriving at Plymouth on 4 February, then travelling on to Paddington.They quickly headed north

On 8 February at the *Theatre Royal* Newcastle accompanied by Gracie's mother. They went to see Dougie Wakefield her brother-in-law was appearing in *Cinderella*. Gracie was in a box and started repartee with Dougie on stage, resulting in an impromptu concert, when she sang *Umbrellas, Danny Bo*y and *The Biggest Aspidestra in the World* to the delight of the audience[140] It all ran over time so much that they left by the 1.30 am train to London instead of the 11.10 pm !

On Saturday 12 February, by concert probably in the Town Hall of Mountain Ash Glamorgan with Harry. Apart from *Little Old Lady, DannyBoy* and others Gracie sang to an estimated crowd of 10000 who joined her to sing *Sally in Our Alley.* She concluded by singing the first verse of the Welsh National Anthem, *Mae Hen Wlad Fy Nhadau* in Welsh. [141]

They both made another recording 17 February for Regal Zonophone featuring *Umbrella Man.* Almost immediately from 20 February, Gracie

---

[140] *Newcastle Evening Chronicle* 9 February 1939
[141] Lassandro, Sebastiano, *Pride of Our Alley*, 2019, BearManor Media vol 1 p 363

and Harry had a week's booking at *Empire* Nottingham filling in at short notice with a variety of performers, but as usual topped by Gracie, because when a circus had cancelled.[142][143]

During the stay there on 21 November, they travelled to Derby for Gracie to open the *Arthur Barlow* ward, an extension of *Derbyshire Royal Infirmary.*, promising to return after their show in Nottingham. They arrived at the Derby Assembly Rooms and started straightaway with Harry playing *Sally*, while the Mayor introduced the dancers there to Gracie. She followed on by singing *Umbrella Man, Mrs Binn's Twins, Music, Maestro, Please* and *Sally*. this was followed by more dancing.[144]

While there, Harry went with Gracie to visit a nearby mining community at New Ollerton on the afternoon of 24 February with a view have a look round and for fund raising for he *Ollerton Colliery Electrical Clinic* there. She said *her bit of knitting* to help things along was her singing at the *Ollerton Picture House*. With Harry at the piano, she gave the first British performance of a Cuban song *'Ay-de-day*. Harry commented that it was a big hit in America, *and Miss Fields thinks the song will be a big hit in England*. This was followed by *The Biggest Aspidistra in the World;* then she as ever up-to-date gave a selection from the Walt Disney film, *Snow White and the Seven Dwarfs*.' It ended with the inevitable *Sally*, before the film was shown, *The Queen of Hearts*.[145]

This was followed by a week beginning 7 March at the *Empire* Holborn.

Band Waggon.

On March 23, a Gainsborough film, *Band Waggon* was released. It was a vehicle for Arthur Askey and fellow comedian Richard (Dickie) Murdoch, the mainstays of BBC Radio series of broadcasts of the same name. It was directed by Marcel Vernel Basically a loosely framed road film, if mildly subversive, it allow ed for lots of comic incidents, solo spots for stars like

---

[142] Lassandro, Sebastiano, *Pride of Our Alley*, 2019, BearManor Media vol 1 p 386

[143] *The Stage, 23 February 1939*

[144] Lassandro, Sebastiano, *Pride of Our Alley*, 2019, BearManor Media vol 1 p 369

[145] *Daily Sunday Telegraph*, 25 February 1939

Patricia Kirkwood, and is finally spiced up with some anti-Nazi thriller business.

In the film because the comic pair are ignored by the BBC, they move off to Sussex, gathering other performers on the way. They all stop at a supposedly haunted castle which in fact houses television equipment capable of sending messages to the enemy. They hi-jack this for a broadcast of a variety show by Arthur and company which triumphantly blocks BBC transmissions to the nation.

Harry was the most notable of the group of composers who provided music, arranged by noted BBC broadcaster, Louis Levy. On 18 May, he brought Harry at *Gaumont Cinema* Lewisham to play *his brilliant little impromptu act, in which he (Louis), while Harry played Gracie Fields song numbers on the, piano Louis conducted the orchestra and led community singing.*[146]

His song *Heaven will be Heavenly* to sentimental lyrics from his current staple lyricists Barbara Gordon and Basil Thomas is a ballad in imitation Hollywood style. The recording made at the time features Pat Kirkwood (for whom it was written) and a chorus singing in a style which came to be known sarcastically as 'the MGM heavenly chorus'. In fact it is a very run-of-the–mill love song.

Shipyard Sally

Also early in the year, finishing before June, preparations for what would the last film of Gracie's for which Harry worked on musically were in hand. Its script was by Karl Tunberg, Don Ettlinger and its director was by Monty Banks for 20th Century Fox. It was a typical Gracie film with a social message of uplift for the workers. The plot shows how the years after the Depression have affected working people i.e. little money, poor morale. After footage showing activity on Clydeside, it shows an uncle (Sydney Howard) and niece (Gracie) a couple of failing music hall artists. Using her own money, Uncle buys a pub for her for the benefit of unemployed Clydeside shipyard workers. Gracie heads off to London to challenge the attitude of politicians and the shipyard owners. Her Uncle

---

146 *The Era*, 25 May 1939

keeps on bungling things, but she always rallies. She allows herself to be mistaken for an American singer/dancer, Linda Brown at a well-to-do reception.

She performs a jazzy number *I Got the Jitterbugs*, after that a Latin American vocal medley of dances written by Harry *In Pernambuco*, (indeed Gracie learnt the rumba for this section of the film).

The result is the building and launching of a new liner.and a cue for Gracie to sing *Wish Me Luck as You Wave Me Goodbye*. The film was released a month after war was declared on 16 October and it became with Vera Lynn's wartime songs one of the nation's war anthems. The song has words by Phil Park, who often supplied lyrics for Harry's work at this time. Harry and Phil Park were in the drawing room at Greentrees. Gracie wanted a new song-in fact another song of farewell for the film. Phil played a few notes on the piano. Harry lying underneath it remarked that it sounded like a bugle call (there had been one in *Sing as We Go*). Harry made this into the rallying beginning of the song's chorus. The introduction and verse Harry keeps to a minimum as if hurrying towards the uplifting and tantalisingly memorable refrain. This is a brisk swinging march constantly surging upward, being faster and more determined than the verse. After a brief contrasting section, it ends triumphantly. It seemed to sum up the response people to all that would happen in the immediate future.

For the rest of the year Gracie was enveloped by financial physical, emotional and marital difficulties. They were to have an effect on Harry as well as everyone else around her. First of all Harry's accustomed London refuge with Gracie's household at 'Greentrees' disappeared, when Gracie sold it to pay for accumulated unpaid income tax at the end of May.[147]

Harry played the organ for the wedding of Margaret Elizabeth Livsey, Gracie's housekeeper when she got married at Telescombe Parish Church Peacehaven on 4 June. Sadly Gracie was awaiting surgery. [148]Having felt unwell during the film shoot of *Shipyard Sally* Gracie was sent to have a biopsy. This showed cervical cancer. She underwent surgery to remove this as well as a hysterectomy as part of the treatment in 14 June 1939 at the

---

[147]   Fields, Gracie, 1960, *Sing as We Go, The Autobiography of Gracie Fields,* Frederick Mulle, p. 99

[148]   `*Rochdale Observer,* 7 June 1939

Chelsea Hospital for Women. Nearing 40, it meant farewell to her having any thought of having children in the future.

More important for her future happiness, the application for her divorce from Archie was presented on 22 July. This allowed Archie to marry Annie, and Gracie to marry Monty. A few days before she went off to Capri with Monty, to have some private time and still convalescing, she broadcast from the BBC a tribute to her audiences with Monty in attendance on 30 July. saying to Harry *Come on Harry, lad, do yer stuff* i.e accompany her on 30 July as she sang Paul Rubens 1917 song *I Love the Moon.* She recorded it with Harry on the next day 31 July.[149]

Later as a likely affectionate salute to Gracie while away, in 1940 Harry wrote unusually for him a purely piano (or orchestral) piece, *September in Capri, an Italian Picture.*

In fact for Harry the time he had spent so close to Gracie now was drawing to a slow end. Her interests and future choices allowed him to emerge more and more as a performer and composer in his own right. While Gracie was convalescing he kept on writing music, viz,. for 2 revues for George Black. Harry moved into *Grosvenor House Hotel.* This suited him as it was a hotel with a large ballroom, where resident band leader Sydney Lipton and his *Grosvenor House Band* played from c. 1931 to 1967. Dating from that time is a song, *The Pretty Little Quaker Girl.* by Harry to words by Roma Campbell-Hunter, Harry's regular lyricist at the time. It was recorded by 15 year old singer Celia Lipton, Sydney Lipton's daughter. She was hailed this side of the Atlantic as the 'British Judie Garland'.

> The naive sentiments expressed in this song were very much of an innocent age about falling in love. The verse questions how Quaker youths meets. A reply is received in the refrain of how a couple communicates, meets and weds. Harry provides a simple almost child-like gently flowing tune perhaps owing something to Lionel Monkton's popular musical *The Quaker Girl.*

---

[149]   *Aberdeen Press and Journal* 31 July 1939

CHAPTER 14

SECOND WORLD WAR AND BLACK REVUES (1939-40)

At the beginning of the Second World War i.e from 3 September 1939 onwards, all London theatres were closed as a sign of the national emergency. It was an unpopular move. A change in the Government's official attitude meant that by Christmas entertainment came to be seen as an essential morale booster. So, theatres in London and the provinces once again opened their doors.

George Black

George Black was a British theatrical impresario who controlled many entertainment venues during the 1930s. Born in Birmingham, he as a young man helped his father set up some of the first permanent cinemas in Britain. By 1928, he had taken over the management of *General Theatre Corporation*, a chain of theatres, cinemas and dance halls headed up the Corporation most important theatres, the *London Palladium* and *Hippodrome*. He rebuilt the latter in 1937. Both these theatres under Black during the next few years would play a significant development in Harry's life as a composer.

In 1931 Black organised *Crazy Week* there, gathering acts together which later grew into the *Crazy Gang*. He continued to promote shows and revues for them at the Palladium until his death. Many theatre programs of the 1930s had the words *Produced by George Black* on their cover. He presided over the merger of GTC with *Moss Empires* in 1932. This put him in control of a new company *Moss Empires Group* with a chain of 53 theatres. In 1937 and 1938, he directed two films; *The Penny Pool* and *Calling All Crooks*.

Harry now moved from being an effective writer of songs either for Gracie or others in films or for publishers, to writing for theatrical revues. He was required tomato a more sustained musical effort, i.e. compose musical sequences of different moods and tempos, suitable for the variety of characters in different situations, all in the one show. After Black's death in London in 1945, Val Parnell as will be seen, who had been his booking manager, took over the running of the Group.

British Revues

Revues had remained fairly popular throughout the 1930's and underwent a renewal during the war years, largely due to George Black promoting them as a superior variety concert with definite themes and popular artists from stage films and using the vital communication link BBC Radio. Noel Coward summarised very graphically putting a review together; *Writing for a revue is a difficult delicate art as is directing a revue..... A sketch for a revue must be quick, sharp, funny (or sentimental) and to the point with a really good exit line. The finale of the first half would already have been agreed upon, but all the numbers had to build, and build to the number before the finale and that number whatever it was had to be sure-free. The second number of the second half was, still is, and always will be, terribly important. It has to be strong, or so funny, or so spectacular or whatever that the audience ...... will be comfortably in their seats, happy in the knowledge that the second half is going to be even ore brilliant than the first.*[150]

---

[150] Noel Coward, p. vii in Raymond Mander and Joe Mitchenson, 1971, *Revue – a story in pictures* Peter Davies

Harry as one of the song-providers had to provide these highlights. His was a comparatively sudden appearance on the revue scene at the end of 1939 writing the music for 2 West End revues. This provided him with the opportunity of moving away from the more formulaic patterns of British popular music scene. He came to write solo songs of a more flexible structure, often with engaging melodies created with specific voices in mind. Responding to war-time feeling, his songs are often sentimental and nostalgic, at other times taking a quirky or comic turn. He was in preparation for dealing with the more extended requirements, which musicals would make of him from 1942 onwards.

Black Velvet

This revue subtitled *George Black's Intimate Rag.* was in 2 acts covering 18 scenes. It opened in 14 November 1939 at the *London Hippodrome*. The show's roster included Vic Oliver as a roving Master of Ceremonies, vocal impressionist Afrique, Teddy Brown (a 5' 2", 26-stone virtuoso xylophone player!), Pat Kirkwood, Roma Beaumont and Carol Lynne as the lead female beauties, the South African duo- Max and Harry Nesbitt and versatile bit-part actor, Cyril Smith. Black encouraged Harry to do the music. As usual, during 1941 it went on tour, being for instance at Nottingham Empire Theatre for 21 August.

> *Bubble Bubble* (lyrics by Roma Hunter-Campbell) was the introductory number sung by Patricia Kirkwood.

> Harry substituted *How Beautiful You are,* more sentimentally sophisticated when sung by rising star, Patricia Heywood. for the Shirley Temple song by Cole Porter, *My Heart Belongs to Daddy* which he disliked on the out-of-town preview in Brighton. This number is an expressive song (in E flat major to a slow fox-trot tempo). Its use of a repeated dissonance anticipates David Raksin's *Laura.* Harry simplifies the structure to an introduction and a long languorous melody. This ends with a coda extending a figure already heard in the introduction. Later

programmes reverted to the Porter song when out on post-London tour – cf. 2 week run beginning 20 May 1940 at *Empire Theatre* Newcastle.

The final number, written by Ralph Butler lyricist (of *Run Rabbit Run* and *Hey Little Hen,*) gave a comic song *Crash! Bang! I Want to go Home.* It closed the show and became a popular hit. It is basically a quick march with 2 strong beats in the bar introduction to start 'celebrating' the blackout to verses verging on the farcical. There are 3 refrains telling of the singers predicament (the rhythm is similar to Noel Gay's 1932 success *The Sun Has Got His Hat On,* (also with lyrics by Butler!), (Ironically Harry was during the war fined for breaching the black-out regulations !!) He in addition contributed a sung dance scene called *3 Shades of Blue* and more unattributed music for other scenes.

Debroy Somers and his Orchestra played the music which Summers arranged. The show ran for 620 performances and it put Harry among the popular musical elite of the day. As the curtain fell on the first night Black called his young composer to the front of the footlights telling the audience, *Here is a young man you'll hear a lot of in the future.* Perhaps the mantle of being only Gracie's pianist and composer was beginning to be cast off.

Come Out to Play

After a try-out in Stockport in November 1939, This typical lavish revue was written and devised by Eddie Pola and Peter Watson. The show was primarily a vehicle (with supporting cast) for comic compère Sonnie Hale, (who directed it) and for singer/dancer Jessie Matthews (his second wife). It included: *Palais de Danse* with Jessie Matthews as a professional dancing girl having to dance with inept partners as wells performing several other dance numbers; *For the Duration* was a burlesque on the

BBC's efforts at entertainment in the early war days; Sonnie Hale appeared as a tourist in Paris sampling absinthe for the first time., Peggy Rawlings as a policewoman in *Close Arrest* and as a *Glamour Girlie*. Other sketches included *Land Ladies*, a sketch lampooning aspiring society land-girls and a medley of music hall memories. It opened at *Phoenix Theatre*, London on 19 March 1940 (the day Monty and Gracie got married), closing in December. that year It subsequently went on national tour.[151]

Harry was among a group of lyricists and composers - Eddie Pola, Sonnie Hale, (also the director) and Ben Frankel. Harry contributed 3 items, the title song, *Come Out to Play, Things are Going to be Different* and *Lucky Me, Lucky You.*

> This last song for which Harry supplied words and music (again in E flat and 4/4 time) is a perky number, well suited to the light cabaret style of Matthews. It has a 5-bar introduction, picking up a down stepping phrase from near the end of refrain, which ends with a short flourish. The verse has 2 long phrases starting off-beat, but running along around the tonic. The 32-bar refrain continues with a more jaunty beginning, which settles into longer phrases to return in the last bars to key. Altogether more 30's in style with no undercurrent of yearning, but without the vigour Gracie gave Harry's songs.

Haw) Haw

Black's next wartime review was to be *Haw Haw*, which opened on 22 December 1939 at *Holborn Empire*. He wanted something loud, cheerful and *risqué* and above all he wanted was the very popular comedian Max Miller as chief crowd puller. Max Miller did a variety of character scenes. He burlesqued the treasonous William Joyce, (nicknamed Lord Haw Haw, who broadcast Nazi propaganda on the German overseas radio service and so became a figure of derisive fun nationally especially to radio listeners. Max followed this up with his own version of Hitler. Then he acted as an old

---

151   www, overthefootlights.co.uk> London Revues 1940-44

soldier, who had once slept in Anne Boleyn's bed and yet another soldier in the army trenches. Interestingly later Max Miller said that taking part in scripted sketches was not his cup of tea, preferring the stand-up gags he plundered from his blue joke book!

Added to all this was Bebe Daniels and Ben Lyon more lively entertainment featuring can-can dancers and tuneful songs which the public could take away with them. Haryy wrote 4 songs for the show. As *'Round and 'Round We Go, Ho-dle-ay Start the Day Right, It's wonderful* and *Your Company's Requested* This latter song in particular shows Harry at his peak. Phil Park's words sound mildly hallucinatory. After a calm verse the refrain is in a kind of schottische tempo, desiring and imagining the lover's presence. It emerges as a quirkily effective cabaret number.

The show proved, despite its provocative title a great variety favourite of the time and it stayed at the Holborn Empire.

Harry wrote words and music for this another waltz song which Gracie recorded, *Love Never Grows Old.* It is a gently flowing waltz, reminiscent of Romberg's *When I Grow to Old to Dream* giving a slightly faltering nostalgic effect to the words of reminiscence. The refrain follows the same kind of flowing tune with a strong 1st beat typical of 1930's waltzes. It was well-enough received to feature in 2 evening band concerts featuring dances, including waltzes at Woodvale Park, played by Reid Memorial Silver Band on 12 June, (it also played *Wish Me Luck, Crash! Bang! I Want to Go Home* and *There Always Be an England;* then in Alexandra Park Belfast on 15 August 1941 fby *Willowfield Unionist Silver Band*

American actors, husband and wife team, Ben Lyon and Bebe Daniels both with Hollywood experience behind them decided to stay in Britain on the outbreak of war. They were a popular couple, who played in the radio feature *Hi Gang.*

He wrote them a pleasant folksy nonsense number during 1939 *The Little Swiss Whistling Song* set to his own words. Like *A Catchy Little Tune* for Gracie and the later *Pedro the Fisherman,* it incorporates phrases for the singers to whistle. The Lyons do this well in their recording of the song. *The* introduction taken from the beginning of the refrain, is placed an octave higher to contrast with the ump-pah sound in the bass and mimicking the higher wind instruments in a pseudo-Swiss accompaniment. The verse has phrases telling why whistling is overtaking yodelling. The refrain launches into a strict time number, with cadences to whistle instead of yodelling. The middle section is in more varied time, before the repeat and snappy ending. The pair took part in the 1941 revue, *Gangway.*

CHAPTER 15

ENSA (1939-40)

At the beginning of the war Basil Dean the film director, together with spirited comic actor and producer Leslie Henson had founded the *Entertainment National Service Association* (ENSA) with its headquarters at Drury Lane Theatre. ENSA's object was to keep up the morale by inviting artistes of all types - comedians, popular singers, classical musicians - to travel out to whereever the forces were, either at home or abroad.

Many entertainers responded, including George Formby, Arthur Askey, Vera Lynn and of course Gracie. During the later part of the year, Gracie was still convalescing and Harry was in the middle of composing for his revues. Furthermore he was now required to register for the draft, in other words was 'called up'. He was to join the Irish Guards, where training for new recruits was to be held on Coulsdon Common, near Caterham, Surrey. [152]

Despite her needing further convalescence, she was asked by Basil Dean to go to entertain the forces out in France. Harry was of course being called up. She baulked at performing without Harry, so she put pressure on the military and he was deferred for a year. [153]

Thus the pair thus came back together. This reunion was compounded by further recordings for *Regal Zonophone* on 17 November., The programme was typical, Gracie sang to Harry's accompaniment *Wish Me Luck, Walter, Walter, When I Grow too Old,* and *Old Violin.*

---

[152] There is no archived record of Harry enlisting in the Irish Guards
[153] BBC Interview with 'Billie' David, 1990

They set off with Monty and Marry Barrett, Gracie's companion for France. Staying overnight in Folkestone before crossing the Channel. They arrived in North France south of Dunkirk. *It was bitterly cold and as we drove along the French roads, the car getting stuck in the mud and slush.*[154] When their vehicle broke down on the way, to the delight of troops already there Gracie stopped to give impromptu concert near Lens.

On Christmas, Day 1939, Gracie with Jack Payne and his Band, with Harry as usual at the piano gave a concert for RAF in *Rheims Opera House*, with a large imposing late Victorian front, but with an art deco interior. This concert was broadcast by BBC.

Gracie (and presumably Harry) returned to UK on 5 January as Harry travelled to Bristol to play solo in a Henry Hall variety concert at *Colston Hall* on 2 February.

At 12.30 pm, 7 February, for half an hour, Harry gave a *BBC Home Service* interview to Leslie Perowne, BBC Head of Light Music.[155] He describes Harry at this time as being tall dark and welsh, with horn-rimmed glasses and a cigarette in his mouth. During the interview Harry talked about the influences on his development in composing and playing music, Seymour Perrott, Sir Walford Davies, Gracie of course and Craxton and Farjeon. Various records were played, by way of illustrating, *I Hate You', Croon to Me, Love is Ev'rywhere* and other items from films. What is notable about Harry's speaking voice is how close it is to Perowne's, namely mainly standard clearly articulated BBC Kensington without any South Walian lilt. Occasionally there is very slight variation showing his Welsh background, but no more that his sister 'Billie' in later interviews. [156]

Gracie for her part went off to Capri for rest before her wedding to Monty, held in California on 19 March.

To France and Back

Gracie and Harry returned to France despite the *Phoney War* coming to its conclusion for a fortnight's tour there. During first week in April.

---

[154] Fields, Gracie, 1960, *Sing as We Go, The Autobiography of Gracie Fields*, Frederick Mulle, p. 138-9

[155] *Dundee Evening Telegraph, Derby Daily Telegraph* 5 February

[156] *Radio Times*, issue 853, 4-10 February 1940

they met up with Arthur Askey, and they did a show in the Paris Opéra on 25 April with Harry playing. They next day travelled north east to Valenciennes.close to the Dutch border Returning to Paris for more contact via concert to the troup, they were suddenly advised to return home. Harry, Gracie Monty and Jack Hylton were pushed as VIP's to the front of the boarding queue to get aboard a 4-engined De Havilland plane and landed at Northolt. From May onwards through to June the Germans were occupying France, surrounding British and French troupes, which of course lead to the Dunkirk evacuation.

On the 30 April safely returned home, they went to Drury Lane for the planned concert there;[157] then to the Brighton Hippodrome for the week beginning 1 June before [158]Gracie and Harry were quickly off to cross the Atlantic on their return to Britain.

[157] Lassandro, Sebastiano, *Pride of Our Alley*, 2019, BearManor Media vol 2 p 22-4
[158] *Worthing Gazette*, 5 June 1940

CHAPTER 16

WAR BRAKES OUT (1939)

Back home in Britain, *Black Velvet* started a provincial tour on 21 August at Nottingham *Empire* Theatre.

Top of the World

It opened in London on 4 September. For this Charles B Cochrane revue by George Black at the London Palladium, Harry joined with experienced composer Kenneth Leslie-Smith. His contribution was: *Alone with You, Fount of Wisdom, Love Stay in My Heart, My Kind of Music, My Wish,* * *We'll Go Smiling Along,* (words by Phil Park*) What Would You Do, Where the Blue Begins* *, Why Worry* *, Yet Another Day.* * [159] Essentially a vehicle for the Crazy Gang with Pat Kirkwood and Tommy Trinder, it was a sure recipe for success. The story line was somewhat topical about a barrage-balloon squadron where a balloon broke loose and drifted to another planet ruled over by an extra-terrestrial queen played by Pat Kirkwood. Although it opened on 4 September, due to heavy bombing it closed d 4 days later; the songs marked * were salvaged and used in 1944 musical *Jenny Jones*

> *Love Stay in My Heart* is one of Harry's most haunting melodies. After a slow introduction and verse, it moves into a Viennese waltz for its refrain. It looks forward to other waltzes in later musicals.

---

[159]   The numbers asterisked were salvaged and used again in *Jenny Jones*..

Gangway

Produced by Robert Nesbitt, the show premiered on 4 December 1940 had 8 items, an intermission and a further 9 items in a variety of sketches, solo acts and set dances. It featured Bebe Daniels and Ben Lyon, performers from BBC Radio series, comedian Tommy Trinder again, the husband and wife singing duo soprano Anne Ziegler and tenor Webster Booth. Harry contributed 3 numbers with lyrics by Barbara Gordon and Basil Thomas, plus a Chopin arrangement. Veteran songwriter Noel Gay had two songs and lyricist Phil Park one. The first two of Harry songs was the title song *Gangway,* for the company followed by a song for Daniels and Lyon, *You Annoy Me.*

A change in mood for the 4th item - a sketch called *Shangri-La.* features Webster Booth is cast as *The Wanderer* and Anne Zeigler as *His Heart's Desire*, surrounded by *Maidens of the Pool.* For this Harry provides the duo with *My Paradise.* A sumptuously romantic song, it starts off with a short loud introduction. The voice quickly enters its long line of melody, outlining his quest. The refrain is a tango (which would not be out-of -place for the Red Shadow in *The Desert Song).* It shows a mood of determination., changing its tempo and key until a climactic note which resolves into a repeat of the refrain. The sheet music puts it firmly in the tenor-high baritone range as a solo. The recording however which sounds as if taken directly from the show. It has a long entrance cadenza for Anne to sing rather shrilly before the verse gets under way with Webster's tenor entry. The tango refrain becomes an acceptably harmonised duet with Webster singing the harmony.

Harry also provided a vocal duet arrangement for them of a Chopin Étude, Opus 10. No.3, Tristesse *How Deep is the Night* as part of a medley of music popular at the time for the Act 1 finale. [160] The music for this revue was arranged by Debroy Somers, who conducted his own Orchestra.

---

[160] Cf.20 December HMV record D 9247, *So Deep in the Night.*

Sailors Three

This was an Ealing Studio's film vehicle for comedian Tommy Trinder released on 14 December. He portrays Tommie Taylor) in farcical situations similar to those in George Formby films. It was directed by Walter Ford and produced by Michael Balcon. Its screenplay was by Austin Melford a frequent writer of comic material, John Dighton and Angus McPhail. Made to seem semi-documentary, it featured a number of established and up-and-coming character actors: Jeanne De Casalis (Mrs Pilkington), Claude Hulbert (Llewellyn Davies 'The Admiral'), John Laurie (McNab), and Michael Wilding (Johnny Wilding). Music was composed and conducted by Ernest Irving with Harry and Noel Gay each contributing a song.

> Harry's song was to Phil Park's lyrics, *Singing a Happy Go Lucky Song,* yet another jollification song made for Trinder's bluffly cheery personality and voice.

Harry wrote another Capri song, published sometime during 1940, *My Capri Serenade* with a mild Latin flavour. It would be easy to read this to be from the words he wrote a lament for not being with Gracie any longer. With a slow Latin American beat, it has no verse, but a short introduction which is repeated throughout the song as a kind of musical mantra - *Play my Capri Serenade.* The whole vocal line is repeated, leading to a coda with a new phrase repeated to make a sustained climax.

More unexpected was another song *The Grandest Song of All* was a tribute to Her Majesty Queen Elizabeth with words by Phil Park *Here's to the Queen (God Bless Her).* This could well have stimulated by Her Majesty's *sang froid* in the teeth of her home Buckingham Palace being bombed on 13 September. It is very much in the British style of vocalised slow march, particularly reminiscent of Eric Coates and William Walton. After the slow introduction, the melody rises with sonorous chords. The verse is a slow almost ponderous melody. The refrain has a much more regular pattern, followed by drum roll pattern in the melody, before it returns to the first tune again, which is repeated with a brief roll-call.

For the New Year 1941 Harry wrote music for yet another new Black review.

Harry only seems to have written the one published song this year, the well written nostalgic *It Always Rains Before the Rainbow* to words by actor Gordon Orbell (a relative of Gracie's) and himself. The verse with some effective echoing effects has sentiments about the sunrise. The refrain in a fox-trot tempo takes up the title as prefiguring future hope for the future when the absent lover returns. For the next five years he wrote no more individual published songs, he was so busy.

CHAPTER 17

CANADA TOUR (1940)

The Dominion of Canada supported the UK and of course came to be actively involved in World War II. The *Naval League of Canada* formed in 1898 was now under its President D.H. Gibson. The league actively sought to operate 24 hostels in various port areas, such as the *Sea Gull Club* in Halifax as well the provision of amenities for both the *Royal Canadian Navy* and *Canadian Merchant Navy* supplying special clothing for visiting seamen. [161] Gracie and Harry were to enter on a fundraising tour for the League. Gracie paid all her own expenses and raised in the event £2000.

She had already arrived in Canada on 14 June. sailing on the Canadian Pacific Steamships ocean liner, *Duchess of Richmond*.[162] [163] To meet up with her, Harry boarded the *Canadian Pacific* liner, *the Duchess of Bedford* in Liverpool on 24 June 1940, bound for Montreal and on to New York. to met Monty and Gracie.

Gracie stopped over at Toronto give a couple of concerts *for the Canadian Red Cross*.[164] Doreen Berry from Toronto accompanied them as secretary for this tour. In Toronto a welcome was given by Mayor and populace on the afternoon of their arrival. The press focussed however on Johnny Weismuller visiting a hospital. Their indifferent attitude was further revealed. when Gracie (and (Harry) were only given a 15 minute spot in the concert. Harry smouldered with rage. *If it were me,* he said icily, *I'd give*

---

[161]   Cf. www.navyleague.ca
[162]   *The Argus* (Melbourne) 15 June 1940
[163]   cf. graciefields.org/housekeepers-secretaries etc.
[164]   *The Argus* (Melbourne) 15 June 1940

'em oompah oompah, stick it up your jumpah, and walk straight off. ....
Gracie more wisely remarked afterwards *I sang with all the confidence and
courage I'd been given that afternoon. I sang with everything I had in me to
give. At the end of fifteen minutes I just stood there and let the applause roll.
Then I went to my dressing-room.* Harry then timed the actual applause, it
lasted 10 minutes. He became very angry again. *You think of nothing but
your blasted audience.* Eventually he was soothed down.

Before starting the tour proper, the three went to Santa Monica California
to stay with her parents in the house she had bought for them They needed
a break. They then travelled up the west coast to British Columbia to do
the first concert in Victoria.They were about to embark on own exhaustive
tour of more than 30 concerts, arranged by ENSA Director Basil Dean,
moving west to east across Canada. This entailed a lot of travel by plane
and train, which tired both of them. Harry provided accompaniment for
the more unpredictable moments in her performance, although bands
also accompanied her and there were frequently other performers on the
programme. *Throughout the tour, Harry introduced Gracie to an advanced
form of 'Solitaire'* Harry provided his usual accompaniment skills for the
more unpredictable moments in Gracie's performances, although bands
also accompanied her and there were frequently other performers on the
programme. Frequently other performers appeared on the programme. as
at home - they were either locally available or were on tour at the time.

British Columbia

Their first venue was on 2 August on Vancouver Island at the 1913
Royal Victoria Theatre. Included in the show's roster was British film
personality Anna Neagle, who had gone to Hollywood after her success in
1939 in the *Edith Cavell Story,* She now changed to lighter musicals, like
Youman's *No No Nanette* (1940) and *Sunny* (released as recently as 10 May
1941). Harry accompanied Gracie of course, and perhaps Anna Neagle,
(he made later contact with her providing music in her British musicals
and films) as well besides playing in his own right. Also playing or this
event was the distinguished Canadian concert pianist, Gertrude Huntley
Green a past pupil of Moszkowski and Medtner. Finally, there was dancer
and choreographer, David Thiman, with Gracie topping the bill.

On 5 August, Harry and Gracie had moved to the mainland to Vancouver. Flying to North Bay Toronto on 7 August, they did a special concert for the *Toronto Star Fresh Air Fund* - a wide based charity started in 1877 in the USA with fund raising group on each side of the border to give holiday time to disadvantaged children - an aim close to Gracie's heart.

Alberta

The tour continued across sparsely inhabited country of variety and beauty. Flying to their destinations, they visited Rocky Mountain settlements and small towns in Alberta where they gave a concert *Jasper National Park* on 9 August to an audience of 66 guests, raising $1200. opening with *The Sweetest Song in All the World.* from her 1938 film. *We're going to be Rich.*

Moving south again, they gave a concert to the same number on 12 August in Banff at the *Springs Hotel.* raising the same amount again. On 13 August. there was a concert in Calgary followed by landing at Blatchford Field airport Edmonton to perform on 14 August in its open air *Arena.* There was *a record crowd of 1800 people with songs, dialogue and satiric patter.* Although Harry is not mentioned, he is likely to have been on the raised platform in front of the crowd for her as usual. *The audience included....... 1500 soldiers, sailors, airmen as well as nurses and wives of the men,.... Long before the 42-year old star of stage and screen appeared the call of "We want Gracie" echoed through the theatre. While they waited the ropes were entertained by the scarlet-coated band of the 2nd Balloon, Edmonton Regiment, the Kiwanis Glee Club, and noted Calgary Baritone Glyndwr Jones.* [165] Members of the *South Alberta Regiment* sang their own regiment song and other tunes, from WW1.

Gracie was introduced to the audience by area commandant, Lt-Colonel J C Brown with the usual noisy acclaim. She then began her8 numbers with *Sing as We Go,* followed by *Mrs Menzies' Twins.* and *The Woodpecker Song. After each song, rolls of applause echoed through the building..... All the troops joined with her in singing* When I Grow Old to Dream *and*

---

[165]   teacher at *British Columbia Institute for Music and Drama*

When Irish Eyes are Smiling. *Then she swung in to a humorous ditty* When are You Going to Lead me to the Altar, Walter? *in her high falsetto voice.*

The theatre was hushed as she sang the first verse of There'll Always be an England, *then everybody joined in. They sang it through twice and meant every word of it.*

Dressed in a replica of the uniform worn by men of the South Alberta Regiment, *11-year old Doris Thomas..... walked from the wings to present Fields with two bouquets of multi-coloured sweet peas. Fields accepted the flowers from the ladies 'auxiliary of the* South Alberta Regiment, *and by the* Edmonton Garrison. She sent them to soldiers' wing of the University Hospital. After singing *Sally,* she left, signing autographs at the stage door. [166] This newspaper account gives good idea of the typical reception grace received on this tour.

Saskatchewan.

Continuing eastwards they gave a concert at the *Major Forces' Training Centre, Dundurn Army Camp* at Saskatoon. and then in the indoor wooden Arena. On 16 August they arrived Regina to give a concert for a local branch of the Navy League. on 17 August at the large brick built Armouries building[167]

She told them she was going to appear at the *Massey Hall* for the *Navy League* and proceeded to give 5 concerts there. Later during a radio interview, Gracie told the interviewer that Harry had been her accompanist for 10 years. He in a finicky frame of mind, felt compelled to correct her and the interviewer by saying it was nine and a half years. *So you want to split hairs.*

Continuing eastwards they gave a concert at the *Major Forces' Training Centre, Dundurn Army Camp* at Saskatoon; on 16 August arrived Regina for 17 August concert for a local branch of the Navy League.[168]

---

[166] *Edmonton Journal.* Chris Zdeb, 15 August 2015, Aug 15, 1940; *Record Arena crowd spellbound by Gracie Fields,* The accompanying photo shows only the front of the platform.

[167] from concert programme

[168] from concert programme

Manitoba

Crossing to the next state, on 17 August they gave a concert in Brandon. [169] This was followed on 18 August, travelling 35 kilometres east of Brandon to Shilo - another Canadian Army facility - to participate in a concert with the local Scottish Piper Band. Returning to Toronto, but for a different charity, 6 concerts were given at the *Massey Hall* from 4 to 9 September. - each night was a sell-out. Later during a radio interview with them both, Gracie told the interviewer that Harry had been her accompanist for 10 years. He was still in a finicky frame of mind and felt compelled to correct her and the interviewer by saying it was nine and a half years. *So you want to split hairs. Yes,* Harry shouted, childishly for all the radio network to hear.[170] *He also grumbled about the poor quality of the pianos.*

Quebec

They moved north east on towards Quebec, via Peterborough, appearing there at the *Armouries* in 10 September.[171] Almost inexorably, they moved on 11 September to Kingston, [172] followed by concerts on 13 and 15 September at the *Auditorium* in Ottawa. Gracie was warned that Ottawa audiences were cold. She laughed and said she would be scared. On the Thursday afternoon of her arrival, however, she quipped, to the paparazzi, *I have 2 real cousins in Toronto and about 15 in Edmonton that I think may be cousins!*

Sir Gerard Campbell, the `British High Commissioner for Canada presented Gracie to the audience saying she was here in aid of the Navy League, remarking on other splendid work in England and France in entertaining the troupes.

Any initial chilliness faded with the vocal acrobatics of her first song and dissolved in mirth at her second. Assisting Miss Fields ....were members of "Let's Go to the Music Hall Group" and the Royal Canadian Mounted

---

[169] probably in the Westminster United Church with its magnificent acoustics

[170] Gracie Fields, *Sing as We Go, The Autobiography of Gracie Fields, 1960,* Frederick Muller p. 148

[171]

[172] likely to have been at the *GrandTheatre*

Police Band under the leadership of Inspector J T Brown and of course Harry. She called the band *lads in red jackets*, made her pearls choke her in the middle of a bar, then after a lot of applause told the audience *it's the first time here, but I tell you it won't be the last.*

She entered into a more serious phase, with Harry accompanying her, and after trills and runs, came to a dead stop. *i bet my mother couldn't do that* continuing the song to the end. then followed *The Biggest Aspidistra in the World* performed with her usual vocal and body antics. The list of numbers continued with *Walter* (she invited the audience to sing with her), *Kerry Dances, the Organ, the Monkey and Me,* interspersed with comic recitation in dialect, a Negro spiritual, *'No More Plowin'*

At the close of the evening, Gracie asked the hall to sing with her a number of the old favourites which she had sung to the boys in France 'When Irish Eyes are Smiling', 'Love's Old Sweet Song' and others. Harry unusually gets an honourable mention *Songs and patter were framed by Gracie were framed in a delightful music al background provided by Harry Parr Davies at the piano who gives splendid support.*

There were dance numbers from Jimmy Devon and Irene Hughes and more songs from Yvonne Miller. At the end of the evening Gracie linked arms with other artists including the *Let's Go to the Music Hall Group,* singers Pat Rafferty and 'Red' Newman, in acknowledgement off the applause.[173]

Finally, when the pressmen came to her and Harry in the hotel suite. she was playing solitaire. *I play it all the time, but it very seldom comes out,* she lamented. *Mr Davies (her pianist) plays it too and has better luck, because he cheats. She refused any more invitation s to perform in Ottawa, because she was so weary.* She entered into a more serious phase, with Harry accompanying her, and after trills and runs, came to a dead stop. *i bet my mother couldn't do that* continuing the song to the end.; then followed *The Biggest Aspidistra in the World* performed with her usual vocal and body antics. The list of numbers continued with *Walter* (she invited the audience to sing with her), *Kerry Dances, the Organ, the Monkey and Me,* interspersed with comic recitation in dialect, a Negro spiritual, *'No More Plowin'*

At the close of the evening, Gracie asked the hall to sing with her a number of the old favourites which she had sung to the boys in France

---

[173] This rambling article in Ottawa Journal of 13 September 1940 has been abridged by author. Original text in Italics

'*When Irish Eyes are Smiling*', '*Love's Old Sweet Song*' and others. Harry unusually gets an honourable mention *Songs and patter were framed by Gracie were framed in a delightful music al background provided by Harry Parr Davies at the piano who gives splendid support.*

Ontario

They went on 17 September to former mining town of Schumacher; (now part of the city of Timmins) in the *Macintyre Community Building.* Then they were three nights 19-21 September in Montreal. Going back west a little to Ottawa, they performed in concerts for an audience 14000 on 22 September. hey moved on to do concerts on 22 at Kitchener.

New Brunswick

For the final stage of their tour in New Brunswick, they moved on 24 September at the Mechanic's Institute in St John on the bay of Fundy; on 25 at Moncton High School on 25. They went on to the peninsula state of Nova Scotia on 27 they gave a concert in Sydney and two concerts on 27 at Glace Bay Miner's Forum.

Nova Scotia

Crossing the Cabot Strait they came on 29 to Capital Theatre, Halifax to end this tour. They to date had raised £99, 306 : 48d [174]

---

[174]   Lassandro, Sebastiano, *Pride of Our Alley*, 2019, BearManor Media vol 2, p 52-3

CHAPTER 18

USA TOUR (1941)

Leaving St Croix, New Brunswick on 30 September, they crossed the river St Croix into the USA at small town of Vanceboro, Maine where the USA Canada custom post had been there from 1871. Harry and Gracie were to embark on another busy whirlwind concert tour of USA during 1941 They went to Gracie's parents in Santa Monica

Flying in from Los Angeles, the first USA concert featuring them both was at the Salt Lake City Tabernacle on 6 December [175] Utah

They flew from Los Angeles on Friday 3 December up to Salt Lake City. About 100 people greeted Gracie and they joined her in war songs, such as *Wish me Luck* and *There'll Always be an England*.[176] The next night, they were at the Latter Day Saints (Mormon) Tabernacle, sponsored by the Utah chapter of the *British War Relief*, providing the usual songs. After the Christmas period they started the tour in earnest.

Los Angeles

On 14 January , they were at the *(? Mason) Opera House* in *A Night at the English Music Hall.* sponsored again by the *English Speaking Union for bombed children of the British Isles.*

---

[175] *Salt Lake City Tribune* 4 December 1940
[176] *Salt Lake Telegram*, 30 November 1940

Lincoln, Nebraska

On 7 March 1941, a concert was given by Gracie, with Harry accompanying, as a Benefit for the *Relief of Bombed English Children* in Lincoln Nebraska, presented by the *English Speaking Union* in *Lincoln. University Coliseum* at 8pm. [177]

March 8 they gave a number of concerts in Dallas Texas

Then more concerts:-

12 March in Youngstown Ohio [178]

18 March at Salt Lake ITabernacle, Utah

24 March at Oakland Auditorium 1

26 March at the Shrine Auditorium, sponsored by the *Lancashire Society of Los Angeles*

Ogden, Utah

They were at Ogden, about 100 miles north of Salt Lake City on 22 March at 8.30 pm at the auditorium of the High School Ogden under the auspices of *Bundles for Britain*[179]

24 March -Back to California to the massive Oakland Auditorium

26 March and the *Shrine Auditorium*, Los Angeles

17 April Toledo Ohio, probably in the Valentine Theatre;

Oakland

Arriving by plane at 5.20 pm on Sunday 23 April at Oakland airport where she was greeted by members of by the *Bay District Lancashire Society*, who are sponsored the concert and taken to her hotel. The next evening *Oakland Municipal Auditorium* greeted them for a concert held by the *English Speaking Union*, Jess Stafford and his Orchestra and

---

[177] *Lincoln Nebraska State Journal*, 7 March 1941

[178] Laasendro doesn't specify which Youngstown, presumably the one in Ohio.

[179] *Ogden Standard Examiner*, 20 March

the *Caledonian Bag Pipe Band*, ballet troupe an others were featured with Gracie, accompanied by harry doing her usual songs and some in Lancashire accent, but topped the bill with *Wish Me Luck'*. [180]

New Jersey

Harry and Gracie gave a concert in *Carter Theatre* Princeton New Jersey for the same cause starting at 8pm on 25 April. The concert started with *God Save the King* and *Star Spangled Banner'* played by the *Princetown High School Orchestra*. There was music from the *Philadelphia Ulster Pipe Band*. Gracie was given 2 solo spots, accompanied by Harry. [181]

14 May at the *War Memorial Opera House* in San Francisco again for British relief
15 May New York to the Madison Square Gardens [182]

Back Home

Criticised by the British press again, this time for not spending more time in Britain touring, and after some difficulty getting an approved flight home, Gracie (probably with Harry and Monty) left New York to fly to Lisbon, boarding RAF plane to London, arriving on 8 July. Gracie went off on a whirlwind tour, but without Harry, Ivor Newton would now play for her during on a hectic 6 week tour of Britain, finishing at the Albert Hall (see below next chapter). He had to go through the process of joining the army.

[180] *Oakland Tribune 24 April 1941*
[181] Princetown Daily Princetownian, 25 April 1941
[182] Lassandro, Sebastiano, *Pride of Our Alley*, 2019, BearManor Media vol 2, p.

CHAPTER 19

'TROOPER' DAVIES (1941)

The close working relationship between Harry and Gracie maintained during 1940 in France Canada and USA was entering a final phase. The delay from his doing compulsory national military service now came to an end.

An application for enlistment 1 August was sent to the *War Office* from Lieutenant-Colonel Francis Gordon Lane Fox, Scots Guards, Household Cavalry Motor Training Battalion at the Hyde Park Barracks. He wrote:-

Harry Parr-Davies

Authority is required please for the enlistment of the above-named man into the Band of the Life Guards. He has been medically examined and graded A.2., which precludes him from enlisting into the Household Cavalry under the existing regulations.

As this man is an accomplished musician(he in fact Composer an Accompanist to Miss Gracie Fields), I fell that his service would be an asset to my band and, although there is no vacancy in the Band at the moment, I am prepared to transfer an A.I man from the Band to duty.

I should be grateful if this matter could be treated as urgent

(SD.) F LANE FOX [183]

---

[183] *Household Cavalry Museum and Archive Records* of Harry's enlistment August 1941

The process to enlist him had been started by Captain Albert Lemoine, the Band's Director of Music from 1938. He wished to incorporate able musicians into the Band. Two other musicians came from the London Symphony Orchestra, - Jock Ashby, its principal trombone and Dennis MacManson, violinist.

On 13 August 1941, Harry now 27 years of age was enlisted (as no. 295736) and posted to *His Majesty's Lifeguards under Lemoine. Captain Lemoine, now with the opportunity of enlisting top civilian musicians, transferred four junior members to line regiments to create vacancies. One of the new intake was Harry Parr Davies. ... Musician Parr Davies was highly thought of by Captain Lemoine and was given the doubtful privilege of being permitted to smoke during rehearsals.*

Harry gave his address at the time, not as a London hotel nor at Swansea with his family but Penmaen Hall, a small residential Hotel on the Gower Peninsula, where he had gone for peace and quiet to work on his music.

As it turned out his army residential base was handily in Knightsbridge. In addition he remained close to the West End for whatever revue (or later musical) he was in the process of seeing safely launched on the stage. Nationally and locally, they were important morale boosters not only for the beleaguered Britain.

Harry in trooper uniform with Gracie at Albert Hall

Even before he started an initial drill training of 5-6 in weeks, he was playing at a concert in aid of the *Red Cross* in the Albert Hall on 17 August with different bands and popular soloists. Gracie sang as top of the bill, accompanied by Harry now listed as a Trooper. Almost symbolic of the future, during Gracie's recital Harry exchanged places with the brilliant concert pianist. Ivor Newton. [184]

As he was not part of the mounted section of the band, he had no need of further cavalry training. Indeed Harry at this point of his career was rather devious. He booked in at the *Dorchester Hotel,* bribed a Corporal to clean his boots and buttons. This stopped of course when his Colonel-in-Chief found out. [185]

A decision was made to move the Life Guards:-_In late 1941 the Band moved west to Combermere Barracks, Windsor, but still carried out engagements in the London parks and seaside resorts, now wearing the drab khaki battledress. [186] The band produced gramophone records during the war. Furthermore, they broadcast frequently throughout the war on the BBC Home and Forces Programme and later on the Light Programme.

After joining up, the earliest broadcast he could have been involved as a member of the Band was at 2-2.30 pm 2 October on the BBC Forces programme. Such a half-an-hour spot was typical. However, Harry was ill during November, which meant a re-scheduling of 7 November BBC Forces Programme until later 21 November.[187] Then he made a BBC Home Service at 9.20 *The Story of Gracie Fields* with Bert Aza. [188]

Gangway

Early in the next year Harry was involved with yet another new Black review, which was first played at the small Ambassador's Theatre, Charing Cross Road on 9 March 1942.

[184] Lassandro, Sebastiano, *Pride of Our Alley,* 2019, BearManor Media vol 2, p. 63-4/8

[185] Gracie Fields, *Sing as We Go, The Autobiography of Gracie Fields*, 1960, Frederick Muller p. 108

[186] George R Lawn, 1995, *Music in State Clothing the story of the Kettledrummers, Trumpeters and Band of the Lifeguards*, Lee Cooper, p.45 and 6

[187] *Nottingham Evening Post*, 7 November

[188] *Yorkshire Evening Post*,21 November; *Radio Times* 2-8 November 1941

It was produced by Robert Nesbitt with a variety of sketches, solo acts and set dances of 8 items, an intermission and a further 9 items. It featured Bebe Daniels and Ben Lyon, performers from BBC Radio series, popular comedian Tommy Trinder, the singing duo Anne Ziegler and Webster Booth. Harry contributed 3 numbers with lyrics by Barbara Gordon and Basil Thomas plus an arrangement. Veteran composer Noel Gay wrote 2 songs and former lyricist Phil Park one. Two of Harry's songs opened the show – the title song *Gangway*, for the company followed by a song for Bebe Daniels and Ben Lyon *You Annoy Me*.

> A change in Mood for the 4ᵗʰ item – a sketch *Shangri-La*. where Webster Booth is cast as the Wanderer and Anne Zeigler as His Heart's Desire, surrounded by Maidens of the Pool. For this Harry provides the duo with *My Paradise*. A sumptuously romantic song, it starts off with a short loud introduction and the voice quickly enters its long line of melody, outlining his quest. The refrain is a tango, which would not of been out-of -place for the Red Shadow in *The Desert Song*, its melody making the mood one of determination, changing tempo and key until a climactic note. This resolves into a repeat of the refrain.

> The sheet music puts it firmly in the tenor-high baritone range as a solo. The recording however sounds as if taken directly from the show has a long cadenza for Anne to sing rather shrilly before the verse sets under way with Webster's tenor entry. The tango refrain becomes an acceptably harmonised duet with Webster singing the harmony.

He also provided a vocal duet arrangement for them of a Chopin Étude, Opus 10. No.3 Tristesse *How Deep is the Night* as part of a medley of music in the Act 1 finale. [189]

---

[189] Cf.20 December HMV record D 9247, *So Deep in the Night*.

Again the music was arranged by Debroy Somers who conducted his Orchestra. It had its London premiere on 17 December at the much larger London Palladium with 534 performances until 24 October 1942.

Harry on occasion featured as a soloist with the military band or more likely played as part of the dance band formed from its members, when not involved with ENSA and Gracie.

> True to form, he penned a couple of songs - one by his former lyricists, Roma Campbell-Hunter, *Lonely Serenade*. This ballade was featured by Lew Stone who led a 7-piece band at the Dorchester Hotel. It is a typical waltz tune of the time in C for the verse, Harry provides a repeated rocking motif. Unusually for Harry, he changes to another key (F) for its refrain ending on its repeat with a partly hummed, partly sung final 8 bars.

> Similarly, he finds another way of using the contemporary idiom, where he asks for the refrain to be 'in a ballad style' in *It Always Rains Before the Rainbow*. Gordon Orbell (Gracie Fields brother in-law) and Harry provide the conventionally uplifting lyrics. He opens the phrases echoed an octave higher. He repeats this eco effect when the voice enters. This leads by contrast into a more strict tempo refrain which is similar to earlier upbeat numbers for Gracie.

CHAPTER 20

HM LIFE GUARDS BAND AND WEST END (1942)

Once 1942 was ushered in, Harry was busy with a round of films, revues and as well as band duties and was at the height of his powers compositionally and pianistically. The Band's Broadcasts on BBC while Harry was enlisted with them usually lasted 30-45 minutes. As they do not include programme details, it is can't be known whether Harry played during any particular broadcast. However they do not clash with other known dates where he was performing other than band duties. For instance there was a half-hour Band concert on BBC Forces Programme on 12 February.

Happidrome

Harry contributed lyrics to the stage version of the radio comedy show *Happidrome* put on `at the *Prince of Wales Theatre*. This was produced by Jack Buchanan. It starred Mr. Lovejoy (Harry Korris) the theatre proprietor Ramsbottom (Cecil Frederick) his stage manager, Enoch (Robbie Vincent) the gormless call-boy, plus Leslie Hutchinson (as himself) and "Two Ton" Tessie O'Shea, another virtuoso ukelele player a kind of female George Formby. This had as musical director Paul Fenouhlet who also wrote some of the songs.

It had a longer than usual out of West End try-out, appearing on 23 November at *New Cross Empire*. Harry wrote 2 songs for Hutch to sing as a guest performer in a variety programme in the farcical stage helter-skelter background to the show a pleasant enough slow fox-trot in Harry's more automatic style, tailored for Hutch's voice and range *You are My Love Song*. This is followed as a mild contrast by a brighter quick-step, *Take the World Exactly As You Find It*. It was filmed by MGM and released on 11 March 1943 as 'Boys in Blue' 3

Full Swing

At the end of 1941, despite axis hostilities being at their height, Harry was invited to develop further his musical range, his first musical(since the *Curfew* in his youth. Joining experienced fellow composers George Posford and Kenneth Leslie-Smith, Harry contributed the lion's share of songs. Posford did 2 and Leslie-Smith did 1 to Harry's 7 numbers, therefore not the full score as in many subsequent musicals. The lyricists were Barbara Gordon and Basil Thomas.

Under the management of Tom Arnold and Lee Ephraim with costumes by Doris Zinkeisen, it opened for the usual provincial test run at the *Opera House*, Blackpool 18 February 1942. It moved then for 2 weeks of performances to Liverpool, 2 in Manchester, 2 in Glasgow before returning to Blackpool on 11 April. It quickly transferred on 16 April to *London's Palace Theatre* for a successful run of 468 performances, closing on 29 May 1943. This musical was created primarily to showcase the lively West-End husband and wife comedy partnership, Jack Hulbert (Jack Millett) and Cicely Courtneidge (Kay Porter) They played a married film star team, playing the same characters from a earlier success, *Under Your Hat* which had music by Vivian Ellis. The script in this musical as in the earlier show gives them scope to enter into a number of disguises when they are set to work on an implausible secret mission for the War Office. This involves tracking down state secrets and missing dossiers of villainous Dr. Carlos in Rio de Janeiro, where most of the musical is set. Harry provided the title song *Full Swing* for the Hulberts on stage at the Palace Theatre, London – they used the device of a theatre in a theatre – and again in the finale scene is placed in the Estoril Theatre in Rio.

Harry wrote 2 comic numbers for Jack Hulbert, *Shopping,
Eating and The Nine O'Clock News* and *You Only Want
It 'Cos You Haven't Got It*. The latter is a witty and lively
song, basically the well-tried formula of an introduction,
comic verses and a tag-like refrain incorporating the title.
With lyrics from Max Kester and Barbara Gordon, Harry
gives Cecily, *Music Makes Me Mad*. For Gabrielle Brune
(Sally) he has 3 songs to lyrics by Barbara Gordon and
Basil Thomas *Follow My Dancing Feet*. A charming tale
of uplift is provided by a songbird, which causes the singer
to start dancing in the refrain to a folk-like tune, saying
how beneficent nature is to tunes reminiscent of earlier
folk songs like *Over the Hills and Far Away*. Then there
was *Love is Love Everywhere* and *Mamma, Buy Me That* -
a kind of torch song with an apparently innocent child-like
pseudo-classical beginning, with some ominous phrases
in the bass-line. This moves into the refrain which is
song absolutely about getting what you want, the insistent
ironic style akin to Kurt Weill's *The Saga of Jenny* in
the musical, 1941 *Lady in the Dark*, but made somehow
typical of Harry at his wittiest.

After this, the show again went on provincial tour during early 1944
with Jack Warner and Marie Marion in the Hulbert leads. [190]

During 1942, he was given a London posting, which meant he could be
nearer the heart of the West End scene. He possibly bought his mews flat
11 Harriet Walk, Knightsbridge around this time in order to have a place
of his own. With regards to future musicals, Harry would provide complete
scores on his own, except for a Cicely Courtneidge vehicle in 1949. In
addition to this first musical, Harry now collaborated on two more revues,
wrote a song for a film and another for inclusion in a musical revival in
addition to any required band duties.

---

[190]   Kurt Ganzl, 1986, *The British Musical Theatre* 1915-1984, Macmillan Press,
        p. 516-7/520-1

Big Top

The first revue was another Charles B Cochrane very extensive production in 25 scenes in 2 parts. after a provincial try-out as usual, starting at Royal Court Theatre, Liverpool on 18 March, it opened on 8 May at *His Majesty's Theatre* London. It had all-rounder singer-actress Patricia Burke with established favourites - in particular Fred Emney, Australian character actor and singer, Cyril Ritchard with his wife and long time partner Madge Elliott, Gretchen Franklin and especially transatlantic comedic performer Beatrice Lillie and a young Pearl Carr in bit parts, (who later teamed up with Teddy Johnson as the popular vocal duo).

Harry as usual was one of several contributors of music including Nicholas Brodzsky and Geoffrey Wright (with whom Harry wrote the opening song *Getting Rid of It* to lyrics by Herbert Farjeon). His more usual lyricists at this time Barbara Gordon and Basil Thomas and they wrote the other words in the show for Harry's songs. In Scene 3, *Tin Pan Alley*, there was *Pluggers Lament* for Patricia Burke. He had nothing more until Part II, Scene 19, quickly paced *Hey Ho* for Patricia Burke and singers Cyril Ritchard, Madge Elliot.

> The next scene 20, *the Lady in Grey*, featured one of the best of Harry's more serious songs for Beatrice Lillie., *Wind Round My Heart*. The verse meditates on the winter weather which chimed in with singer's mood of isolation. The refrain is more dynamic about the wind portrayed as emotional pain with restless changes of tempo and key and the restless harmonic shifts which are particularly effective. Not to lose the intensity, the refrain is not repeated. The song subsides on a long held note.

For scene 24, he gives Patricia Burke a song with a male chorus *When I Hear Music*. There was much additional music from USA and elsewhere arranged by Ben Frankel, the distinguished composer who conducted the Orchestra.

Captain Thornberrow conducted the Life Guards at Jephson Gardens in Leamington Spa on 29 May with many band members playing solo including Harry on the piano [191]

Suspected Person

This was an *Associated British Picture Corporation* thriller.film released in June 1942. Following a $50,000 bank New York Robbery, suspects Franklin (Robert Beatty) and Dolan (Eric Clavering) are acquitted by a USA court. They journey to England in the belief that the money is in possession of crook-turned-reporter Jim Raynor (Clifford Evans). He has tried to exchange it from dollars to sterling. Inspector Thompson of Scotland Yard (David Farrar) knowing the suspects are in Britain, goes undercover by moving into Raynor's apartment let by Raynor's sister, Joan (Patricia Roc). Harry provided a song *Every Night at Seven*. This is a typically film noir night-club slow swing number, like David Raskin's *Laura* to words by Barbara Thomas.

> It is a simple piece in structure, simply introduction, no verse or refrain just a long melody in which the words *Every Night at Seven* of the title are repeated as a kind of mantra. Such a well-crafted song shows how Harry was developing his compositional techniques. The song deserves to be better known.

Bedford

The aim of the Band's activity was to keep morale up among the public therefore, besides all his compositional activity, Harry appeared as a soloist with the Band Firstly he appeared with them at the Granada Cinema Bedford on 26 July.

---

[191] *Leamington Spa Courier*, 29 May 1942

Cheltenham

Then he was at the Gloucestershire festival from 2 to 8 August held in the gracious Montpellier Square Cheltenham. *The Band of His Majesty's Lifeguards* gave concerts conducted by Lieutenant-Colonel Albert Lemoine (their Bandmaster from 1938 to 1959) on Sunday 2 August and each afternoon, Harry played the solo piano part in Richard Addinsell's popular wartime piece *The Warsaw Concerto.* [192]

This was followed by two days as part of a *Military Band Festival* at Jephson Gardens Pavilion at Leamington Spa, where there was a 3pm and 7 pm concerts. *HM Royal Marines Band* were on Sunday to Tuesday, (30 August-1 September) *HM Life Guards* were playing on Wednesday and Thursday, (2 and 3September) with Harry as solo pianist followed by the prestigious Kneller Hall Band on Friday to Saturday 5-7 September.

At 8 until 11 pm of the Wednesday the Dance Orchestra of HM Guards played at the Leamington Town Hall for a 'Military Ball'.[193] Harry may well have played for this also. He was granted leave for a week from 14 to 21 September, whether this was holiday due to him or some bout of illness, the purpose is not given in his record.[194]

Performing Rights Society

He was elected to the committee of the *Performing Rights Society* to replace Arthur Tate, who had retired due to ill-health and is remembered chiefly for the charming ballad *Somewhere a voice is calling.* [195] The Performing Rights Society had been formed in 1914, by publishers Boosey and Hawkes to protect the rights of musicians lyricist and publishers. Harry could well have joined the Society in early 1930's. There was Band recording, this time for Columbia, done on 21 October with a two-part title, *Tommies Tunes.*

---

[192] *Cheltenham Chronicle*
[193] *Coventry Standard*, 29 August 1942
[194] Household Cavalry Museum and Archive Records of Harry's service
[195] News in brief, 7 August 1942

There was an early press notice in October that Harry was to provide music for a spoof mediaeval musical with the title *Kiss the Girls*. [196]

Best Bib & Tucker

This revue opened on 7 November [197] at the London Palladium in the usual 2 acts, with 6 scenes before intermission and 7 after. It was developed by Black as a vehicle for self-centred comedian Tommy Trinder. It was notable for Trinder's 'take off' of Carmen Miranda (Carmen Minranda!); - a song *No, No, No, Columbus,* written by Val Guest with Edmundo Ross and his orchestra in a Cuban setting. Comic stalwart Nat Jackley Jack Clifford and the Cairoli provided individual acts of humour. and Harry provided the music for the 2 opening numbers, the title song and *Gentlemen of Leisure.* There was a stylistic survey of American musical style in song and dance from black Afro-American music, Sousa marches and the blues. This was followed by another scenario with music by Herman Finck and based on the Rev. Richard Harris Barham classic Victorian poem, *the Jackdaw of Rheims.* The whole revue ran for 490 performances.

HM Life Guards Band recorded Columbia DB 2081 *Tommies Tunes* in 2 parts and gave a further concert for BBC Forces Programme at 10-30 -11pm on 12 December.

Belle of New York

This was a revival of this early American musical by Emile Littler which opened on 23 December 1942 at the London *Coliseum,* featuring Edith Stamp-Taylor and Evelyn Laye, the female lead. Harry was one of two who provided music, his being an insert waltz song, *Love Alone Will Remain* for the heroine. It is a quiet exposition of contented love for Evelyn Laye.[198]

A period of more easy going rest was not to be.his. Unfortunately 1943 saw even more activity for Harry on all fronts, films, musical and band programmes.

---

[196]   *The Stage* 15 October 1942
[197]   *The Stage, 12 November 1942*
[198]   Radio Times, Issue 992, 4-10 October 1942

CHAPTER 21

3 NEW MUSICALS (1943)

1943 saw even more activity for Harry on all fronts, films, musical and band programmes.

We'll Meet Again

Released by *Columbia British Productions* on 18 January 1943 in UK, this was an unsophisticated showtime vehicle featuring Vera Lynn and her singing, directed by Philip Brandon with screenplay by James Seymour and Howard Thomas (script contribution), The plot is a simple tale of success in World War II London for a young female dancer named Peggy Brown, (Vera Lynn) who very surprisingly finds she can sing! She nevertheless entertains a packed theatre during an air raid, singing one of her early classics, *Be Like The Kettle And Sing*.with a friend's help, Peggy, she ends up singing it on a recording with Geraldo's Band. She is soon introducing a weekly radio series (as in real life her radio series entitled 'Sincerely Yours'.) As an agony aunt,Peggy manages to get a formerly engaged couple back together after they have differed. The girl has a baby while he is serving away. Sending her good wishes to the couple on the air, she hears he has been killed in action. - a – cue for Harry's *All the World Sings a Lullaby.*

Harry finds another way of using the usual song structure.
It is a slow waltz, with an introduction, a short verse, but

a long refrain. It is written in F major in slow waltz time (providing a gentle swinging motion therefore). He keeps range comparatively narrow. Vera Lynn's voice is very clear in both tone and diction and accurate in pitch, but can sound rather hard in its upper reaches. Harry avoids this by keeping it in the warmer lower part of her voice. After a gentle rocking almost Mozartian introduction, not related to what comes after in the vocal line, like a mantra the first part of the refrain is repeated 4 times before going on tovary the rest of the melody. The initial rocking figure underpins the bars leading to repeat of refrain,. The repeat and final bars have an upward flourish. It makes a charming number, akin to *Tree Top Lullaby* 10 years before. The lad in fact has just been injured not killed. The film naturally ends with Vera singing *We'll Meet Again*.

Police Ball

On 6 March, a Ball was held in Gloucester Guildhall for Gloucester City Police. This was in aid of the *Red Cross Prisoner of War Fund* and *Longford Children's Hospital*. The band played, with Harry as soloist for the 300 guests. It raised £60.[199] The band had a busy year with 15 BBC Radio broadcasts. It is not clear how many times Harry actually appeared with the Band or its dance band section and of course how much rehearsal time he was involved with for both of these as well for all the individual songs, revues and musicals he composed.

Musicals

Writing a musical was for Harry a much more elaborate venture task, than filling scenes for revues, indeed more akin to his early work with the *Curfew*.

---

[199] *Gloucester Citizen*, 6 March 1943

During a very busy year in 1943, he produced 2 more musicals but this time as their sole composer. To make the musical work, he had to deal with a wider range of people. Even more than revues, musical comedies (or musicals for short) were intended as a means for telling a story, using the wide variety of talent available. Musicals derived from the earlier lighter forms of opera as structures. These in turn came from many European sources usually with their own national 'flavour', but could be transferred and popular elsewhere. They included 18th and 19th century Ballad Operas (English and not readily transferable), More widespread were Singspiels (German), Opèras-comique and -bouffes (French) and opera buffa (Italian with harpsichord or piano accompanied recitative based on speech patterns, but stylised). During the 19th century, the operetta (French and Austrian) developed as a more sentimental variant. Musical comedy evolved particularly in USA as a way of incorporating the vigour of revues into a more sustained narrative with the music in the hands of European emigrés or their descendants.

Outline Scheme of a Musical

Origins – i) a play or a novel;

ii) contemporary or historical theme

iii) a biography

iv) a vehicle for a popular entertainer

Available experts Director to oversee; Producer to co-ordinate stage presentation; Costume and scenery designer; Lighting; Choreographer; Musical director to coordinate the music required and often orchestrate it. Composer and lyricist able to accommodate and exploit available musical resources, especially singers, chorus conductor and orchestra

Overture Usually this consists of a pot-pourri of salient melodies (as in many opera overtures) linked to form a striking set of contrasts intended to get the audience in the mood for what follows.

Dialogue This is sometimes a pruned version of an earlier original play. Its function is to reveal further aspects of character or explain situations within the plot, to introduce and link musical numbers as well as push the action on. Usually, the emotion in situations is developed in the music. One artifice, melos (or melodrama), used sometimes in mid-19th century French opéra-comique and sparingly in Italian opera), is used where speech instead of singing with an underlying orchestral theme of significance used to heighten a scene's dramatic effect, e.g. the letter scenes in Verdi's *Macbeth* and *La Traviata* and Catherine's recollection of her dead mother in Meyerbeer's *L'Étoile du Nord*. It came to be used in a similar way in films.

Songs, duets, trios and ensembles – The range of the melodies are tailored to be well within the compass of the singers. Their function are often to heighten the emotion, humour or characterisation of situation.

Dance is often a feature to provide local colour either of place or time, usually devised by a well known choreographer

Jack Hulbert the experienced director, singer and dancer summed up the whole background needed for a musical: *Opening a big musical is always a daunting task. A straight play is difficult enough in all conscience but with a dancing chorus, a singing chorus, trick lighting, setting up new complicate sets for the first time, making necessary adjustments, band calls and principals, it is no picnic.*

The Knight was Bold

This his first solo musical comedy had a scenario written by Harriett Jay (authoress of the original farce of 1907 *When Knights were Bold* - itself close to Mark Twain's novel *A Yankee at the Court of King Arthur*). *-It had further* plus contributions from Emile Littler and co-author Thomas Browne. Its lyrics were put together by Barbara Gordon and Basil Thomas with a dialogue too full of mock mediaevalisms e.g *Thee* and *Thou*.

The first provincial performance was at *Theatre Royal*, Newcastle-upon-Tyne on 26 April 1943, at this stage with odd title of **Kiss the Girls** - making it sound more like vaudeville than musical comedy. Its scenario was It was intended as a vehicle for popular West End comedy and musical revue star Sonnie Hale, who frequently appeared with his sister, Binnie Hale

It was the tale of a hard up feckless Knight, Sir Guy De Vere (Sonnie Hale), who dreams he is back in the Middle Ages. He sees himself battling against Ballymote (Frances L. Sullivan). The costumes by Doris Zinkeisen and Norman Hartnell among others.were by accomplished and elegant. There were a further set of performances in *Hippodrome* Coventry (3 May for week- well received [200]), Grand Theatre Blackpool, Grand Theatre Leeds, Theatre Royal Birmingham, Liverpool and Edinburgh, finishing on 19 June. It opened on 10 July at the *Piccadilly Theatre*. After a favourable opened night, the show now retitled as *The Knight was Bold*in fact only lasted a 10 further nights.

Harry wrote all the music for the songs:- *If this is Love; I Go on My Way Whistling; I'm Telling Thee; In Summer When the Trees be Green; Kiss the Girls* (hence earlier title)*; Mother Nature; Tradition (the Good Old Days); Well Done, Dean; Where the Rainbow Ends; Whoopsy-Diddly-Dum-de-Dumm; You and the Moonlight and Who Knows.* Another song *Halfway to Heaven* was dropped during the provincial tour. The music for the show seems to have disappeared.

Fortunately, the next musical would be one of his key-works and was very successful.

---

[200]   *Birmingham Mail*, 4 May 1943

CHAPTER 22

LISBON STORY (1943)

George Black gave it an ambitiously produced contemporary war-theme musical with scenario and lyrics by Harold Purcell, who used his film experience to give Harry musically a variety of situations by which he could to display compositionally different and imaginative styles. Apart from the songs and dances, the score included much *melos* both to underpin the dialogue and anticipate later numbers or reprise earlier numbers. Its use derived from Harold Purcell's experience with filming. Backdrop stills were shown, presumably intending to make the atmosphere more realistic and immediate.

Debroy Somers did the necessary musical arrangements; - hence, the conventional pot-pourri overture, arranged from 8 of the show's songs with the waltz song as a climax. The opening scene of Act 1 shows Gabrielle's studio in July 1938 Paris where friends and associates having cameo parts to create a suitable artistic atmosphere around Gabrielle Girard, (Patricia Burke) a famous Parisienne singer.

> After a brief orchestral introduction (no. 1 in C and in common time) based on part of the first song. Her friend Gorelle picks up this tune on the piano and hums the tune Panache another friend (Noelle Gordon) sings the first song no.2) – a bright soubrette number, *Happy Days*. To Gorelle's piano accompaniment. it has little runs for the verse, and a refrain in a strict tempo quickstep, setting out the sentiments of the title. Gabrielle loves Englishman,

David Warren (a non-singing part for Jack Livesey). who works in the Foreign Office.

No.3 is a melos, introducing Gabrielle's first song (no.4) a waltz (in C), *Someday We Shall Meet Again*. In the verse, she ponders on the present (in 4/4 time) which changes to waltz time for the big tune reminiscent of Ivor Novello and Franz Lehar). This ends with a coda based on music for verse, arranged as a cadence to end scene. The entr'acte repeats no.4 as an orchestral interlude.

The scene changes to Garielle's villa in neutral Lisbon in summer 1942. She.has escaped from the German Occupation of France. Songs dances and music are now geared to give an Iberian atmosphere.

The chorus sing sings a mock-Latin American comedy song *Madame Louisa* (no.5) with many off-beat entries from Lola (Margaret McGrath) a local singer retailing Madame Louisa's many faults and international escapades in verse 1 and 2. The crowd disperses while the music for the verse is played as a dance. The scene changes to a Lisbon street, Gonzalez a fruit seller (high tenor Joseph Dollinger) sings (no 6) a nostalgic waltz-song (in F) *Never Say Goodbye* (no.7) which Gabrielle hears and embellishes with graceful runs at the end, Gabrielle (no. 7a) reprises the verse, expressing regret for the present. (in E). A brief melos with the tune under dialogue by von Schiner's and his assistant Doctor Hoffman.

This dialogue continues over the introduction of the next song (no.8) with a vaguely tango rhythm which Ramon, (Ronaldo Mazar) a street singer joined by mixed chorus in 4-part harmony, sing *Music at Midnight*. The scene ends with another melos (no 9.), which repeats under the dialogue orchestrally (now in D) of *Someday We'll Meet Again*.

Gabrielle has been approached by Nazi Carl von Schriner from the *Berlin Cultural Department* (Albert Lieven in another no-singing part- he often played Nazi officers in British wartime films). If she returns Paris, he will arrange for her to appear in a suitable piece of musical theatre in an operetta, *La Comtesse*. She agrees to this because it can provide a front to assist the escape of a French scientist and his daughter. He is developing an important new metal, but will act the role of her designer in the operetta.

During a scene change from the Lisbon street to the quayside using a harbour back-drop, the *Vincent Tildsley Mastersingers* dressed as Portuguese fisherfolk mending their nets etc sang, *Pedro the Fisherman*(no.10). (The need for this emerged during the out of town trail run, which started on 3 May at Imperial Theatre in Brighton for 2 weeks. By the 3rd night the time taken to do the change from Paris to Lisbon was noticeable. Purcell and Davies wandered back to their hotel in a blitz warning, with the composer whistling a mite disconsolately. Why not have out a whistling song to cover the scene change. Apparently written on scraps of paper by the fourth night in Brighton, the resultant chorus *Pedro the Fisherman* went into the show.) The chorus is fulfils its function of filling in scene change, in having a core set of verses and tunes about 4 mins long (in the vocal score these can be added to, should more time be needed). The show is now best remembered for this whistling tune, which sold 50,000 song copies in a week. The record of the basic set of verses made by the *Vincent Tildsley Mastersingers* was radio's most frequent request at the time.

An organ is heard off-stage playing a religious andante (in E flat and a hymn-like 4/4); the fisherfolk enter the church. His repeated with a 4-part harmonised chorus (no.11a) for the procession to bless the fleet. (no.11b). Once this done, Carmelita (Nora Savage) a singer of coloratura ability sings a short Spanish-flavoured waltz (in Bb flat) *Carnival Song*. There is followed a sequence of ballet pieces with an Iberian flavour, in fact nearer to Latin America than Portugal (no. 11c) for the *cor de Ballet*. They are given a lilting Spanish waltz (in D) in a slower version of the same (now in A) which leads to an increasingly noisy climax changing key twice (to F and then G) on the way.

This is followed by a Festival dance (no. 11d) for 2 of Gabrielle's friends (the distinguished Polish duo Alicia Halama and Ciesław Konarski), another dance sequence, starting slowly and lyrically, changes to a bolero followed by a slow waltz, which accelerates and comes to a lively conclusion. The villagers leave (no. 12).

Von Schriner finds out who the scientist is. He will turn a blind eye, if she becomes his lover. The well-used device of a show within a show is staged in the shape of the first performance of the operetta at the *Théâtre. Mogador.*

The act concludes with a set number (no. 13 in C) to start with and common time throughout) for Gabriel *Song of the Sunrise*. The verse views the present in a hesitant line, while the refrain indicates hope for the future to a typical flowing tune by Harry. The key changes when the 4-part chorus enter (to G flat), allowing the parts to le more easily within their compass. Gabrielle leaves with von Shriner.

Act II begins in a railway station setting on the border between Spain and France. Ramon now sings *Serenade for Sale,* (no. 14) a vocalised tango in (A flat) in a tongue-in-cheek style reminiscent of Friml's *Donkey Serenade*. Gorelle, Gabrielle's friend picks it up in a burlesque way (no.14a), which the chorus take up and harmonise briefly (no. 14b). As Gabrielle departs a melos (no 15) reprises the waltz, *Someday We'll Meet Again* and the scene ends

with the chorus reprising (No 16) *Never Say Goodbye*
followed by another melos starting with another reprise
of *Someday* and then a change portraying the train in
motion, but with the vibraphone of Radio Berlin sounding
through.

Gabrielle now takes the place of the scientist's daughter in the operetta,
thus allowing the scientist and his daughter escape to England. There is
another change of scene music (no. 18 called 'Mogador Theatre'). Now
also back in Paris, Gabrielle's friends Panache and Gorelle, reprise *Happy
Days* as duet (no.19).

The scene changes to the theatre and the operetta. It is the
Finale of Act I of 'La Comtesse' (no.20) entitled somewhat
grandly 'Napoleonic Scena'. It is starts with the men of the
chorus marching into a festive Paris.this to a rythmic tune
(in E flat) in Romberg style, *So Paris wears Her Easter
Dress*. There are solos by characters as interludes during
the march, a Soldier (high tenor Joseph Dollinger) talks
about dreams, Milkmaid (high soprano Nora Savage) sings
a waltz about Paris being special, Innkeeper (baritone Kurt
Wagener) sings for people to encourage drinking, Flower
Girl (Eleanor Fayre) reprises *Never Say Good Bye* as a
duet with the Soldier. A brief fully harmonised reprise of
Someday We Shall Meet Again follows. A reveille is sounded
the Drummer Boy (Patricia Burke) enters with a march,
Follow the Drum which the Chorus take up. There is a brief
piece, reprising *Happy Days* followed by ballet as a type of
morality play in which *Evil* (Konarski) tempts and seduces
Innocence (Eleonor Fayre), despite the presence of *Piety*
(Alicia Halama) and *Wisdom* (Patricia Burke). *Wisdom*
steps forward at the end to point up the moral of the ballet.

Because her deceit has now been discovered, Gabrielle is shot dead by von
Schriner, while the cast sing the *Marseillaise*. It ends with a triumphant

Someday We Shall Meet Again as a final curtain making a thrilling and moving *coup de théâtre*.

The musical's first London showing was at the *London Hippodrome* by George Black on 17 June 1943 and drew large audiences, running for 492 performances. Rather ironically as a kind of German reply to it, it ended its run abruptly on 8 July 1944 when the devastation resulting from German V-1 'flying bombs' forced the majority of London's theatrical venues to temporarily closed. Nevertheless, after only three months on tour it returned to the *Stoll Theatre* on 17 October for a further 54 performances with Maria Eisler as Gabrielle and other small cast changes closing on 2 December 1944. For its provincial tours in late 1945 Harry wrote 2 new songs, *April in the Spring of Love* and *Very Odd Fish*.

Besides the stage work and in a way backing up his increasing reputation as a composer, Harry's music was broadcast on the BBC Home programme on 26 June at 1.30pm a half-an hour-selection of Harry's music at 6.30 pm, presented by Sam Heppner, the war time broadcaster on matters musical. Later on 12 August, in its monthly series presenting outstanding personalities and memorable incidents from the life of Wales. gave Harry's music an airing courtesy of *BBC Welsh Light Orchestra and Chorus*, conducted by Arwel Hughes. Sam Heppner again was playing host for to a BBC Programme for the Forces at 2.30pm 27 October, featuring Harry's music

CHAPTER 23

THE LATER WAR YEARS (1944)

During 1944, Harry provided music for 3 songs for a film, 3 extra song ballet and incidental for a musical and 1 for a play. as well as appearances with the band at home and in Northern Europe

Bell Bottom George

This is a typical Formby situation comedy very much in the style of earlier Formby films - a kind of *It's in the Air* for the Navy. It was directed and produced for British Columbia Films by Marcel Verney with Ben Henry as co-producer. Charles Williams was the conductor/arranger. Harry was given 10 days to complete his contribution to the score. [201] It was released on 7 February.

The plot concerns Navy club steward George who because of a low medical grade is turned down by the navy. Yet, he gets in by mistake when a sailor friend borrows his only suit of clothes and he is obliged to wear the sailor's uniform. Following a case of mistaken identity, he becomes involved with enemy agents based in a taxidermist's shop, and foils their attempts to blow up a British warship. Harry put music to 3 songs with words by Phil Park *Swim Little Fish, If I Had A Girl Like You* and *Bell Bottom George.*

---

[201] Bret, David, 1999, *George Formby*, Robson Books Ltd p. 129 (he gets the name of the forces band wrong!)

The first is a quirky serenade to a gold fish Egbert, as a symbol of George being love lorn; the second a typical little love song the third is the usual strophic song for George the introduction based on the 'sailors hornpipe', the verse not quite as sharp as those provided earlier for him by Haine and Harper) but ending of each verse having the title repeated. There is room for having the inevitable banjolele solo.

The Rest is Silence

He also wrote more songs. Firstly. *I'd Like to Share My Love for You* for BNP film, *Candle at Midnight*.released on 18 January 1944 Then there was the only song that Harry wrote for a play (he did write fo radio plays later for which Harold Purcell also wrote the lyrics). *The Rest is Silence* by Harold Purcell, staged for the first time on 20 April featuring Ann Todd, directed by David Lean. It was about the trial of Madeleine Smith, accused of poisoning her French lover with arsenic. Lawrence Olivier's talented cousin, Sheila Burrell made her debut as Rose It featured the song *We Shall Always Have Today.* Both had words by Harold Purcell.

HM Life Guards Concerts

Harry appeared from as solo pianist on 9 April with the H M Life Guards Band, conducted as usual by Captain Le Moine in afternoon (3pm) and evening (7.30) concerts at the Town Hall, Leamington Spa. [202]He was in similar concerts as solo pianist from Monday to Friday 22 to 26 May with the HM Life Guards band giving an afternoon (3pm) and evening (7.30) concerts this time with another soloist Australian dramatic soprano Mae Craven at Jephson Garden Pavilion in, Leamington Spa. [203]

---

[202] *Leamington Spa Courier,*31 March 1944
[203] *Leamington Spa Courier,*19 May1944

Jenny Jones.

He became involved in writing the complete music for his next musical *Jenny Jones*,[204] another George Black promotion, due for the Autumn. *Jenny Jones* was another George Black promotion. Harry must have written all the music from March to August, before he went off to Europe. The lyrics were again by Harold Purcell and scenario by Ronald Gow (author of the famous play *Love On The Dole*). He based it on short stories about South Wales coalfield by the Welsh poet Rhys Davies. The result was quite episodic e.g. in 2 acts and 12 scenes:-

Act 1	Scene 1	Morgan Jones Cottage
	Scene 2	The Ice Cream Parlour
	Scene 3	The Hill Above the Town
	Scene 4	St Ceiriog's Abbey
	Scene 5/6	A Village Street

Unlike the realistic sets for the film *How Green was My Valley*, the show's scenery was criticised for not having sight of a coal mine or slag heap and being very clean-looking no coal-dust anywhere. Verisimilitude was not a requirement in a lavish production.

The plot tells of Morgan Jones, (Sidney Bland) a Welsh miner in Aberdowlais[205], a father of 18 children, who wanted to make them 21 in number and seeks to find a new wife. The first act opens in the family cottage with Penry who loves daughter Jenny (Carole Lynne) and Morgan's his young son David who sings *My Wish*. Morgan's children come in to sing Henry Purcell's *Nymphs and Shepherds*.

Capri Serenade, is a play featuring Ugolini, Marie, Dai and Jimmy. Light relief is provided by a Geordie miner Jimmy Armstrong (Jimmy James) and his mum who become involved with the family. Dilys and her lover Paul sing *Where the Blue Begins*. There is the usual ballet sequence derived from an Anatole France book *The Story of Saint Ceiriog*, (Tommy Linden) with the reliable Wendy Toye choreographing the spectacle.

---

204 There is a handwritten copy in Parr-Davies collection.
205 Is this a corruption for theatrical purposes of Aberdulais, near Neath?

Morgan Jones marries and the finale of act 1 has Jenny leaving her lover Penry (Ronald Millar) to go to London.

Act 2	Scene 1	A Herbalist's Shop
	Scene 2	The Market Place
	Scene 3	A Dressing Room
	Scene 4	The Stage of the Theatre at Aberdowlais
	Scene 5	The Hill Above the Town
	Scene 6	Backstage of the Theatre at Aberdowlais.

Act 2 opens with more from the children and Dilys and Paul in *Merry Go Round*. Dilys, Jenny's sister and Paul sing another duet, *After All*. Jenny comes back with an operetta (this device of an operetta in a musical yet again) called *An Episode in Havana*, It was an historical romance (derived from a Doris Leslie book, possibly *Royal William; the story of Democrat*). about the future King William IV, Lord Nelson and a Local Cuban girl. Jenny wants people locally to perform it put on at the Aberdowlais Theatre Royal (see Act 2 Scenes 3 4 6). During its playing, Ugolino (baritone Kurt Wagener) sings *Don Vasco Salano* and the chorus (Vincent Tildesley Mastersingers) sing *Annabella*. Dilys and Paul sing yet another duet *Yet Another Day* and after a dance David sings *Ar hyd y nos*. The Girl acrobats *The Three Wallabies also* perform. The music for this typically lavish and spectacular Black production was orchestrated by Debroy Somers and played by the *Cranbourn Light Symphony Orchestra* conducted by Bobbie Howell.

It had a short pre-London tryout (once again at the *Brighton Hippodrome*) from 12 September. It did not appear to be cohering very well so some of the show met with disapproval. Ronald Miller the romantic lead in it helped to reshape before it opened at the *London Hippodrome* on 2 October.[206]

---

[206]   He became speechwriter for Margaret Thatcher and creator of her famous catchphrase *The lady is not for turning.*

It had a modest success running for 153 performances, closing in December. There was a BBC Home Service broadcast for excerpts on Friday 24 November at 8 pm.[207]

Being in N W Europe, Harry was not on hand to deal with the show's music, so never saw it as a complete entity. Indeed four numbers by Harry to words by Phil Park were brought in from the review, *Top of the World* (which had been bombed out 4 days after its London first performance in 1940).

The musical director was Bobby Howell. The costumes were designed by Norman Hartnell and Digby Morton. *The Observer* sniped that the Welsh episodes were as much like the real thing as the Rhondda is to Leicester Square. However, it ran for 153 performances.

> Harry would be aware that D-Day was looming, indeed then officially launched on 6 June. This meant that he had to get ready for a possible future posting. He stayed in the *Sheriff's Private Hotel* in Bath on 10 June, possibly on the way to Swansea to see his family before embarking. [208]

He took part in a concert by the orchestra for HM Life Guards in the Town Hall, Lewes on 10 July. It provided a good illustration of the variety of music he played at the time and what was in their repertoire and how much Harry was valued as both composer and pianist:-

Fanfare Albert Ketelby

Overture *Die Fledermaus* Johann Strauss the Younger

1st movement of 1st piano concerto o by Peter Illych Tchaikovsky (solo pianist - Harry)

Viennese Memories of Lehar - selection made by Henry Hall

Arrangement of *A Nightingale Sang in Berkeley Square* Manning Sherwin, Made by Harry

Warsaw Concerto Richard Addinsell

Rhapsody in Blue George Gershwin (both with Harry as solo pianist)-

Meditation *Thäis* Jules Massenet (solo violinist - Dennis MacManson)

---

[207] *Radio Times issue* 1103, 19-25 November 1944
[208] *Bath Chronicle and Gazette* as dated

Lo Here the Gentle Lark Sir Henry Bishop (adaptation of The Comedy of Errors)(solo flautist -Corporal J G Thornburrow and clarinettist Lance Corporal L Hazel)

Stepping Out (Simpson) and *Red Hearts* (solo xylophonist - W Connor)

Laughing Song- Die Fledermaus Johann Strauss the Younger

If My Songs Were Only Winged Reynaldo Hahn

The Pipes of Pan The Arcadians Lionel Monckton (all solo soprano - Pamela Woolmore)

The Blind Ploughman Robert Connisby Clark

The Yeoman of England (Merrie England) Edward German

Old Barty (all solo baritone - Harold G Williams)

A selection from Harry's musical *The Lisbon Story* was played by soloists and orchestra with Harry at the piano.[209]

It Happened One Sunday

This was an ABPC film released on 28 July starring Robert Beatty, directed by Czech Karel Lumac, with Charles Williams as music director/arranger.

> Harry contributed 2 songs, a quasi-naval ditty, *All Ashore* and a more romantic number *Valley of Dreams* with a slight Irish nostalgic flavour nostalgia, as befits the heroine, an Irish servant girl Moya Malone (Barbara White). She is working in Liverpool and mistakenly believes that she has a secret admirer working at a hospital and while seeking him out accidentally meets and falls in love with a serviceman Tom Stephens (Canadian actor Robert Beatty). She spends the rest of the day going around Liverpool with him and they eventually decide to marry.

---

[209] *Sussex Agricultural Express*, 18 August 1944

CHAPTER 24

AFTER D-DAY (1944-5)

Harold Purcell provided lyrics for a song, *One Song Shall Ever Remain*, featured in the film *2000 Women*, published in 1945.

In N W Europe in the aftermath of D-Day

On 19 August, Harry got orders to go with the *Life Guard's Band* to the Western Front in Northern France. They embarked on 22 August. The impetus - Operation Overlord - by the Allied Forces breakout after the D-Day landings on 6 June had freed Normandy carrying them eastwards to liberate Paris on 24 August.

The British Red Cross had arrived as early as 7 July to support wounded and sick soldiers not only medically but providing *morale boosting comforts, from jam to books and chess sets* .... and *cheerfulness and dedication,* [210]

The role of the Band was similar i.e. to rally fellow troops, but give musical support to the local people devastated by what had happened to them. Harry would now see much more of the effects of war than he had earlier with ENSA. What had happened not only affected military personnel, but ordinary people in the different Nazi-occupied countries. The musical efforts led by Captain Lemoine, which the Band made (including Harry) were more than mere morale-boosters for the forces and local people, but had a special significance in showing there was hope for the future.

---

[210] *BBC History Magazine* July 2019, p 32

The band initially moved from the eastern part of the D-Day Landings inland to Calvados in the Bocage south and west of Caen in Lower Normandy (now relieved of German occupation by the end of July) travelling mainly to its villages and townships. The tour was extensive, (one newspaper stated an unlikely 25000 miles) but logistically the tour left a lot to be desired as will emerge more clearly below. [211]

Harry was now a long way from the comforts of Gracie, her family, his own family or of an hotel or his won flat in London. Colleague musician Norman Bearcroft left a record of the band's tour in his diary (quotations from him are in italics):-

The tour had initially mild autumn weather, which began to cool off in late September and through October.

21 August ....*the first step was a move to a camp near Gosport on the 21ˢᵗ. The following day the Band boarded an American tank landing craft, 'Ops Neptune', manned by British seamen. At 9 o'clock the craft was packed with tanks and lorries, the only passengers being The Life Guards Band and the band of the 'Shiny Tenth' Hussars* [Prince of Wales' Own].

22 *Six or seven hours later the craft moved a little way of Portsmouth, where it waited for the convoy to assemble by midnight, then mover off round the Isle of Wight.*

Lower Normandy

23 *Landing on Juno Beach Normandy at 6.45 pm* [where British and Canadian forces had disembarked on D-Day] .... *the musicians' first task was to help with the loading of British casualties and German prisoners on the landing craft they had arrived in while waiting for transport to St Aubin-sur Mer.*[nearby village just off beach 10 miles N of Caen] [212] *The camp at St Aubin was a rest camp for soldiers from the front.*

---

[211] Harry's army record laconically has *Embarked for NE Europe – 22.8.44*

[212] Lawn, George R, 1995, *Music in State Clothing the Story of the Kettledrummers, Trumpeters and the Band of the Life Guards,* Lee Cooper, p. 50 George Lawn uses musician Norman Bearcroft's diary, about what happened to the bandsmen. in NW Europe. The author has corrected spelling of place names and used [] to add relevant detail including locations.

26 .. *the Band moved to St. Germain du Crioult,* [small village about 25 miles SW Caen in the Bocage], *only to find they were not expected and had to sleep under hedges with only greatcoats for bedding.*

27 *The following day instruments were unpacked, oiled and later played in a concert, given in Condé-sur-Noireau* [a crossroad village on main road, two and half miles miles E] *for the 'Guards Armoured Division'* [part of XXX Corps].

When how and what Harry played during this tour if not clear. The Band obviously carried around portable instruments. even possibly such percussion keyboards as xylophone, celesta or glockenspiel, but not a piano. However, there may have been pianos available in the villages on the tour. Here Harry's ability to adapt and transpose would stand him in good stead, especially if the instrument was off-key. It is always not clear where the Band played in the villages visited, but each village usually had a reasonably sized parish church. here his previous skill in organ playing would have been available,…

28 ..... *concerts were played at Galigne,and Vassy, before moving to Lande Patry* [all villages west of cross roads.]

31 [moving 10 miles SW] *Concerts at Tinchebray* [a small town]

1 September .... *and St Clair De Halauze* [a small village further SE 12miles]

2 *was spent travelling to Flers* [NE about 12 miles.Allies had strategically bombed this small city with 80% destruction] *and very rough accommodation in a German barracks.*

3 *a concert played in a local cinema.*

The band in the following week moved east about 75 miles to wooded Upper Normandy.

11 *to Morgny-la Pommeray* [a small village 11 milesNE of Rouen]

12 f*or a concert at Notre Dame d'Isle* [nearby Village]

13 *A day of general cleaning up, change of clothing and a mobile bath...*

14/15/16 *concerts starting at Etrepagny* [small city further 30 miles SE], *then playing for civilians at Limerick* [about 40 miles cross-country] *to Limetz-Villez and St Pierre d'Autils and in the evening for the Royal Artillery at Bonniéres-sur-Seine* [nearby villages]

20 *A brief period of comparative luxury, spent in the Three Merchants Hotel* [timber-framed Hôtel des Trois Marchands} *in Les Andelys* [25 miles SE of Rouen]

22 *After playing for local civilians, the Band provided the music....* *for a swank (i.e. inspection) parade of the Scots Guards, followed by a long journey to give a concert the same evening for the Grenadier Guards.*[213]

23 *spent entertaining at a local hospital*

24 *playing at a sports meeting.*

Belgium

The band now made its way to Brussels, 250 miles to the NE. The city had been relieved a month before on 4 September.

3 October *leaving Les Andelys, they arrived in Brussels to enjoy the Splendid Hotel* [in North Brussels].

5/6 *Broadcasting from a Belgian studio*

7 *Concert at the Théâtre Royal de la Monnaie.*[Brussels Opera House]. The typical programme included ;-

> *Steps of Glory [Aubrey Winter]*
> *Orpheus in the Underworld [Offenbach]*
> *Charm of the Waltz,*
> *The Chocolate Soldier [Oscar Strauss]*
> *Excerpts from 'Aida'[Giuseppe Verdi]*
> and *Five minutes with Cole Porter.*

Harry could well have played the excepts from *Chocolate Soldier* and Cole Porter. on the piano.

---

[213] Both were constituent Corps of the *Guards Armoured Division.*

24 Several more performances were given in Brussels before leaving at 12 midnight. They were moved on where *During their short stay in Holland the Band lived under canvas, four or five miles from the front line which was the River Maas.* – near the so-called 'Battle of the Dykes' liberating towns south of Maas.

25 *arrived at 8.30 am .... concert for ... Welsh Guards .... at the Divisional Club* [214] [215]

26 *The Band played for their own regiment*

27 *concert .... for the Grenadiers*

28 *return to Brussels*

29 *to take the Royal Corps of Signals to church.*

November brought even cooler clearer weather. Eventually this changed to more and more cloud until snow and frost appeared in December, a harbinger of increasingly severe winter weather in early January 1945. It did thaw afterwards.

4 November *the Band now known as 'Monty's Pets', played for him at a dinner he gave for all the senior officers who had taken part at the Battle of El Alamein.*

8 *concert given at the Ancien Belgique* [large Brussels concert hall]

9 *rehearsals began for a parade on 11th at the Palais de Beaux Arts finished 2 in the morning;*

10 *this was followed later in day with another, then a performance in the evening*

11 *concert in the presence of Her Majesty Queen Mary the Queen Mother.*

13.... *a concert given at Renaix* [40 miles W, close to French border]

14 *the band said goodbye to the people of Brussels and moved to Tessenderloo* [town 50 miles E of Brussels]. *There the accommodation was a disused house, very dirty and no beds.*

17 *on the road for Asse a medium sized town SW of Tessenderloo with a Corporal Major was detailed as navigator, but Captain Lemoine insisted*

---

[214]   Another constituent Corps of the *Guards Armoured Division.*

[215]   War diary *1ˢᵗ Battalion of Welsh Guards* for 25 October 1944.

that he was in charge and would therefore navigate. Some hours later the Musicians were asking why all the road and shop signs were in German.

They had moved steadily east into Germany! rather than NW towards Asse.

Holland

After this there was 100 miles SW journey to a strip of Holland between the Belgian and German borders close to Maastricht:-

18 *to Geleen* [coal mining city] *to live in a theatre.*

19 *Church parade on Sunday*

20/21/22/23/24/25 *c oncerts played every day.*

Although there were grumbles from the Band, the comments also reveal the hardships of the local people, especially as the weather was getting colder:-

26 *to Brunnsum* [another coal mining town a few miles SW of Geleen] *The trip was so badly organised that they had done only about quarter of the playing they might have done .... They were billeted with civilians.....* e.g. a back kitchen with a stone floor .... *There was nothing to eat and the toilet facilities were down the garden*

27 30 November/1/2 December in area *including eating in a café 2 miles away, playing in a cinema 6miles away and having a bath down a coal mine.*

3 *concert in Hoensbroeck* [a village few miles S near Hasselt]. They travelled all the way back to Asse.

5 *played for the 2nd Household Cavalry Regiment*

9 *played again or the 2nd Household Cavalry Regiment at Waterschei* [a mineing area within the city of Genk in the Hasselt area] *and afterwards slept on the floor as usual. More Concerts, inspections and prize-givings were undertaken in the next few days.*

15 *dance band played for the US Air force on the night Glen Miller died.*

19 *A concert .... was cancelled five minutes before starting time, when the Regiment, as part of the Guards Armoured Division, were ordered up to assist the Americans at the Battle of the Bulge.*

Belgium

25 December to 1 January *completely free. A concert in a Casino in Belgium started the ball rolling again.*

Despite the weather, they now moved back into Holland about 90 miles NE.

8 *to snowy Eindhoven [[large city in Brabant[into civilian digs and concerts given in the local hospital and theatre. Nijmegen [a city 50 miles NE on German border] was the next stop, living in a hospital, then a brief period of leave in Brussels.*

There is a lull in the account during the early weeks of the New Year. The Band returned to England on 9 March.[216]

---

[216] This date is confirmed in Harry's war record.

CHAPTER 25

FINAL ARMY DAYS (1945-6)

The month following his return to UK, Harry played at a concert in Donnington Hall on Saturday 14 April with an augmented orchestra:-

Land of Hope and Glory likely no 1)	Edward Elgar
Selection *Rose Marie*	Rudolph Friml
Glorious Devon (Maid of the Mountains)	Fraser-Simpson

A Perfect Day (Carrie Jacobs-Bond) baritone Herbert Morrison
(both above songs accompanied by pianist Mary Durkin)
violin solos by Michael McMenemy
popular tunes banjoist George Morris
arrangement (by concert organiser G Cruikshank) of *Fantasia on British Sea Songs* SirHenry Wood
Yeoman of England (Merry England)Edward German
(again Herbert Morrison and Mary Durkin)
Selection of *Lisbon Story*
*Rhapsody in Blue*George GershwinHarry and orchestra
Community singing
(OHM Life Guards Band or orchestra are not mentioned as orchestral source).[217]

---

[217] *Sevenoaks Chronicle and Kentish Advertiser*, 20 April 1945

Gracie and he not only cooperated musically over the years since 1932 on many enterprises even if they argued over details. Harry could be touchy if he felt he was not being properly acknowledged (as was seen in Canada). Both were compulsive workers. Gracie despite her considerable charm was quite a driven character.

Sadly in May 1945, things came to a head between Harry and Gracie He disagreed with her and her wish that he accompany her on a tour to Australia and the Far East He baulked at the idea deciding he did not want to do war work anymore. He claimed that he had seen enough of uniforms ;he had done enough military service to last him a life time.

Misreading the intentions behind his words, later Gracie wrote to her sister rather cynically about the break-up being financial, *Harry - didn't mind going to Australia, but he wanted a nice remuneration in American dollars, which of course we couldn't afford. The upshot was that he did not go to Australia and finally accompanied Gracie no more.*

The situation was more complicated that either made out. Logistically, Harry still had responsibilities for concerts with and for the *HM Life Guards Band* and would have needed permission for such an extensive tour. He also had West End commissions. On a more personal level, Harry had only recently returned from an exhausting tour of duty in NW Europe for 8 months. This must have pushed him well out of every 'comfort zone' he had previously experienced - physical mental and social. He had viewed at first hand all the horrific after-effects of total war. on military personnel and the citizens of the countries he travelled through beside the privations suffered by the Life Guard's Band.This meant he had now exhausted himself e.g.as before at the end of 1943. In fact he was not demobbed until the next year.

In the event any way on 6 June 1945, the Band was ordered to take part in August in the Victory parade in Paris. *The busiest section of the Band at this time was undoubtedly the dance band, celebration dances being a regular excuse for good times.*[218] He had also songs to get ready for the Tom Arnold revue *Fine Feathers* mounted for Jack Buchanan due to be premièred in London in October.

Despite this breach between them in fact the pair continued to communicate after they had returned from their respective tours of duty.

---

[218] Lawn, George R, 1995, *Music in State Clothing the Story of the Kettledrummers, Trumpeters and the Band of the Life Guards,* Lee Cooper, p. 55

She continued to sing his songs and the pair appeared occasionally together and Gracie's letters to him remained warm.

Cheltenham

Then Harry appeared again as a soloist in the Cheltenham Festival. The music provided by the band was part of a whole group of wide ranging activities – dog and horses shows, cricket and tennis matches, water polo, rambling, swimming, wrestling at a Sports festival, held as before in early August. Beginning on 4 August for the week it ended on following Sunday. There were afternoon (3pm) and evening (7pm) concerts on the Sunday and each day during the rest of the week.[219]

The music provided included recitals by Louis Kentner the distinguished pianist, the *Spa Orchestra* as well as *The Band of His Majesty's Lifeguards* under Lieutenant-Colonel Albert Lemoine. A number of band members played solos, also in the evening On Saturday at the inaugural concert was held in Montpellier Gardens. The extensive programme was:-

Overture *to Orpheus in the Underworld* (Offenbach)-
Selections of music by Ewing, Lehar, Debussy and (?Max)
Friedman
Agostine
(Three trumpeters - B J Clarke, Harry B Dunsmore and
L-Corporal E D Mirams)
*Clair de Lune (*Debussy)- and
*The Warsaw Concerto (*Richard Addinsell)
(both played by Harry).
Solo items by Dennis Macmanson (violinist originally from
London Symphony Orchestra)
Demarare - Cleopatra (cornetist Harry B Dunsmore)
Lo! Hear the gentle Lark (Henry Bishop)-
(Clarinettist L-Corporal L Hazel and flautist Corporal RG
Thornburrow)
– *'Twixt Heather and Sea* (Geldard)

---

[219] *Gloucestershire Echo* 3 and 6 August 1945

(xylophonist W Connor)
Further selection were from Sullivan's *Iolanthe,*
Friedmann's or Dvorak's *Slavonic*
Rhapsody No. 2, Wagner, Tchaikovsky, Raprecht and
Monti

To Paris

The band on 14 August crossed over to Paris. Harry embarked with
them on 20 August. They were present on 25 August for the anniversary
parade, commemorating France's liberation from the Nazi occupation.
They returned on 1 September.

Fine Feathers

A Tom Arnold revue, this was devised by Robert Nesbitt starring
veteran Jack Buchanan with experienced dancer/actress Ethel Revnell,
exotic dancer Marqueez and experienced character actor 'Duggie'
Wakefield. It had 2 acts with 8 individual sections each. There were a
number of writers and composers. The doyen was Vivian Ellis, Ethel
Revnell wrote a song she sang herself, despite taking a diversity of roles
in many of the sections. Phil Park furnished not only lyrics for the four
songs Harry penned, but wrote 2 songs one to his own lyrics and another
to words by Alan Melville. Harry wrote the song incorporating the show's
title, *Fine Feathers Make Fine Birds* setting a scene linking and aviary
and fashion house. For the finale of Act 1, Harry provided Jack Buchanan
with a deep South number to one of Park's better lyrics. It mimics a deep
south minstrelsy number. The orchestra was again conducted by Bobbie
Howell with musical arrangements were by George Melachrino. After the
usual provincial try-out, this time at the *Hippodrome,*Brighton from 11
September and week; at the *Palace Theatre Manchester* for a fortnight
from 25 September, before being transferred on 11 October 1945 [220]to the
Prince of Wales and ran for 578 performances.

---

[220] *Manchester Evening News*, 30 August 1945

In late November, 12 players from the dance orchestra section of HM Life Guards band played, for the Victory Thanksgiving Ball in the *Temple Speech Room*, prompted by the Rugby Rotary Club, with Harry and Macmanson both appearing as soloists.[221]

---

[221] *Rugby Advertiser,*23 November 1945

CHAPTER 26

'DEMOBILISED' (1946)

The Lisbon Story – the Film

British National Film company made a film version of his 1943 musical *The Lisbon Story*. Retaining many of the original stage cast, the film displays fundamental changes in the presentation of the story line. It becomes more of an anti-Nazi thriller with a lot of extra expository scenes and dialogue to little real effect. It strips out a lot of its music in two ways, cuts it out or puts it out of original context. This dissipates the tension accumulated especially in the second act of the musical. Patricia Burke becomes more decorative and prettily vocal than in the musical where she has a key role musically and dramatically. This is removed and her music is made into set numbers, not integrated into the story through appropriate music and the use of melos. The *rive gauche* flavour at the beginning goes and melos and the ballet sequences are much reduced to one dance. At the end, Gabrielle is spared the assassin's bullet, her accompanist is shot instead!

There is a guest appearance by Richard Tauber singing *Pedro the Fisherman*. He does this well enough but without the life the original chorus had given the number. Harry provided a new song for Patricia Burke a pleasant set number *Paris in My Heart*. The musical director of the film was fellow-composer/conductor Hans May and orchestral arrangements were done by Wilfrid Burns. Released on 21 February 1946, it was only a limited success as a film.

Now Harry became involved with 2 further revues on the cusp of being discharged from the Army.

High Time!

This Val Parnell revue opened on 20 April at the Palladium. It featured a many popular stars of the time, especially Tessie O'Shea in her first review and regular Polish dance duo Alicja Halama and Ciesław Konarski. Harry only contributed one song to no 7 on the programme -*Yukon Nights - Down the Trail*, to words by Dick Hurran- major contributor of words and music to the revue The orchestra was the RAF band *The Sky Rockets* conducted by Paul Fenoulhet who did the musical arrangements.

'Demobbed'

Papers were prepared from 9 April to release Trooper Harry Parr Davies 295736 quaintly given as being *Musical Adviser to Associated British Picture Corporation Ltd* – now only a partial truth. He was 'demobbed' officially by Captain Gordon on 18 May 1946 from *His Majesty's Life Guards.*[222] He moved back in to his own mews flat at 11 Harriet Walk Knightsbridge. He got ready 7 items and ballet music for a revue.On his first day as a civilian, he was one of the guest stars in the hour long popular BBC Radio show *Welsh Rabbit* at 9 pm on 20 May.

Last public encounter

Probably staying with his parents as part of his re-adjusting to 'Civvy Street' he met up with Gracie one again, in August during her 1946 UK summer tour when she arrived in Swansea. He played for her as she sang *Pedro the Fisherman*. It was sad that Harry never got to write the a proposed musical for her.

The Shephard Show

This 2 Act revue subtitles *A Medley of Mirth and Music* opened on 26 September at the *Princes Theatre*. It had 8 numbers in each act. It featured

---

[222] Household Cavalry Archive records 1946 for Harry Parr-Davies

4 talented comedians, Eddie Gray (one of the original Crazy Gang, now solo), Richard Hearne (character actor), Arthur Riscoe (also a singer) and Douglas Byng (female impersonation in scene 2 as Madame Touchée). Harry was as usual one of several providers of the necessary music as were John Blore (who conducted BBC Orchestra) and Michael Treford. Harry teamed up again with Harold Purcell.

They gave scene 4 *Mary Must Have Music;* No 5 *Passports for Two* for Marie Burke and bass singer Gavin Gordon; No 7 *Disconcerto* for singers and dancers including Marie Burke, Jeanne Ravel and others. In Act II, he went on to do the three final numbers 14 15 and 16. 14 *A song and a Story* is for comedian singer Arthur Riscoe; 15 looked like a ballet with vocals, *Chanson de Paris* (as Wendy Toye the experienced choreographer was involved) and *Bubbling Over* ended the show.

The programme includes 3 pieces published as sheet music, *It All Comes Back To Me Now*

(possibly from No.7); *Counting Sheep.* This is a deceptively simple, but charming song in Harry's accomplished nursery rhyme vein, about love stopping the singer going to sleep, after repeat of the refrain, he doses (z-z-z-z-)and piece ends quietly and *I Shall Always Remember.* This revue turned out to be the last revue with which Harry was involved.

35 minutes of excerpts were broadcast at 5.10pm for 35 minutes on 11 November on BBC Light Programme.[223]

---

[223] *Radio Times*, Issue 1206 10-18 November 1946

CHAPTER 27

SETTLING IN 'CIVVY STREET' (1947-8)

Harry's career once he was demobbed showed some slowing up of musical activity.

The Savage Club

He was recorded in 1947 [224] as being a member of the *Savage Club*, then situated at Carlton House Terrace.[225] This exclusive club was founded in 1857 and was named after Dr Samuel Johnson's fey friend Richard Savage and had remained a gentleman's club for those belonging to the public professions i.e. connected with Art, Drama, Music, Literature, Science and Law and are acceptable to the their fellow 'Brother Savages'. When Harry was a member, it included members of the Crazy Gang, Arthur Askey, Webster Booth, Charlie Chaplin and HRH the Duke of Edinburgh. It has a fortnightly dinner and as well as obtaining daily meals and other forms of refreshment. Members could be called on to entertain fellow guests – it all sounds an arrangement very suitable for Harry. He spent time with Savage Club socialising with his lyricist friends, Basil Thomas and Harold Purcell and then Christopher Hassall.

---

[224]   *Who Was Who 1947*
[225]   *Now at 1 Whitehall Place*

His family back in Swansea continued to give Harry with some of the warm and security he needed. 'Billie' was particularly close to him, always having his favourite 'treat', a Custard Slice' ready for him to tuck into when he came back to Swansea. He wrote few songs during 1947 and 1948, and they were without apparent connections to stage or film. or musicals

Glen Echo was published on 16 January. 1947, reminiscent of Andy Stewart songs is competent, purporting to be Celtic or Scottish. The melody is typically Harry's, i.e pleasantly enough worked out. Its introduction is the nearest he gets to a 'Celtic' flavour with its slightly eerie figure and harmony. His verse and refrain are much blander. The only Scottish feature is 'ye' in the lyric. The best feature is the gentle 'echo' effect in the accompaniment after the words of the title are sung. As usual, it is a vehicle for the singer to make effective.

Royal Command Performance

He had picked up his friendship with Gracie and they came together for a *Royal Command Performance* performing for King George VI and Queen Elizabeth on 3 November 1947 at the Palladium Theatre.

There were 2 further songs set as exercises in gentle nostalgia :-

The years to come, to words by Douglas Furber, was the only other song published in 31 December 1947. This is more romantically personal with a verse and refrain with interesting rise in the first phrase and its easy listening refrain. *Angela Mia,* published 31 March 1948 *Annette* and *Peter the Penguin.* were published in 1948

> The latter *Peter the Penguin* is an almost Mahlerian lament for the past, using a three part nursery rhyme structure. The first part is about Peter love for his lady bird, and her rejection of him leading to his passing away. The middle is the reaction of his friends in the zoo, with an ironic return to the first tune as a summary.

British Music Week,

This was held at the Dominion Theatre,London during the week of 12 February and featured apart from Harry a collection of light music talent - the prolific and versatile Haydn Wood, the lyricist Douglas Furber, the populist composers Noel Gay and Eric Maschwitz.[226]

Her Excellency

His return to writing a musical for a summer 1949 première, was with Manning Sherwin on a new musical which in reality did not have a lot of music. It was more a series of comic situation for Cecily Courtneidge's talents. It was a British precursor to Irving Berlin's very successful Ethel Merman vehicle, *Call Me Madam,* even as far as the sub-plots. The book was by Archie Menzies and Harold Purcell provided the lyrics.

Her Excellency Lady Frances Maxwell is the first lady British Ambassador to the South American Republic of *San Barcellos.* Act I deals with her reception at the hotel she is staying at there. She pursues getting a meat import contract for Britain in return exporting British pianos. The contract is to be obtained from forceful Señor Riazza 'the Meat King' (Austin Trevor). Martin Nash (Patrick Barr) plays, the suave American Ambassador. She appears to favour each of these 2 men initially. but accidentally gets engaged to Riazza *Congratulations on your joint effort* wired the Ministry of Food to her!!

A double secondary love interest occurs when Jimmy Denham, (young Thorley Walters as the British commercial attaché is pursued by Margaretta Riazza, (Sandra Martin) the 'Meat King''s daughter who eventually falls for Bill (John Probert) a Texan cowboy. This leaves Jimmy free to woo Mary Cresset (Margaret Mc Grath), the embassy secretary. Musicals like this needed plenty of incident. Billy Dainty, an experienced comic singer and dancer plays a puzzled toreador with a song *Steak and Samba.* He is subdued by the redoutable Frances.

Of the 7 musical numbers, there were 2 for Jimmy and a duet for Frances and Jimmy, Harry wrote only one of Frances' numbers *Sunday Morning in*

---

[226] *The Stage 12 February 1948*

England, a quasi-nostalgic number for Courtneidge to include her comic character impressions of folk back home. It was the best remembered song of the show.He also wrote *Diplomacy*. (and possibly *A Man about the House*, and *I Wonder* and some of the dance and incidental music [227])

As part of the usual provincial try-out of 2 weeks in each place, the show started on 19 April at the Alhambra Glasgow, followed by Birmingham, Nottingham, (from 6 May), Southsea (from 23 May Coventry from 5 June and Brighton, where it closed on 11 June. Its London première was on 22 June at London Hippodrome was not well received and only became a success later, running for 252 performances. There was critical and audience acclaim for Courtneidge's comic versatility and Harry's number for her gained the most plaudits. The show was broadcast as a TV movie and released as a black-and white film by BBC TV on 23 September 1949.[228]

On 20 May Harry was a guest star on BBC Home Programme weekly 9pm Radio show, *Welsh Rabbit*. with the BBC Welsh Variety Orchestra (Leader, Morgan Lloyd) produced by Mat Jones.[229]

Maytime in Mayfair

Harry was asked to provide the title song for an Anna Neagle musical, *Maytime in Mayfair was* given performance on first performance on 24 May. It features suave penniless man-about-town Michael Gore-Brown (Michael Wilding who has inherited a dress salon whose chief designer is Eileen Grahame (Anna Neagle) They decide to make it work, but are hindered by rival D'Arcy Davenport (Peter Graves) who fancies Eileen. Character actor Nicholas Phipps plays Sir Henry Hazelrigg, Gore-Brown's cousin, a clubland military bore but who is betraying the fashion secrets to Gore-Brown's rival. There is much Astaire-and-Rogers style of dancing from Neagle and Wilding on the way to all ending happily. This title song was set by Harry as a fairly typical lushly scored ballad song of the period.

---

[227] There is no complete score extant and only sheet music for *Sunday Morning* and *Diplomacy*

[228] *Radio Times* TV edition 15-21 May 1949

[229] *Radio Times* Issue 1335,23 May 1949

Sauce Tartare

A revue *Sauce Tartare* in 7 parts, mounted by Cecil Landau began at the *Cambridge Theatre London* on 29 August. It featured another leading lady the popular singer/ dancer Jessie Matthews, with whom he had worked earlier. Other artistes in the show, were Muriel Smith the American contralto.and the comic actor Claude Hulbert. Harry wrote the title song for the 7th part entitled *An Englishman in Love* which Zoe Gail and Claude sang. The revue was a moderate success.[230]

230

CHAPTER 28

MORE MUSICALS (1950)

February marked the release of the score of *The Lisbon Story* for amateur use. [231] More intriguingly. Harry and Harold Purcell travelled to be present at a production of *The Lisbon Story* by the *Midland Bank Operatic Society* at the *Scala Theatre. Eastbourne on 15-18 February.* They appeared during the final curtain call and Harold Purcell commended them on an able production.

Vanity Fair proposal for a musical

March provided an intimation that there was to be musical version of Thackeray's *Vanity Fair.*[232] There was surmise during the summer that Harry and Harold Purcell were to be involved, but nothing materialised.

THE HOUSE NEXT DOOR

This was a serial half-hour radio broadcast by BBC Home Service 9.30 -10 pm on Tuesdays evenings on 2/16/23/ 30 May 1950 Cicely Courtneidge was in the lead.as Cis. The other players were

George: Wilfred Babbage

---

[231]   *Eastbourne Herald,* 22 February 1950
[232]   *Birmingham Daily Gazette,* 17 March 1950

Michael:	Brian Roper
Mr Perkins:	John Stevens
Mrs Frobisher:	Doris Rogers
Mr Frobisher:	Leslie Bradley
A Civil Servant:	Olwen Brookes

Written by David Climie, it was billed as about *the adventures of a family who might live next door to you,* Lyrics were by Harold Purcell and music by Harry with, BBC Variety Orchestra, conducted by Rae Jenkins with production by Tom Ronald.[233] The melody Harry provided went through permutations during the series.

Harrys' health

There is some indication that Harry began to suffer from a gastric ulcer which caused him to go eventually to see his local GP in 1950. The causes for this can only be conjectured. Smoking had become an ingrained habit. The effect the Band tour after D-day had on him well have played its part. His 'demob' thrust him back like many another into 'civvy' life without much psychological preparation for the change.

Dear Miss Phoebe

At the same time notices appeared that about a new musical *Dear Miss Phoebe* by Harry with lyrics by Christopher Hassall, he who had served Ivor Novello so long and well with memorable verses. for his musicals. This musical was an adaptation of Sir James Matthew *Barrie's Quality Street* (1901)with much of the original dialogue in place, only separated by appropriate musical numbers, some developed from ideas with in the play's dialogue.

.In 1938. knowing Coates was searching for material to set as a musical, Hassall had offered him his version of Barrie's play as a musical.

---

[233] *Radio Times* Issue 1389, 28 May - 3 June 1950

Eric Coates did indeed set some of Hassall's verses [234] In the event, Harry took up Hassall's skilful re-ordering of the play. Aiding in setting the musical up were director Charles Hickman and Doris Zinkeisen with costumes and scenery.

Harry responded to this text with a more refined, less exuberant score. It is nearer to the Edward German model of musical comedy/operetta than previously, using waltzes, marches and period pastiche ballet music. Being closely based on the play makes gives it a solid structure, Although the music slows the action down to give the dialogue point, much of it is underpinned with key melodies played either before they appear or in reminiscence of them, as a way of revealing often what is going in the character's mind. The story is set during Napoleonic war (1805) in gossipy Quality Street, where Phoebe and Susan Throssel live. Young doctor Valentine Brown (Peter Graves) has met 20 year old Phoebe Throssel, (Carol Raye) on several previous occasions and they like each other. [235]

The overture (no.1) is a mixture of the main melodies. It leads to a minuet being played on a harpsichord as the curtain rises. Set in a blue and white drawing room, there is with a view through a wide window of the street. The Throssel sisters' friends, Fanny and Mary Willoughby and Henrietta Turnbull are there with Susan. Fanny is reading from a thrillingly romantic novel, about which the orchestra comments. After more gossip during the introduction to next number (No.2), set to a slow, but regular gallop during which Phoebe comes in. She goes on to relate in her song, (arranged from the original dialogue), how when out shopping she met *A Certain Individual.* Susan interjects short comments and exclamations. It is about Valentine, a young doctor who is coming to see her this very afternoon.

Reilly the Irish recruiting sergeant for the Infantry (or Redcoats) (baritone Bernard Clifton) now enters. Phoebe and he exchange banter. He says he has a new recruit. Using a line from act II of the play, Hassall inserts a drinking song in the form of a duet, (No. 3) between Reilly and Phoebe, *Cowslip wine.* - he toasts in the song a barmaid, she the fighting

---

[234] Self, Geoffrey, 1986, *In Town Tonight,- a centenary study of the life and music of Eric Coates*, Thames Publishing, p.88

[235] like Gabrielle in Lisbon Story this role requires a lyric soprano with a good top register

men,.After this, Phoebe eventually shows him the door to a postlude based on the song's main melody. It is a rollicking song in the tradition of Lionel's *Porterlied* in Flotow's Martha.

Susan, who had prepared a wedding dress in a blighted hope of getting married,-offers it to Phoebe, who now enters a reverie about love (No.4), a charming waltz song, *I'm Living A Dream*. Valentine now calls. He tells Phoebe much to her disappointment that he has enlisted, (the one the sergeant had mentioned). After a flourish on the harpsichord he tells her that (No 5), *I Leave my Heart in an English Garden*. She is the garden he leaves behind (again Hassall develops a short paragraph in the play into the musical's best known number. Verse I tells about what Valentine likes about the garden, but verse II reveals that he has done the Grand Tour of Europe. Phoebe joins him and the piece ends as a duet. Susan learns of the result of the meeting with a reprise of *I Leave* as a melos under the dialogue. Phoebe weeps with disappointment.

Here Hassall adds a very effective scene to the original play. A reveille sounds as the scene changes to the street outside and Reilly reads a proclamation over military music (No.7). This is followed by (No.8) *March of the Redcoats* [236] a lively quick march. Reilly sings of the people he has enlisted the men join him in chorus and then tells them what they will experience in war. The ladies of the chorus join in to bring the scene to a triumphant close.

.Scene three occurs ten years later (1815) in the same room but now changed into a school room. The soldiers' march is briefly heard (No.9) before moving into the children's ballet (No. 10). This refashions and amplifies the school part in the original. The children are assembling. It starts with a *Skipping Theme* and using the ropes as reins is transformed into *Horse Theme ballet*, the Throssel's outspoken maid Patty (Gretchen Franklin) bustles in. There is a knock and she rushes to open the door. Some more boys enter to a gallop – a variant of later Act II song (No.24) *I Can't Resist the Music*. Another knock and the girls come in shyly to a jumpy variant of another act II song *When will You Mary Me* (No.22). The tune becomes more flowing as they become bolder. A boy plays 'Chopsticks' on the harpsichord, then the *Blackboard Theme* a snatch of

---

[236]   The sheet music and programme erroneously gives the soldier on the right side of the cover a blue uniform!

Cowslip Wine followed by drawing a cat on the board. Phoebe in plain clothes and with straight hair starts a French lesson, *Après vous*, Susan similarly dressed enters and the children practise the minuet (heard at the curtain rise of Act I). An Algebra lesson occurs, the music of the melos shows Phoebe thinking of the evenings Waterloo Ball by anticipating its waltz song *Whisper While You Waltz*. This continues through the Latin lesson.

To the tune of *I Leave My Heart* (No. 13) Valentine (now a Captain) comes in. He has lost his left hand. Phoebe and he converse awkwardly. When he has gone, Phoebe and Susan discuss the situation to the background music of (No.14) *Whisper While You Waltz* and *I'm Living A Dream*. She sees herself as too old for romance. Susan remains and the orchestra plays the beadle's night watch song *All's Well To-night.* (No.15). Patty now confesses to Susan that she would loves to have a lover in a song with a jig-like rhythm. (No.16) *The Love of a Lass.*

.Phoebe sings a short reprise of *I'm Living A Dream. (*No.17) and now decides on her plan. She will outwit and partly avenge herself on Valentine by appearing as 'Livvy' her own (fictitious) niece dressed in the old bridal gown of Susan's and with ringlets to make her look younger when she goes to the ball. The music under the dialogue continues her reprise and then turns (No.18) to *Whisper While You Waltz* as she thinks about the ball. Valentine comes in and is courteous to, but not deceived by 'Livvy' and together they sing and dance (No.19), *Whisper While You Waltz*, the chorus joining in to provide a climax and curtain call.

There is an intermission piece based on this latter tune (No. 20) before the curtain goes up to reveal the ball room. Charlotte, loved by Blades and Spicer, both ex-pupil soldiers, Patty and the ladies of the chorus in Wallflowers, bemoan the way men behave to women. The next number puts the lie to this as Patty collars Reilly and asks him (not coyly) *When Will You Marry Me and Carry Home*, a tune to a steady gallop. He replies to her reluctantly at first, but gets caught up with her insistent liveliness.

The situation changes to 'Livvy' and her flirting with Ensign Blades and Lieutenant Spicer in a light hearted skittish trio, *I Can't Resist the Music.* (No.24) discussing how 'Livvy' can't resist dancing with a number of beaux. The other men in the chorus join in.

Valentine enters and 'Livvy' and discusses the meaning of love, obliquely outlining their love for each other. He breaks out with a reprise (No.25) of *I Leave My Heart*, now recast as *'I Found My Love'* but it is not 'Livvy', but the real Phoebe.

Hassall adds another scene at this stage not in the play. The beadle as a kind of night watchman tries to make sure the young bucks all get off home. Harry writes one of his most haunting melodies, *All's Well Tonight* (No. 26) under the dialogue ; it had been already heard briefly in the ballet music. There follows a numbers of reprises (No.27) as the men of the chorus sing the recruitment song of Act I, the whole chorus sing (yet again) *Living a Dream, Whisper While You Waltz* and *I Leave My Heart* finishing the scene in a climax. This is presumably so the audience will become even more familiar with the music - a kind of contemporary plugging!

All's Well Tonight (No. 28) is now vocalised by the beadle and harmonised chorus at the end of which they slowly disperse. The gossipy friends, Fanny, Mary and Henrietta not realising Phoebe's trick has been unmasked tell about Livvy Is Having *One of Her Turns* (No.30) to a slow gallop. This allows the scene to be changed back to the Throssel's front room where a charming ballad is sung *Spring Will Sing a Song*, (No.31) first by Phoebe and then taken up as a duet with chorus by her and Valentine. Strangely the dialogue supervenes in the final section, with I Leave My Heart being played by the orchestra.

Despite the overplaying at time of some of the numbers, this is the most satisfying complete of Harry''s musicals and with *The Lisbon Story* demonstrates his skills in a viable genre of theatre. His melodies, the musical characterisation and context as provided for him are consistently worked out.

The musical first opened at the *Theatre Royal, Birmingham* under Emile Littler on 31 July 1950, followed by 2 nights in Bournemouth, then at Swindon, Folkestone, Southsea Exeter Theatre Royal (4-9 September)[237] and Oxford (twice nightly and a Saturday Matinee) from 25 to 30 September [238]when it opened a London run at the *Phoenix Theatre* on 13 October 1950, running for 283 performances until 16 June 1951.

---

[237] *Exeter and Plymouth Gazette, 8 September 1950*
[238] *Banbury Gazette,* 20 September 1940

Tired of the one way traffic of musical into London from USA, a group of theatre managers composers and writers formed an association to push British musical in other countries, particularly America. Among those concerned were Messrs Emile Litttler, Guy Bolton, Harold Purcell, Harry Parr Davies and Christopher Hassall It was 20 years, i.e well before the war that a British musical, *Bitter Sweet* had been exported to the states. A musical based on Mendelssohn and Jenny Lind was being prepared.

A start was made with *Music at Midnight (His Majesty's Theatre)*. The opening was attended by theatre representatives from Stockholm, Germany, France – their version was nearly ready – and Lee Shubert's man from New York. Harry (and Christopher Hassall) must have been gratified that all were going to see *Dear Miss Phoebe* to test the possibilities there. [239] Unfortunately, it took other later composers to make an impression on the international musical scene. Harry's musicals, songs and revues have remained at best tied to the British stage only.

'Blue For A Boy or What shall we do with the Body?'

Harry's other 1950 musical (a musical romp of 8 pieces in a show more like a loosely connected farcical revue and really consequently much less demanding. musically. Harold Purcell was the lyricist in what was to be the last musical they did together. Its source was a German comedy *Hurrah! Eine Junge!* by Franz Arnold and Ernest Bach. There had been an English version in 1930 originally directed by Austin Melford, who again directed and played a comic role in this new piece. Emile Littler was again the manager.

The piece was written to exploit the cigar-smoking, rotund comedy star Fred Emney, dressed in blue baby rompers. It is set in the Bompard's villa in Deauville. He played gambler Fred Piper the mischievous loud and large stepson (dressed in a blue huge romper suit) of Dudley Leake (Austin Melford). He wants to keep the existence of Fred a secret. Dudley

---

[239] *Evening Telegraph Perth* 13 November 1950. This initiative could well have come from the Songwriters Guild of Great Britain. Their annual concerts started in 1950 and went on until 1964 usually being held in 2nd week of March (see Chronology)

is to celebrate the first anniversary of his remarriage to lovely Mary Leake (Hermene French). Hercule (Guy Fane) and Emily Bompard (Bertha Belmore) are her parents. She and the female chorus open the musical with *A Year Ago Today*. Visiting guest lady novelist Anita Gunn (Eve Lister) joins them to sing the title song *Blue for a Boy*. This is in Harry's quasi-nursery rhyme vein Emily appears (she is eager to see her grandson) and joins Anita and Mary, *You've Got Him where You Want Him* to close act 1.

Fred has chosen to make himself known to his stepfather's new wife. Mary with the girls, wch Fred loves to have round him sings *I Fancy My Chances*. Fred is aided in his pranks by the unlikely named solicitor Dickie Skippett (young comedian, Richard Hearne). Fred and Caprice sing *A Little Bit on Account* and Anita sings *At Last It's Happened*; a song about not believing love can happen and then realising it has. This is followed by Anita singing the very beguiling *Lying Awake and Dreaming* another of Harry's numbers about loving and dreaming. It starts off with the emptiness of a house at night, then the refrain recounts how yearning can affect sleeping or not. This leads to a dance by eight chorus girls and a male principal dancer (Terence Theobald). They all work through various farcical predicaments, where even Fred and Dudley each takes off the lady novelist in drag i.e. Anita. After a reprise of *At Last It's Happened*, there is a finale. There are some peculiarities in the show e.g. no male chorus and a division between the farcical and the romantic mainly through Harry's songs for Eve Lister hardly nd integrated show, but it did well.

Following opening at the *Theatre Royal*, Birmingham, it underwent the further adjustments, before a 16 week preliminary to London tour. It went to Bournemouth, Glasgow and Newcastle for 2 performances, and then on to Blackpool, 2 more performances in Liverpool, on then to Sheffield, Nottingham and 2 more in Manchester until 20 November. Its London opening at *His Majesty's Theatre* on 30 November and ran for 664 performances, closing 28 June 1952 before going off on a further provincial tour. Like other musicals of Harry, it was broadcast on BBC Light Programme at 8.30pm on 25 April 1951.[240]

---

[240] *Radio Times* Issue 1432 25 April 1951

CHAPTER 29

ESTABLISHED
(1951- 1954)

In November 1950, there was a triumphant production by *Neath Operatic Society* of *The Lisbon Story* in the previous November in Neath, This was followed by a warm hearted reception and a celebratory dinner given by the Mayor, his tutor's brother. This must have been an occasion of pride to the family and even some of his schoolteachers like Miss M T Harvey, his French teacher at the Grammar School. Harry replied to tributes from various members of the Council by commenting that a composer must have knowledge of Bach and Handel before he could himself write a tune, and it was Mr Perrott who had given him the courage to go on and try to get somewhere. Afterwards, he expressed his gratitude to Miss Harvey by writing out for her a poem by Goldsmith.

Sadly shortly after this on 23 January 1951, Harry's father died at 9 Lôn Cadog, the family home at Swansea. He was 71. He was interred in what was the family grave at Oystermouth cemetery on 29 January. The request for gentlemen only for the obsequies no doubt included Harry and Billie's husband Geoffrey and cousins from Pontypridd, who would attend Harry's funeral 4 years later. His father had helped Harry with his career by proudly sending regular pieces to the *South Wales Evening Post* over the years about the progress his son was making.

Harry continued to have a number of inter-related physical and mental strains probably further exaggerated by his father's death and the overseeing of scores launched for major musicals in the West End as well as his heavy cigarette smoking and large intake of alcohol.

He wrote two songs which were published to words by Harold Purcell.

He set *Lero-Lillibullero,* a march known for its many different word settings from the days of the Battle of the Boyne (1690).from Marlbrough's campaigns in early 1700's. It now becomes a celebration of the *Festival of Britain i*n 1951 *The Song of the Festival Fires.* The verses talk about Britain in a lightly jingoist frame of mind in a simple and clear musical arrangement.

The other song *Love Calling Me Home* was a waltz for duo Anne Ziegler and Webster Booth, a more muted number than earlier *My Paradise,* Popular singers e.g.tenors Lester Ferguson and John Hanson took it up also.[241] It is a pleasant if slightly dated Rombergian number, suitable for the duo.

Ranch in the Rockies

This was Harry's major compositional work for 1952. It was billed as Chris Langdon's summer show (in association with Henry Hall) held for its premiere at the Empress Hall on 5 June.It was a 2 act Western musical,The whole was all presented in a spectacular fashion on stage and on ice.

Unfortunately, no musical score either vocal or full, nor did BBC TV broadcast survive. The original programme is still extant. It gives an account of the structure of the show in detail, being divided into 7 scenes, 4 in the Rockies, 3 being in Brazil. There is however no extant account of the story line, just lists of players, their characters and individual musical numbers. Harry ic credited as composer, Confusingly some of songs appear to have been written by others (but they may have only provided the lyrics). It would seem that Harry coordinated the whole thing, and as with other musicals, Harry Rabinowitz providing the orchestration.

The set was 290 ft long by 57 deep and had 5 stages 4 built in to the set, the fifth an ice stage. It had 4 tons of specially made glass fibre curtains

---

[241]   *The Stage* 27 September 1952

made for the show, worked from tracks in the roof, driven by motor. Eve Bradfield was the producer (she had already done 3 ice pantomimes). The linking character featured 32 year old comedian/actor Jon Pertwee [242] as a 'hokum' i.e a comedy spoof detective Hemlock Soames (the near spoonerism-name says it all !!) and that he has arrived in the Canadian Rockies.

The whole ensemble comprised of

> a corps de ballet with 12 women/4 men,
> 22 women as a skating corps de ballet
> 4 The Skating Starlets and 4 The Dashing Blades
> 6 Precision Girls (? acrobats)
> 4 women/7men doing horse riding routines
> Captain Younghusband's Rangers and G C Mossman's Horses

the Empress Hall Orchestra and 16 voice Empress Choir conducted by Harry Rabinowitz.

There are 25 numbers in the show with Harry being credited as composer. in programmes and other publicity.[243] However, the Congress Library Washington has three numbers attributed to other composers (see below). it is difficult to know the whole picture until more information is available.

ACTS, SCENES, NUMBERS AND DRAMATIS PERSONAE (in italics): - (possible alternative lyricists and composers to Harry in brackets based on Library record). [244]

Overture

ACT ONE
Scene 1   **The Russell Ranch**

Opening chorus   Empress Choir (8 women./8 men)

---

[242] later famous for BBC radio comedies -e.g. The Navy Lark' and BBC TV's 'Doctor Who'. and Thames TV 'Wurzel Gummidge'.

[243] *The Stage* 15 May 1952

[244] Items and their scenes are a guesstimate

Barbecue Day (Mervyn Saunders -words and? music)	*Judy McBride* (Anna Mac) and Ensemble
Ranch in the Rockies (Frank Williams words and Patricia Nash)	*Tod McBride* (Gordon Needham - baritone) and Ensemble
I'm Not That Kind of Lady (Frank Williams and Barbara Gordon - words)	*Caroline Russell* (Barbara Shotter) and Ensemble
Speciality	Alice Farrar and James Gordon

Scene 2   **The Saloon**

I Can Always Get a Man	*Belle Bailey* (Lucille Gaye) and Ensemble
Speciality	Conover and Suzy
It's Spring (Phil Park)	*Caroline Russell* (Barbara Shotter) and Ensemble

Scene 3   **The Russell Ranch**

Caribou Road (Mervvn Saunders music and Patricia Nash)	*Tod McBride* (Gordon Needham) and Ensemble
Any Friend of Yours (Frank Petch)	*Caroline Russell* (Barbara Shotter) and Ensemble
Indian Ceremony (Leonard Morris)	*The Company*

ACT TWO

Scene 1   **The Club Catalan, Rio**

Cavaquinho	Lotus and Ensemble
Jump Through the Ring (Wood, Manus and Cherdak)	*Tod McBride* (Gordon Needham)

Night over Rio

Tod McBride (Gordon Needham) and *Caroline Russell* (Barbara Shotter)

Mr Music Maker (Sy Cromwell)

Belle Bailey (Lucille Gaye) and *Aristide Beaujolais* (Maurice Baquet)- French comedian

Speciality

Alice Farrar and James Gordon

Our Melody (David Heneker music and Christopher Hassall words) *Tod McBride* (Gordon Needham) and *Caroline Russell* (Barbara Shotter)

Speciality

Kodall

Scene 2

The Saloon

*Saturday Night (*Tommy Connor music and Sy Cromwell)

Judy McBride (Anna Mac) and Ensemble

Precision Stakes (Leonard Morris)

The Skating Starlets, The Dashing Blades and Precision Girls

Scene 3

The Club Catalan, Rio
(later the same day)

Mine All Mine (Mervyn Saunders music and Sy Cromwell words)

Caroline Russell (Barbara Shotter) and *Tod*

McBride (Gordon Needham and Ensemble

Scene 4	**Back to the Ranch**
Skip to Ma Lou	Judy McBride (Anna Mac)
	and Ensemble
The Musicians	Zany (Marion Rivers) and
	Sam Pryce (Jimmy Lee)
Square Dance	The Company

Other characters were:- *Jim Palmer* (Donald Careford), *Pete* (Ronnie Brody); *Skippy McBride* (Douglas Chapman), *Josie* (Josie Gray) and *Susie* (Betty Malin)

A special edition of excerpts made for a BBC TV outside broadcast was shown on 8 June, presented by Alan Shivers for a specially invited audience. [245]

The GloriousYears

Anna Neagle won a popular audience for her *Coronation Year* romantic pageant *The Glorious Years*. It featured rather contrived situations to showcase Neagle's versatility. A young London actress (Anna Neagle), knocked unconscious by a bomb explosion during the blitz, who dreams she's Nell Gwyn and Queen Victoria, the inspiration for her own future. (Anna played Nell Gwyn and Queen Victoria again.) [246] Errol Flynn came from Hollywood to join Anna Neagle as her co-star, with David Farrar to play King Charles in the Nell Gwyn episode, and then Peter Graves as Prince Albert (the male lead in *Dear Miss Phoebe* in 1950). In the cast list, Sean Connery again appeared as an extra - a Guard in this first screen appearance.

It had a pre-season try-out in the later months of 1952; at Manchester Palace during August [247]at the *Empire Theatre Nicholson Street Edinburgh*. This was rather surprising, considering its distinctly English flavour; then

---

[245] *British Universities Film and Video Council -bufvc .ac.uk 1952*
[246] She had already played Queen Victoria in the Wilcox film, *Sixty Glorious Years*
[247] *The Stage* 21 August 1952

at the *Coventry Hippodrome* from 14 October for 3 weeks. [248] It was staged at the *Palace Theatre* London from 28 February 1953. It lasted eight months. It had 4 songs characterful songs by Harry the title song, *Glorious Days*, the hyper patriotic *The Song of England* (sung by Lorraine Tunstall), *Up the Hill to Windsor Castle* and a lively pseudo folksy *Hop, Skip and Jigstep.*

> This number is a pleasant country dance creation in common time. After a jaunty 8-bar jig, the voice enters (in mood like *Boys and Girls Come Out to Play)* with more provocative lyrics in a verse about a lady dancing in the town. This is followed by the usual refrain and a coda - and 8-bar jig repeated as a code. This leads to a repeat of verse, refrain 2 and another 8-bars of jig, leading to the 'envoi' of refrain 3 and final instrumental jig.

Besides BBC televising extracts (reduced down to 45 minutes from 3 hours) on 13 April 1953, [249] the show was later not very successfully transferred to the screen in 1954 with a miscellany of songs chosen by Anna's husband the director, Herbert Wilcox and retitled as **Lilacs in the Spring.** The only song of Harry's which survived from the original stage musical was *Up the Hill to Windsor Castle.*

Sometime during 1953, he spent a week in hospital, no doubt the smoking and alcohol excess affected him again.

Metropolitan Police concert

Harry appeared as unusually as aguest conductor with Harry Mortimer at the Festival Hall on October 30 . 1953. It featured a mixed programme:

Singers Grace Nevern (soprano) and Alexander Franks (bass) and the massed *Police Male Voice Chorus,* accompanied by Ann Lewis;

Roger Barsotti conducting the *Metropolitan Police Band* ;

---

[248] *Leamington Spa Courier,* 10 October 1952

[249] *British Universities Film and Video Council* -bufvc .ac.uk 1953

Dick Emery providing the comedy;
John Howlet at the Hall organ
Choir of London Policewomen [250]

The continued popularity of Harry and his music is reflected in a series called *Nights of Gladness,* featuring music from the last 25 years in an hour long tribute broadcast by BBC Light Programme by the BBC Concert Orchestra starting on December 2 with his music. [251]

At 10.30 pm on 7 September on BBC West Programme, there was a concert of Harry music played by the BBC West of England Light Music Orchestra. Harry may have missed this. He had kept contact with Monty's family and had travelled to Italy for a holiday in September 1954, sending a post card home on 25 September: from Rome. -

Sat. Morning.

It is really wonderful. Hot sunshine and wonderful food. I've had a nice few days with Monty's brother and sister - nice people. The plane was one (unreadable) 2 hours and 45 mins. I am going to Sorrento tomorrow. I am going to the film studios tomorrow. I may get a film. B[oy]

Here Harry sounds quite full of life touring Italy. Besides visiting Monty's brother and sister in Cesena, near Rimini and Ravenna in the north east of Italy, Monty had died in 1950 at Arona railway station and after his funeral at Cesena (possibly the Cathedral there) was buried in St Stephen's Abbey complex in Bologna.[252] Harry went off to view recently refurbished Cinecittà, SE of Rome and then on to Sorrento (perhaps to go to Capri to call on Gracie).

---

[250] *The Stage, 8 October* 1953
[251] *The Stage* 20 November 1952
[252] according to late Bill Hanks, noted in Scott Wilson, 2106, *Resting Places: The Burial Sites of More Than 14,000 Famous Persons,* 3d ed.

CHAPTER 30

HIS FINAL YEAR (1955)

Now and Forever

Harry now contributed the title song for *Associated British Picture Corporation* romantic Technicolor film *Now and Forever*, directed by Mario Zampi to a script by R E Delderfield, based on his play, *The Orchard Walls*. Here are two young lovers society girl Janette Grant ('coming of age' Janette Scott) and motor mechanic Mike Pritchard (Vernon Gray) are lovers, much to the disapproval of her father, J Pritchard (Jack Warner) who stops her seeing Mike. She attempts suicide, decides to elope to Gretna Green in a MG midget. This sparks off a nation-wide hunt. There were many cameo roles in the film for Pamela Brown, Sonia Dresdel, Bryan Forbes, Moultre Kelsall, David Kossoff, Wilfrid Lawson, Michael Pertwee and Ronald Squire.

The film music was provided by Stanley Black, but Harry wrote its title song, *Now and Forever*, which Janette Scott and Vernon Gray sing. It is a slow waltz song to simple lyrics by Christopher Hassall. It has an introduction and refrain only which can be repeated, the sentiments being a pledge of long-lasting love - a neatly put together romantic ballad very much of the period.

The film was released in February 1956, after his death although the title song was copyrighted and published in 1955, making it his last known composition.

Final unrealised musicals

In May 1955 [253]Emile Littler announced that he putting on 3 new musicals.[254] the first was to be *Peg O' My Heart*, with Eric Maschwitz with whom Littler had worked in the past. Harry was to provide the music. It was to be an adaptation of *Peg O' My Heart*, J Hartley Manner's 1912 play, popular on both sides of the Atlantic. As well being adapted as a radio play it had both silent and 'talkie' film versions of it notably for Marion Davies in 1937. Harry started work on it causing Littler to comment on the night after Harry died *I was negotiating with them to work with me on a musical version of 'Peg O' My Heart'. We were going to call it 'Marry Me Margaret' We should have met last week to begin work. I had to call the meeting off. We should have met this week. I consider this man a genius. One of the best composers in the business.*

The play concerned love, class and money. A penniless Irish girl Margaret O'Donnell is informed that she has inherited a £2 million bequest from the father-in-law of Pats deceased wife by a London lawyer, Sir Jerry Markham, Unknown to her a placement of 3 years, costing £5000 has been made for her to stay with Lady Chichester and her family. So, she has to leave her father Pat in Ireland who is reluctant to see her go, but is philosophical about it. She travels to England as part of the condition of inheriting a fortune. She witnesses and experiences much there. Eventually until she finds true love with Sir Jerry Markham, the lawyer who had originally brought the news of the legacy.

Harry had in reality a limited social life[255] and had lived alone at 11 Harriet Walk. While he was not particularly party or media conscious, he had a number of close friends arising from his collaborative work with

---

[253]   *The Stage,*5 May 1955

[254]   the other two pieces were *Romance by Candlelight* with Patricia Burke and *The Captain's Lamp* with Oscar Homolka.

[255]   According to Harry's sister, 'Billie' in www. billhanks.co.uk

his lyricists, for instance as Christopher Hassall notes in his letter to his mother after his death:- *It was a happy relaxation to be in his company and my work with him was never a labour, always a joy.* [256]

During mid September in the weekly called 'Red Letter Days', Harry gave an interview/article about Gracie in which he recalled somewhat neutrally anecdotes about their working relationship.

The Inquest

Mrs Alice McPhee his daily help lived at North End Road, Fulham. She testified that she had bought for him a bottle of brandy the day before. He was feeling sick, but would not let call a doctor. Sadly, he had died alone on during the night of 14/15 October 1955 in his apartment. She found him the next day dead lying on his bed with a bowl beside him. She said in evidence *Nearby there were an empty bottle of gin and an empty brandy and an empty mineral bottle.* The press initially reported that his death was due to natural causes.[257] His body was identified by his sister Marjorie, who had rushed to Knightsbridge once she read about it, not realising that his mother Rosina or sister Glenys didn't know.

The inquest on him however was conducted least two stages. It was opened on 16 October but was adjourned until 31 October with the distinguished Hammersmith Coroner Major H Neville Stafford had sent certain body fluids (in the bowl) for analysis to the police laboratory. The final verdict that Harry Parr-Davies, aged 41, composer and song writer, *died from stomach haemorrhage, caused by acute alcoholic gastritis* was recorded at the resumed inquest at Hammersmith on 31 October. [258] His doctor Dr Patrick Warren summed it up clearly, *He had periodic attacks of acute gastritis brought on by anxiety about business and drinking alcohol, which he was not supposed to do.*

There was a certain irony at this time, if had lived he may well have appeared on 29 October in another *Royal Command Performance* at the Palladium, accompanying Gracie.

---

[256] Included in Hanks, www. billhanks.co.uk
[257] *Western Mail* and *Daily Mirror and Birmingham Daily Post*, 15 October 1955
[258] Obituary in the *Times*, 1/11/1955

Harry of course had not heeded medical advice about not having alcohol. Smoking at this time was not made so much of an issue. The added physical, psychological and emotional stress are all factors associated with peptic ulceration. Possibly he had taken even a small amount of alcohol it could cause his ulcer to perforate leading to internal haemorrhage and a subsequent fatal peritonitis. He would have had intense pain which would have prompted physical collapse prior to his death, a situation not made easier by drinking so much alone. It was a sad conclusion to a life dedicated to make people happier through his music.

The body was taken to Swansea, the funeral being held at *Holy Trinity Church* Sketty with the Rev H Wynne Griffiths, Vicar of Trinity performing the funeral rites according to the *Church of Wales.*

Afterwards, he was interred at *Oystermouth Cemetery* at Mumble Head on the west of Swansea Bay in the family plot beside his father. The funeral was an occasion in which the remaining family participated as well as civic dignitaries. The cortege left from 9 Lon Cadog Cwngwyn, Swansea, his parent's home for the last 20 years. His mother was chief mourner, accompanied by brother-in-law Geoffrey David; Leonard Howells of Port Talbot, William and Frederick Davies were cousins from his father's side of the family from Pontypridd; and F Hughes and H. Harrison possibly family friends were also there Local dignitaries present at the service were [259]:

Councillor C.Martin Davies, *representing the Midland Bank Executor and Trustee Company;*

T.J.H. Griffiths *manager of the Wind Street branch of the bank (for whom Harry's sister Glenys worked);*

From Swansea:-

Councillor Hywel Thomas; J Barlow; T J Harries; J D Davies, *manager of Barclays Bank, Uplands;* A Bruce Davies, *manager of Lloyds Bank, Uplands (Geoffrey David worked there so had 'Billie' before she married;*

---

[259] As Davies is such a common name in the area it is difficult to know who are related to Harry, unless explicitly stated.

From Neath:-

G W Knoyle; Derek Pratt; H S Williams; W G Davies; F J Evett; F H Brooks; Owen Joseph; W J Barrett; Miss Joseph.

Rev H Wynne Griffiths, Vicar of *Trinity Church, Sketty* performed the funeral rites according to the *Church of Wales.* Floral wreaths were sent by Gracie, *With deepest sympathy, Gracie Fields* and from *The Song-Writers Guild of Great Britain*, 'in loving memory', directors and staff of Frances Day and Hunter Ltd and from Fred and Doris Day.

Probate showed that he left £7633/14/10d. £5677 net. Apart from £170 death duty, he left his mother £500 and the rest of his estate was divide equally between his sisters. However, 'Billie' later recalled that for years afterwards royalties still came in. Christopher Hassall sent a letter to his mother.

My Dear Mrs Parr Davies,

Though we have not met, I feel very close to you at this time, through my sympathy for your grievous loss, which I deeply share. As you know Harry was an intimate and beloved friend of mine as well as a collaborator in my work. He was one of only two or three people I have ever loved with whom I was completely at ease. It was a happy relaxation to be in his company, and my work with him was never a labour always a joy. Work will never be such fun again.

Within the last ten days (from c. 4 October), we had two of our happiest evenings together; one evening we went to see a musical play [260] at the Piccadilly Theatre and then

---

[260] This was very likely to have been *Romance in Candlelight*. The London show had a good promising cast ;- Sally Ann Howes, Jacques Pils, Patricia Burke, Roger Dann, under the expert musical direction of Alexander Faris, but it lasted for a mere 53 performances from 15 September 1955. The critics agreed with Harry and Christopher Hassall. It was one of the unrevivable flops of 1955.

went on the Ivy [261] *for supper. We both hated the play, which stimulated us into a lot of talk about how we could have done much better ourselves. Then another night he introduced me to his friend Basil Thomas.*

Gracie the next month sent a letter to Glenys, Harry's older sister:-

My Dear Glenys,

Thank you for your letter. I find it difficult to put into words my feelings, it's impossible to express this deep sorrow.

He was too young to leave us.

Harry's musical knowledge and imagination, and most perfect piano execution, made him one of the most outstanding pianists. When he was going through a spot of nervous tension, I was always happy to see him going home to you all he always came back more calm & happy to go on with his work.

I only wish we could have done more for him, poor boy was so mixed inside.

May the Good Lord give his soul Peace and contentment.

Always sincerely yours
Gracie

Harry's mother Rosina outlived him, and died on 29 March 1964, at 4 Broadway Sketty, Swansea. After Harry's death she must have moved to live with either one of her daughter's. She was buried with her husband and son in the joint family grave.

---

[261] The Ivy opened in 1917 is an exclusive restaurant on West Street, which over the years has catered for theatre goers and players.

Family Grave at Oystermouth cemetery

His younger sister, the one who worked for the Swansea branch of the *Midland Bank*, died in 1974 and her ashes were scattered over the family grave.

Marjorie David (or 'Billie' as she was called) lived on until 2011. She showed her deep affection for her brother Harry by providing much information often in the shape of anecdotes about him to Bill Hanks for his web site history and to George Lawn for his history of *His Majesty's Life Guards*. Like her sister, her ashes were scattered on the family grave at Oystermouth.

Gracie's final tribute

The next year, Gracie made a gracious recorded tribute to Harry during Anna Neagle's programme on 18 September 1956. *Our Harry was with me for twelve years. He first played for me when he was seventeen years old. We all loved Harry very, very much and it is really, really sad that the had such a short career.*[262]

---

[262] Lassandro, Sebastiano, *Pride of Our Alley*, 2019, BearManor Media v 2. .p. 373-4

POSTSCRIPT

How to sum up Harry's achievements? There are two main aspects to his life— the personal and the musical.

In purely human terms, his life was short. Through a large part of early life as child and adult, he had been protected emotionally, first by his family who remained devoted to him and his career in music and by Gracie who saw him much as a talented younger brother./ partial chaperon. Even during the war, he had managed a comparatively sheltered existence, working the West End revue and musical scene. This continued even after his call-up.

The major factors that broke into his lifestyle were the earlier ENSA tour and even more so the August 1944-March 1945 tour ofNW Europe received of Nazi occupation after D-day. His health became poorer on his return to UK and despite rallies to produce musicals and songs ultimately didn't prevent the factors which lead to his sudden death. His life was by and large centred arouud the music he made as part of the light entertainment establishment.

He was well-respected and humorous, a hard and generous almost obsessional worker at his craft, mildly ambitious and easily stressed. He was not an expansively social being but had a few close friends in addition to his family.

His music within the light music genre has a surprisingly wide range from sentimental via the whimsical to the comic with some degree of restraint in its expression. He wrote many of his own lyrics throughout his working life. They are at best charming if limited to conventional images from nature or from feelings of nostalgic love. They have little of Cole Porter's, Irving Berlin's or Lorenz Hart's flair and wit being more akin to the British tradition of Horatio Nichols Vivian Ellis and Ivor Novello.

The lyricists with which he collaborated especially Harold Purcell and Christopher Hassall gave him material well suited to his rather romantic-tending abilities. Any piece of his is always well and carefully crafted. His songs weld words to music easily and to the best advantage for the singer.

There is throughout his output a stylistic movement too from the earlier jazz and music hall styles via a trend for operetta type waltzes, Latin American and Swing through to the more serious ballads often nostalgic of WW2 years until the more expressive mood of the fifties. While not adventurous in choosing remote keys or extravagant harmonies, he moves easily and appropriately from major to minor. He supports the vocal line with varied harmonies, traditional sometimes, at others with mild jazz or chromatic sequences.

Although the resulting music can be at times be routine, especially if not stimulated sufficiently by the text or possibly his being overworked, generally Harry's responses to verses and refrain are deftly appropriate. In a large number of his songs, the melodies are indeed memorable. Indeed some have passed into the nation's canon of favourites, others still await discovery as the investigation of light music of 20th century continues into the 21st century.

CHRONOLOGY

Includes list of tours, premières of revues, musicals, broadcasts, concerts, records, and release dates of films.

1914

24 May
born 11 Grandison Street, Briton Ferry, Glamorgan

1919

c. early September
family moved to Tynewydd; Harry started *Dunraven Primary School*, played *I'm Forever Blowing Bubbles* there on piano

c. 1920-1
moves to Neath - 2 Arthur St. Neath and started Gnoll Primary School

1922

February
sent a song/ cantata to Princess Mary on her wedding to Viscount Lascelles

1923

? September
starts *Neath Intermediate School*; wrote c. 30 songs while there

1925
a pupil of Neath Borough organist Seymour Parrott

1926

A foxtrot composed by Harry played at *Empire Cinema* Neath

sends letter to publisher, Lawrence Wright about publishing his songs

1927

? at end of Easter term	writes scenario, words and music for 3 act
First week of April	operetta *The Curlew* given at school
24 May	starts *Neath Grammar School*
Late Spring early Summer	accompanied by aunt toLondon to take Royal College of Organists examination.

1928

8 April	concert at *Bethany English Presbyterian Church*, Glynneath
14 April	concert of his music held in *Wesley Methodist Church* Neath
	works at getting his music published; music played in London and broadcast

1930

30 November	becomes member of *Royal College of Organists*

1931

3rd week December	goes to London to meet Gracie Fields during her revue *Walk This Way* presents her with song *I Hate You*

1932

February	contract for publishing from Horatio Nicholls

March	sits Matriculation exam but leaves school;
Summer	starts a trial season accompanying Gracie in her summer tours
25 July - 27 August	weeks at Finsbury Park Empire,Grand Theatre Blackpool, Empire, Kingston, Empire Liverpool
15 September	***Looking on the Bright Side*** - released - Harry's first film music for Gracie
26 September	weeks at Hippodrome Manchester, Theatre Royal, Chatham, 2 weeks London Palladium,
13 -October	2.30 pm - a matinee - *Metropolitan Charity Show for St Mary's Hospital*;[264]
24 -October	week at Hippodrome, Southend
November	Hippodrome Theatres, in Portsmouth, Newcastle (? Empire) and Stratford Empire Palace of Varieties and Hippodrome, Brighton
December	Empire, Leeds
Boxing Day.	Empress, Brixton

1933

1 January	weeks at Hackney Empire, Shepherd's Bush Empire, Empire Palace Theatre, Edinburgh, Empire Nottingham, Birmingham
early February	a concert at *Queen's Hospital, Birmingham*
13 February & week	Metropolitan, Edgeware Road
14 February	HMV factory Hayes
20 February	weeks at London Palladium, Rochdale, Plymouth Palace;Victoria Palace London, Wimbledon Theatre, Holborn Empire, Empire Finsbury Park

19 June	weeks at Empire Finsbury Park, Garrick Theatre, Southport, Pavilion Bournemouth, for 2 weeks Palladium London
27 July	*This Week of Grace* released
7 August	weeks at, Opera House Scarborough, Grand Blackpool, Garrick, Southport, His Majesty's Theatre Aberdeen, Empire, Liverpool, Opera House, Belfast, Hippodrome, Brighton
15 October	week at Kings Theatre, Edinburgh, Alhambra Bradford
7 December	*The Variety Artists Ladies Guild Annual Dinner and Ball raised £1500*
18 December	A selection of music from *This Week of Grace* is recorded by *Edison Bell Winner* record company
30 December	Gracie starts work on her next film, *Love Life And Laughter*

1934

5 May	BBC broadcast of his music
May	travels to Capri, wrote music for Gracie's
Summer	film *Sing As We Go* moves into Gracie's *Greentrees;* some weekends at Gracie's parents' house at 29, Telscombe Cliffs Way
23-June	weeks at Empire Finsbury Park Empire, Garrick Theatre, Southport
9 July	*Clifton Hall Garden Party* Holgate Nottingham;
12 July	week at Pavilion Bournemouth, 2 weeks Grand Blackpool, 2 weeks - London Palladium

---

[263] *Kensington Post* 7 October 1932

7 September	release of film, *Sing As We Go*
10 September	week at Bournemouth Pavilion, 2 weeks at London Palladium
9 October	a concert at *British Legion Annual Carnival* in Preston.
10 October	Holborn Empire this whole show very enterprisingly was issued by HMV as a 3-record album the next day - 11 October
16 October	weeks at Empire Palace Edinburgh, Alhambra Bradford
26 November	weeks at Folkestone, Rochdale. London Palladium. Palace Manchester

1935

7 -January	weeks at Metropolitan Theatre London, Hippodrome Birmingham Empire Stratford, Empress, Brixton
25 April	ANZAC concert
27 June	pm trade show preview of the film *Look Up and Laugh* at the Capital Cinema Cardiff.
13 July	reception in Neath for father, mother and Glenys who leave Neath for Swansea
4 August	general release of *Look Up and Laugh* and 3 weeks at London Palladium, Brighton, Palace Manchester.
28 October	*No Limit* - George Formby film released
21 November	sets off for tour of South Africa with Gracie sailed out on Union Castle 'Windsor Castle'; gave concert on board
20 December	disembarked at Cape Town

1936

7 January	visits 'East Geduld' Gold Mine and Cullinan diamond mine
27 January	first night of film, *On Top of theWorld*
7 February and week	concerts in Theatre Royal Durban
21 February	concert in Grand Theatre Pietermaritzburg
13 March	boarded *Stirling Castle* for Home
26 March	sails from Cape Town home to Southampton; concert on board *Stirling Castle*
30 March	arrived home; Harry broadcasts on BBC Northern Programme (441 metres) 10 .00 - 10.20pm BBC Variety Orchestra under ou Ross - Gracie sings with Harry at piano
25 May	Gracie broadcasts to Australia with Harry accompanying her.
1 August	*Keep Your Seats Please* - George Formby film
5 October	release of *Queen of Hearts*
4 December	*Variety Artists Ladies Guild and Orphanage* Dinner and Ball
Winter	Holidays with Gracie and her parents at St Moritz

1937

Late January	time in St Moritz
5 February	Gracie attends opening of the opening of *Black's Regal Cinema*, Gateshead
10 February	*I See Ice* - George Formby film
5 March	sails on 'Queen Mary' from Southampton to New York with Gracie (as Mrs Salinger)
17 March	*BBC Western Programme* (373.1 metres) broadcasts a selection of his music, arranged by Leonard Morris and Garfield Philipps and played *by Garfield Philipps Quartet*

24 March	London release of **The Show Goes On** - Gracie film
15 April	return from Hollywood
22 May	9.45 pm - accompanies Gracie in *Starlight* TV programme, broadcast from Alexandra Palace; BBC Television Orchestra conducted by Hyam Greenbaum.
Mid-July	goes with his mother Rosina to see **The Show Goes On**
19 July	Rosina sees him accompanying Gracie at Palladium
August	To Capri to prepare for next film **We're Going to be Rich** broadcasts with Gracie from *Radio Luxembourg*
11 November	*Variety Artists Ladies Guild and Orphanage*
12 November	*Royal Command Performance at Palladium*
17 November	BBC broadcast
25 November,	*A Glamorous Night - 8th Annual Film Ball* at the *Albert Hall*
Late December	crossed the Atlantic to New York by plane

1938

January,	returned to UK
10 February	**I See Ice** - next George Formby film released
13 February	2 charity concerts (Grand Theatre and Central Hall) with Gracie at Derby (Harry joined in repartee)
3 March	left for USA for New York for a fortnight
18 April	2 evening variety shows at Chiswick.
25 April	*Hippodrome Coventry,*
28 May	accompanies Gracie on stage in show finale at *London Palladium.*

3 July	release of *We're Going to Be Rich*-Gracie film
12 August	release of *Keep Smiling* - Gracie fil
23 August	70th birthday reception for Sir John Jackson, Deputy Lord Lieutenant of Lancashire at Prospect House
5 September	release of *Lassie from Lancashire* at Chorley
6 September	release of Formby film, *Its in the Air*
24 September	Release of *Penny Paradise*
8 November & week	Holborn Empire and
10 November	Recordings for **Regal Zonophone** of Gracie with Harry and orchestra
14 November	flight to Rotterdam to give 2 shows
15 November	Royal Variety Command Performance
18 November	*9th Annual Film Ball* at the *Royal Albert Hall*
19 November	sailed from Southampton on SS. *Normandie* with Gracie
Christmastime	at *Coachella Ranch, Near Palm Springs*

1939

4 February	arrived home
8 February	Newcastle Theatre Royal
12 February,	concert in Mountain Ash Glamorgan
17 February	*Umbrella Man* for **Regal Zonophone** recording with Gracie and her brother Tommy Harry (piano) and orchestra
20 February&week	Empire Nottingham
24 February	New Ollerton
27 February	release of George Formby film *It's in the Air*
7 March	Empire Holborn.
March 23	*Release of film* **Band Waggon.**

18 May	Louis Levy and Harry at *Gaumont Cinema,*Lewisham
Before June	***Shipyard Sally*** completed the last Gracie film for which Harry provided songs
4 June,	played organ for wedding of Margaret Livsey
30 July	Solo record released for **Regal Zonophone;** concert with Gracie at Blackburn before she sailed to Capri
16 October	release of ***Shipyard Sally***
14 November	***Black Velvet*** – Harry's first George Black revue
17 November	Gracie and Harry (piano), recording *Wish Me Luck*, *Old Violin* and *When I Grow Too Old to Dream* (with *Walter Walter*) for **Regal Zonophone**
November	Stockport try-out of Jessie Matthews vehicle, the revue ***Come Out to Play***
9 December	- New Year 3 weeks in France for NAAFI, accompanying Gracie's concerts in Douai and Arras
14 December	***Sailors Three*** – a Tommy Trinder film
22 December	***Haw Haw*** – George Black Crazy Gang revue
25 December evening	Gracie broadcasts from war front with Harry as accompanist and Jack Payne and his orchestra to BBC

1940

5 January	Gracie returned from France
2 February	Harry as soloist in variety concert at *Colston Hall*, Bristol
6 February	*BBC Forces Programme* 12.30 am. Half hour music by Harry, billed as 'accompanist-in-ordinary' to Gracie

7 February	at 12.30 Harry told Lesley Perowne some of his life story and some of his music was played
March	Gracie went off to USA to get married to Monty
23 March	release of film **Bandwagon**
early April	toured France with Gracie as part of ENSA concerts
30 April	returned to UK and gave concert at Frury Lane
1 June and week	Hippodrome Brighton
24 June	sailed on Canadian Pacific *Duchess of Bedford* from Southampton to Montreal to join Gracie and Monty. then on to
July	goes with Gracie to her parent's house in Santa Monica
2-5 August	3 concerts in British Columbia and gala in Vancouver
7 August	first night of revue, **Top of the World** (UK)
9 13 August	concerts in Alberta
16 -17 August	concerts in Saskatchewan
17 August - 14 September	concerts in Manitoba
21 August	touring version of *Black Velvet* starting at *Nottingham Empire Theatre*
4 September	**Top of the World**(UK) George Black revue bombed and therefore closes after 4 days
10 15 September	concerts in Quebec
17-22 September	concerts in Ontario
24 -7 September	concerts in Nova Scotia
30 September	crossed into USA at St Croix, Maine
October /November	went to California
4 December	concert in Salt City / also first night of revue, **Gangway** (UK)
14 December	first night of film, **Sailors Three** (UK)

Christmas time	California

1941

14 January	concert in Los Angeles
7 March	concert in Nebraska
8 March	number of concerts in Dallas Texas
9 March	premiere of *Gangway* - George Black review *(*UK)
12 March	concert in Youngstown Ohio
18 March	concert in Salt Lake |Tabernacle, Utah / First night of revue,
24 March	concert in Oakland Auditorium
26 March	concert Shrine Auditorium
6 July	arrived in UK
10 August	officially enlists and is posted to *His Majesty's Life Guards Band* under Col. Albert Lemoine
17 August	ENSA concert at *Royal Albert Hall*, accompanying Gracie
7 November	9.20 - 10.00 pm *BBC Forces Programme* broadcast is postponed due to Harry's illness rescheduled for 21 November
21 November	BBC Home service 9.20 broadcast *The Story of Gracie Field*s recalled by Harry and Bert Asa
6 December	Gracie in Winnipeg
4 December	revue *Gangway* premiered
14 December	release of Tommy Tinder film *Sailors Three*
17 December	*Happidrome* – stage version at *London Palladium*. During war acquires mews flat at 11 Harriet Walk Knightsbridge

1942

18 February	*Full Swing* Harry's first George Black musical co-written with George Posford starts provincial preview
8 May	first performance of *Big Top* George Black revue
June	song for *Suspected Person* David Farrar/ Patricia Roc film
26 July	*HM Life Guards Band* concert at Bedford
2- 8 August	plays piano with *HM Life Guard Band* under Lt.-Col Lane Fox each afternoon in Montpellier Gardens
c. 7 August	elected to committee of *Performing Rights Society*
30 August -1 September	*HM Life Guards Band* concerts at Leamington Spa
14-21 September	given leave
16 September	Writes insert song for *Belle of New York* at *London Coliseum*
7 November	*Best Bib & Tucker* George Black revue
November	*Happidrome* - MGM film of BBC radio series

1943

18 January	song for *We' ll Meet Again* - Vera Lynn film / song for film *Women Aren't Angels*
6 March	*HM Life Guards Band* ball held in Gloucester Guildhall
26 April	premiere of *The Knight was Bold* at Theatre Royal, Newcastle
31 May	*The Lisbon Story* – provincial preview of musical

| 1 July | ***The Knight is Bold*** - George Black musical complete score |
| 11 November | Grand Armistice Ball held in Gloucester by Dance band section of His Majesty's Life Guards, with Harry as soloist. Becomes exhausted again |

1944

18 January	song for film ***Candle at Midnight***
7 February	***Bell Bottom George*** - *George* Formby film
9 April	solo pianist with the H M Life Guards Band
20 April	***The Rest Is Silence*** - Harold Purcell play opens
22 to 26 May	solo pianist with the HM Life Guards Band
10 June	stays at Sheriff's Private Hotel
10 July	HM Life Guards Band concert in Lewis Town Hall
28 July	***It Happened One Sunday*** - Robert Beatty film
20 August	set out from Gosport for 6-month HM Life Guards Band tour of liberated North West Europe, travelling c. 2500 miles through Normandy, Belgium and Holland
12 September	Brighton try out of ***Jenny Jones*** - George Black musical
6 November	song, for film *2000 Women*

1945

9 March	returns from HM Life Guards Band tour of Northern Europe to UK
14 April	concert at Donnington
May	refused to travel with Gracie to Australia and far east;

4-12 August	solo pianist in HM Life Guards Band Montpellier Gardens, Cheltenham
20 August	travels to Paris for 25 August Victory Parade
31 August	returns from France
11 September	*Fine Feathers* - George Black musical
late November	Victory Thanksgiving Ball in the *Temple Speech Room*, Rugby

1946

21 February	*The Lisbon Story* - film of musical
20 April	Revue *High Time* opened
18 May	Demobbed
20 May	guest star in BBC radio programme,*Welsh Rarebit*
8 August	music for radio play-*Dear Appointment*
August	with Gracie in Cardiff
26 September	*The Shephard Show* revue

1947

3 November	*Royal Command Performance* at the Palladium. member of *Savage Club/* 2 songs published

1948

	2 songs published

1949

19 April	*Her Excellency* Cecily Courtneidge musical, co-written with Manning Sherwin
20 May	Harry a guest star in BBCRadio show,*Welsh Rabbit.*
24 May	Release of *Maytime in Mayfair* Anna Neagle musical film
29 August	premiere of *Space Tartare*

1950

18 February	Purcell and Harry attend last night of *Lisbon Story* by amateurs in premiere Eastbourne.
6 March	*Songwriter's Guild of Great Britain* Annual concert
30 May	**THE HOUSE NEXT DOOR** - BBC Home Service radio feature
31 July	premiere of **Dear Miss Phoebe**
14 August	**Blue For a Boy or What shall we do with the Body?** Provincial pre-view tour Fred Emney musical
6-11 November	attended **Lisbon Story**, produced by *Neath Operatic Society*
10 November	Harry at civic dinner in Neath

1951

23 January	Harry's father dies in Swansea and
29 January	is buried in Oystermouth cemetery
4 March	*Songwriter's Guild of Great Britain* Annual concert
3 May	march for opening of Festival of Britain
5 June	musical, **Ranch in the Rockies**

1952

9 March	*Songwriter's Guild of Great Britain* Annual concert
Summer	**Glorious Days** pre-London run in Manchester 6 weeks; then Glasgow; Bristol; Coventry and
November-December	above's final pre-London run in Edinburgh

1953

28 February	*Glorious Days* - opens in London
9 March	*Songwriter's Guild of Great Britain* Annual concert
October 30	Harry appeared as guest conductor with Harry Mortimer, Festival Hall **1954**
7 March	*Songwriter's Guild of Great Britain* Annual concert
23 September	in Italy on holiday
21 December	*Lilacs in the Spring* - Anna Neagle musical film of *Glorious Days*

1955

20 March	*Songwriter's Guild of Great Britain* concert
c. mid September	Article for *Red Letter Days* on Gracie
	Now and Forever Janet Scott film – 1 title song (released **21/2/1956**)
	preparing 2 other musicals, *Marry Me Margaret, Caroline*, plus a possible Ivor Novello adaptation
14 October	dies alone in 13 Harriet Mews of perforated gastric ulcer
18 October	is buried beside his father in Oystermouth Cemetery Swansea

1964

| 29 March | his mother died in Swansea |
| 1 April | buried beside her son and husband Oystermouth Cemetery Swansea |

1973

| February | his sister Glenys dies and |

1 March	is cremated and ashes scattered over burial place of brother, father and mother in Oystermouth Cemetery Swansea

2011

August	Marjorie (Billie) dies aged 99 years and
26 August	is cremated and ashes scattered over burial place of brother sister father and mother in Oystermouth Cemetery Swansea

ALPHABETICAL LIST OF COMPOSITIONS

Vocal **NB** (JJ = song used agin in Musical Jenny Jones)

o.	Name	Type/source	Year
1	A Certain Individual	Musical - Dear Miss Phoebe	1950
2	After All	Musical - Jenny Jones	1944
3	A Little Bit on Account	Musical - Blue for a Boy	1950
4	All Ashore	Film - It Happened on Sunday	1944
5	All's Well Tonight	Musical - Dear Miss Phoebe	1950
6	All the World Sings A lullaby	Song	1943
7	Alone with You	Revue - Top of the World (JJ)	1940
8	A Man about the House	Musical - Her Excellency	1949
9	A Melody at Dawn	Film - This Week of Grace	1933
10	An Englishman in Love	Revue - Sauce Tartare	1949
11	Angela Mia	Song	1948

12	Anna from Anacapri	Film - Look Up and Laugh	1935
13	Annabella	Musical - Jenny Jones	1944
14	Annette	Song	1948
15	Any Friend of Yours	Musical - Ranch in the Rockies	1952
16	April in the Spring of Love	Musical - Lisbon Story (tour)	1945
17	Arrangement of *A Nightingale Sang in Berkeley `s`quare*	solo piano	1944
18	A Song and a Story	Revue - The Shephard Show	1946
19	A Song in Your Heart	Film - The Show Goes On	1935
20	As 'Round and 'Round We Go	Revue - Haw-Haw	1939
21	At Last It Happened	Musical - Blue for a Boy	1950
22	A Year Ago To-day	Musical - Blue for a Boy	1950
23	Barbecue Day (? see text)	Musical Ranch in the Rockies	1952
24	Baritone Song	Revue - Big Top	1942
25	Bell Bottom George	Film - Bell Bottom George	1944
26	Be Refined (cut)	Musical - Full Swing	1942
27	Best Bib and Tucker	Revue - Best Bib and Tucker	1942
28	Binkie's Lullaby	Film - Keep Your Seats Please	1936
29	Bird Cage Walk	Musical - The Glorious Years	1952
30	*Blue Bird of Happiness*	*Words only*	1935
31	Blue for a Boy	Musical - Blue for a Boy	1950

32	Bring Back the Girl in the Old-fashioned Gown	Song	1935
33	Bring in the Prisoner	Operetta – The Curfew	1927
34	Bubble, Bubble	Revue - Black Velvet	1940
35	Bubbling Over	Revue - The Shephard Show	1946
36	Capri Serenade	Musical - Jenny Jones	1944
37	Caribou Road - (? see text)	Musical - Ranch in the Rockies	1952
38	Carnival in Spain	Song	1935
39	Carnival Song	Musical - Lisbon Story	1943
40	Cavaquinho	Musical - Ranch in the Rockies	1952
41	Come Out to Play	Revue - Come Out to Play	1940
42	Cottage of Dreams Come True	Song	c. 1924-8
43	Counting Sheep	Revue - The Shephard Show	1946
44	Cowslip Wine	Musical - Dear Miss Phoebe	1950
45	Crash, Bang I Want to Go Home	Revue - Black Velvet	1940
46	Croon to Me	Song	1934
47	Dearie	Operetta – The Curfew	1927
48	Dear Appointment	Song	1946
49	Diplomacy	Musical - Her Excellency	1949
50	Dirty Song	Revue - Big Top	1942
51	Disconcerto	Revue - The Shephard Show	1946
52	Don't Say Ha-ha to My Heart	Song	unknown

53	Down the Trail	Revue – High Time!	1946
54	Do You Remember My First Love Song	Film - Queen of Hearts	1936
55	Drifting	Song	c. 1924-8
56	Early in the Morning	Operetta - The Curfew	1927
57	Ending in Smoke	Revue - Fine Feathers	1945
58	'Erbert 'Enery 'Eppelthwaite (I want to be a Crooner)	Song	1935
59	Every Night Seven	Film – Suspected Person	1942
60	Farewell	Operetta – The Curfew	1927
61	Father in Heaven	Operetta – The Curfew	1927
62	Fine Feathers Make Fine Birds	Revue - Fine Feathers	1945
63	Follow My Dancing Feet	Musical - Full Swing	1942
64	Follow on Behind the Drum	Musical - Lisbon Story	1943
65	For the First Time I've Fallen in Love	Musical - Lisbon Story	1943
66	For the First Time in My Life I'm in Love	Film - Lassie from Lancashire	1938
67	Fount of Wisdom	Revue - Top of the World (JJ)	1940
68	Foxtrot	Piano solo	c1924-8
69	Full Swing	Musical - Full Swing	1942
70	Gangway	Revue – Gangway	1940
71	Gentlemen of Leisure	Revue - Best Bib and Tucker	1942
72	Getting Rid of It	Revue - Big Top	1942
73	Giddy Up	Film - Keep Smiling	1938
74	Glen Echo	Song	1948

75	Good Night Little Sweetheart	Film - Lassie from Lancashire	1938
76	Hail to Our Master	Operetta – The Curfew	1927
77	Happy Ending	Film - This Week of Grace	1933
78	Halfway to Heaven	Musical - The Knight is Bold	1943
77	Harbour Lights	Song	c. 1924-8
79	Heaven Will Be Heavenly	Revue – Gangway	1940
80	Here's to the Queen God Bless Her	Song	1940
81	Hey-Ho the Merry-O	Revue - Big Top	1942
82	High Hat Time	Revue - Fine Feathers	1945
83	Ho-dle-ay, Start the Day Right	Revue - Haw- Haw	1939
84	Home	Song	c. 1924-8
85	Hop, Skip and a Jig-Step	Musical - The Glorious Years	1952
86	How Beautiful You Are	Revue - Black Velvet	1940
87	I Can Always Get a Man	Musical - Ranch in the Rockies	1952
88	I Can't Resist The Music	Musical - Dear Miss Phoebe	1950
89	I'd Like to Share My Life with You	Film - Candles at Nine	1944
90	If All the World Were Mine	Film - Sing As We Go	1934
91	I Fancy My Chance	Musical - Blue for a Boy	1950
92	If I Had a Girl Like You	Revue - Bell Bottom George	1944
93	If It's Wits that You Want	Operetta – The Curfew	1927

94	If This is Love	Musical - The Knight is Bold	1943
95	I Go on My Way Whistling	Musical - The Knight is Bold	1943
96	I Hate You (arranged from *The Curfew*)	Film- Look on the Bright Side	1932
97	I Leave My Heart in an English Garden	Musical - Dear Miss Phoebe	1950
98	I'm Not That Kind of Lady	Musical - Ranch in the Rockies	1952
99	I'm Peter the Pup amd I'm Twenty One To-day	Song	c.1927
100	I'm Telling Thee	Musical - The Knight is Bold	1943
101	Indian Ceremony	Musical - Ranch in the Rockies	1952
102	In My Little Snapshot Album	Film - I See Ice	1938
103	In Pernambuco	Film - Shipyard Sally	1939
104	In Summer When Trees Be Green	Musical - The Knight is Bold	1943
105	I Shall Always Remember	Revue - The Shephard Show	1946
106	It All Comes Back to Me Now	Revue - The Shephard Show	1946
107	It Always Rains Before the Rainbow	Song	1941
108	It Happened One Sunday	Film - It Happened One Sunday	1944
109	It's in the Air	Film - It's in the Air	1938
110	It's Spring	Musical - Ranch in the Rockies	1952

111	I Want a Kiss From You	Operetta – The Curfew	1927
112	I Wonder	Musical – Her Excellency	1949
113	Joe the Jolly Mariner	Song	1935
114	Jump Through the Ring	Musical - Ranch in the Rockies	1952
115	Just a Catchy LittleTune	Film - Sing As We Go	1934
116	Kiss the Girls	Musical - The Knight is Bold	1943
117	Le Rêve d'Amour	Violin solo	c 1924-8
118	Learn How to Live a Love Song	Film – Penny Paradise	1938
119	Legends	Piano solo	c 1924-8
120	Lero, Lero, Lillibolero	Song	1950
121	Let's Have an Old-fashioned Christmas	Song	1937
122	Living a Dream	Musical - Dear Miss Phoebe	1950
123	Livvie's Had One of her Turns	Musical - Dear Miss Phoebe	1950
124	London is Saying Good Night	Song	1938
125	London Song	Revue - Big Top	1942
126	Lonely Serenade	Song	1940
127	Look Up and Laugh	Film - Look Up and Laugh	1935
128	Love Alone	Insertion in *Belle of New York*	1942
129	Love Finds a Way	Operetta – The Curfew	1927
130	Love Calling Me Home	Song	1950
132	Love is Everywhere	Film - Look Up and Laugh	1935
133	Love is Love Everywhere	Musical - Full Swing	1942

134	Love Never Grows Old	Song	1940
135	Love Stay in My Heart	Revue - Top of the World (JJ)	1940
136	Lucky Me, Lucky You	Revue - Come Out to Play	1940
137	Lying Awake and Dreaming	Musical - Blue for a Boy	1950
138	Madame Louise	Musical – Lisbon Story	1943
139	Mamma Buy Me That	Musical - Full Swing	1942
140	March of the Redcoats	Musical - Dear Miss Phoebe	1950
141	March On	Operetta – The Curfew	1927
142	Mary Must Have Music	Revue - The Shephard Show	1946
143	Mary Rose	Film - This Week of Grace	1933
144	Maytime in Mayfair	Film - Maytime in Mayfair	1948
145	Mélodie	Organ Solo	x 1924-8
146	Merry Go Round	Musical - Jenny Jones	1944
147	Midnight Music	Musical - Lisbon Story	1943
148	Mine, All Mine (? see Text)	Musical - Ranch in the Rockies	1952
149	Moon, Moon	Operetta – The Curfew	1927
150	Mother, Mother, Mother, Mother	Film - I See Ice (not used)	1938
151	Mother Nature	Musical - The Knight is Bold	1943
152	Mr Music Maker	Musical - Ranch in the Rockies	1952
153	Music Makes Me Mad	Musical - Full Swing	1942
154	My Kind of Loving	Film - Women Aren't Angels	1944

155	My Kind of Music	Revue - Top of the World	194o
156	My Love for You	Film - The Show Goes On	1935
157	My Paradise	Revue – Gangway	1940
158	My Lucky Day	Film -This Week of Grace	1933
159	My Wish	Revue - Top of the World (JJ)	1940/ 4
160	Never Say Goodbye	Musical -Lisbon Story	1943
161	Noughts and Crosses	Film - I See Ice	1938
162	Now and Forever	Film - Now and Forever	1955
163	Night Over Rio	Musical - Ranch in the Rockies	1952
164	Nocturne	Violin solo	c 1924-8
165	Oh! Come All Ye People	Operetta – The Curfew	1927
166	Oh! You Naughty, Naughty Man	Film – We're Going to be Rich	1938
167	One Song Shall Ever Remain	Film -Two Thousand Women	1944
168	On Top of the World	Film - On Top of the World	1936
169	Opening Chorus	Musical - Ranch in the Rockies	1952
170	Orchids in the Evening	Revue - Black Velvet	1940
171	Our Melody (? see Yext)	Musical - Ranch in the Rockies	1952
172	Paris in My Heart	Film - Lisbon Story	1945
173	Paris Song	Revue - Big Top	1942
174	Passports for Two	Revue - The Shephard Show	1946
175	Pedro the Fisherman	Musical - Lisbon Story	1943

176	Peter the Penguin	Song	1948
177	Peter the Pup (See *Sing as We Go)*	Song	c. 1928
178	Praise to the Lord	Operetta – The Curfew	1927
179	Precision Stakes	Musical - Ranch in the Rockies	1952
180	Ranch in the Rockies	Musical - Ranch in the Rockies	1952
181	Saturday Night	Musical - Ranch in the Rockies	1952
182	September	Piano solo	1940
183	Serenade for Sale	Musical - Lisbon Story	1943
184	She's Got That Look in Her Eyes	Song	1948
185	Shopping, Eating and the None O'clock News	Musical - Full Swing	1942
186	Sing a Happy-go-Lucky Song	Film - Three Sailors	1940
187	Sing as We Go (reworking of Peter the Pup c 1928)	Film - Sing as We go	1934
188	Skip to Ma Lou (Arrangement)		1952
189	Smile When You Say Good-bye	Film - The Show Goes On	1935
190	Someday We'll Meet Again	Musical - Lisbon Story	1943
191	Song of April	Musical - The Glorious Years	1952
192	Song of the Sunrise	Musical - Lisbon Story	1943
193	Spring Will Sing a Song for You	Musical - Dear Miss Phoebe	1950
194	Square Dance	Musical - Ranch in the Rockies	1952

216

195	Stick Out Your Chin	Film – Penny Paradise	1938
196	Stop! It's Wonderful	Revue - Haw-Haw	1939
197	Success Cockalorum	Film - The Show Goes On	1935
198	Sunday Morning in England	Musical - Her Excellency	1949
199	Sweet Virginia	Revue - Fine Feathers	1940
200	Swing Your Way to Happiness	Film - Keep Smiling	1938
201	Swim Little Fish	Revue - Bell Bottom George	1944
202	Take the World Exactly As You Find It	Film – Happidrome	1942/3
203	Tell me Gypsy	Operetta – The Curfew	1927
204	Tesgar	Organ solo	1927
205	The Angel (Fairy) on the Christmas Tree	Song	1936
206	The Glorious Years	Musical - The Glorious Years	1952
207	The Lady In Grey	Revue - Big Top	1942
200	The Lady with the Mandolin	Song	1952
208	The Little Swiss Yodelling song	Revue – Gangway	1940
209	The Love of a Lass	Musical - Dear Miss Phoebe	1950
210	The Musician	Musical - Ranch in the Rockies	1952
211	The Night You sand 'O Sole Mio'	Song	1934
212	The Pretty Little Quaker Girl	Song	1938
213	There'll Be	Operetta – The Curfew	1927

214	There's a Trail That's Leading Back Home	Revue – High Time!	1946
215	The Shades of Night	Operetta – The Curfew	
216	The Show Goes On	Film - The Show Goes On	1935
217	The Song of England	Musical - The Glorious Years	1952
218	The Sweetest Girl in the World	Song	1938
219	The Sweetest Song in the World	Film – We're Going to be Rich	1938
220	The Trek Song	Film – We're Going to be Rich	1938
221	They Call Me a Dreamer	Revue - Come Out to Play	1940
222	The Years to Come	Song	1947
223	Things Might Have Been Different	Film - Look Up and Laugh	1935
224	Three Shades of Blue	Revue - Black Velvet	1940
225	Thro' Skies that Were Blue	Song	c. 1924-8
226	Tin Pan Alley's Plugger's Lament	Revue - Big Top	1942
227	Tradition	Musical - The Knight is Bold	1943
228	Tree Top Lullaby	Song	1934
229	Underneath the Moon in Old Shanghai	Song	c. 1924-8
230	Up the Hill to Windsor Castle	Musical - The Glorious Years	1952
231	Valley of Dreams	Film - It Happened One Sunday	1944
232	Very Odd Fish	Musical - Lisbon Story (tour)	1945

233	Wallflowers	Musical - Dear Miss Phoebe	1950
234	Wand'ring	Song	c. 1924-8
235	Well Done, Dean	Musical - The Knight is Bold	1943
236	Welcome the Bride	Musical - Jenny Jones	1944
237	We'll Going Smiling Along	Revue - Top of the World	1940
238	We're All Good Pals Together	Film - The Show Goes On	1935
239	We Shall Always Have To-day	Play – The Rest is Silence	1944
240	What Would You Do?	Revue - Top of the World	1940
241	When Cupid Calls	Film -This Week of Grace	1933
242	When I Hear the Music	Revue - Big Top	1942
243	When I was Young	Operetta – The Curfew	1927
244	When Will You Marry Me and Carry Me Home	Musical - Dear Miss Phoebe	1950
245	Where the Blue Begins	Revue - Top of the World (JJ	1940/44
246	Where the Rainbow Ends	Musical - Top of the World (JJ)	1944
247	Whisper While You Waltz	Musical - Dear Miss Phoebe	1950
248	Whoopsy-Diddly-Dum-De-Dumm	Musical - The Knight is Bold	1943
249	Why Did I Have to Meet You	Film - Queen of Hearts	1936
250	Why Worry	Musical - Jenny Jones (JJ)	1944
251	Wind Round My Heart	Revue - Big Top	1942
252	Wish Me Luck	Film - Shipyard Sally	1939
253	Wondering	Song	c. 1927-8

254	Yet Another Day	Top of the World (JJ)	1944
255	You and the Moonlight	Musical - The Knight is Bold	1943
256	You Annoy Me So	Revue – Gangway	1940
257	You are My Love Song	Film - Happidrome	1943
258	You Can't Have Your Cake	Film – Penny Paradise	1938
259	Your Company's Requested at a Dream	Revue - Haw-Haw	1939
260	You've Got Him Where You Want Him	Musical - Blue for a Boy	1950
261	You've Got to Smile When You Say Good-bye	Film - The Show Goes On	1935
262	You Only Want It 'Cos You Haven't Got It	Musical - Full Swing	1942
263	Your Way is My Way	Film – No Limit	1936

Posible joint composition

Title	Comment	Year
The Grandest Song of All		1940
There'll Always be an England	both music and lyrics for these are usually credited to Ross Parker (possibly joint efforts with Harry)	1940

APPENDIX C

THE DRAFT TEXT OF 'THE CURFEW'

"The Curfew"
(transcribed from Harry's exercise book.)[264]
An operetta in Three Acts
Partly based on the narrative poem entitled "The Curfew shall not toll
(sic) tonight" written and composed by Harry Parr-Davies aged 13 years
=======

Dramatis Personae

Marie Blanche .... a village maiden
Jack Courtnay .... her lover
Lord Gerard de Maur .... a callous lord
Oliver Cromwell ....
Madame Grenfell ---------------------------- the Village Gossip
An old Bellringer ....
A Captain of the Guard ....
Judge Barton .... a Judge
Janet, Elizabeth, and Charles
A witness ....
1st Juryman...

---

[264] Repeats are indicated but not written out again. The denouément is as given but
historical anomalies are noted in footnotes. This MSS would seem to be an early
draft rather than a performing edition.

2nd Juryman ....

~~Father Joseph Vaughn~~ .... a priest

A Gypsy

~~An accomplice of Charles I~~

Squire Courtnay .... father of Jack

Papa Oldham .... an old villager

Nan Oldham .... his daughter

Chorus and Villagers, soldiers, Priests, and Jury

Period

The early part of the Seventeenth Century.

Synopsis

When the story opens, it is "Harvest Time" and the villagers are enjoying themselves. Suddenly upon the scene comes a callous French Lord by the name of Gerald de Maur. He is attracted by the looks of Marie Blanche, a village maiden who is in love with the Squire's son, Jack Courtnay. Jack threatens Gerald de Maur with his life if he makes love to Marie again.

Gerald de Maur consults a gypsy, as to whom he loves, and the answer is, that he loves Marie Blanche, but it is dangerous for him to make love to her. That night he makes love to her and is shot. Jack is accused of murdering him, and is put into prison, until he can be tried.

The next day he is tried for his life, and is found guilty. He is sentenced to death at the ringing of the Curfew the following night.

Marie begs the old bell ringer, who is deaf, not to ring the bell that night; but he refuses.

It is nearing the time for the execution when Marie thinks of a plan. Her plan is climb the belfry and stop the bell as it moves.

She carries out her plan, and seeing Cromwell coming over the hills, she falls at his feet and begs for Jack's life. He grants her request, and he also brings with him, proof of Jack's innocence.

Mysteries cleared, all ends in song and dance.

Scenery

Act I (scene I)	The Village Green (Scene II) Same Night
Act II	The Court Room
Act III	Interior of Prison and Church

Act I	Scene I
No. I	Opening Chorus "Oh! Come all ye people"
Chorus:-	Oh! Come all ye people, and join with us in song
	For, we must depart to, the fields ere long
	And then with a rake, and then with a hoe,
	We'll start with our work again, as of yore"
Papa Oldham:-	I am a poor papa old, you'd tell me by my name
	Tho' I am four score five years, I'm not so much as lame,
	For all my troubles, burst like bubbles
	So should yours too.
	Oh! Dance about forget your troubles, as I always do.
Refrain:-	So Follow this way, follow that way but wherever you go
	Mind to call at wheat fields, with a rake and a hoe.
	Come back this way, come back that way but wherever you go
	Mind to pay a friendly call, in at the "Head of the Boar".
(Chorus in unison):-	Repeat refrain
Papa Oldham:-	I had a loved one, but she's gone some twenty years ago
	In joining her, I shan't be long, to love her all the more.
	And she'll come to meet me, and to greet me
	In the heavens above
	Oh! Then how happy will I be, up there where all is love.
Refrain:-	Repeat refrain
(Chorus in unison):-	Repeat refrain and
Chorus:-	repeat 1ˢᵗ 4 lines
Madame Grenfell:-	Stay for a moment, I've some news to tell, '
	'Tis very important, and will not bode us well.

223

Chorus:-	Put down your rake, and put down your hoe.
	And stay for a moment before we go
	Then on to the wheat fields, with song and then a dance.
	So come with your chatter, while you've a chance.

Dialogue I

Chorus:-	Now perhaps, I'll tell you the news."
(excitedly)	
Chorus:-	"Hurrah hurrah, the news, the news."
(excitedly)	
Mdme G:-	"Do not get excited, and I do wish you wouldn't push so."
Papa Oldham:-	"Aye, silence there, silence."
Mdme G:-	"Well, I will continue. As you know, my master, the Squire went up to London last week, and, he has not returned. He has sent e this letter, explaining why he has not returned. I will read it to you. (reads)

Dear Jane,

    I have been here a good while now, and, I hope to return to-day. When I got in London, I was greatly surprised to find the streets deserted; and driving on I came to a crowd of people, standing outside Westminster Hall. I enquired into the matter, and found out that Our Royal sovereign, King Charles I was on trial for High Treason. [266]

I expect this will interest you greatly, and give you a topic for a few days. I am bringing home with me a new friend, by the name of, Lord Gerald de Maur. I trust you will give him a good welcome.

        Your sincere master, and friend,

            Silas Courtnay.

There, what do you think of that?"

---

[265] This occurred in January 1849 not in the Autumn as indicated by the harvest.

Nan O:-	"Positively disgraceful."
Papa O:-	"Most shocking"
Nan O:-	"Terribly alarming."
Papa O:-	"Exactly so"
Nan O:-	"'Tis almost incredible, isn't it? All I hope is, that it will put an end, to this dreadful Civil War."
Madame G:-	"So do I, but here comes our master and his new friend."
Chorus:-	"Hurrah hurrah hail to our master, and, his friend."(enter Squire Courtnay and Lord Gerald de Maur with followers.)

No. 2   Scena   "Hail to our Master"

Chorus:-	Hail to our Master, hail to his friend; Hail to their escorts, whom, Liberty defend. Welcome are they in, our village small; On this jolly harvest day, come and join us all.
Squire Courtnay:-	Yonder stands a noble peer, He is worthy of your cheer, In your praises never fail, never fail; Hail him as you'd hail a king, Aye and make the welkin ring, To his praises gladly sing, Aye gladly sing.
Chorus:-	repeat above
Gerald de Maur:-	Just across the silv'ry sea, In sunny France; There how happy will I be In sunny France; For all my servants love me well, Their gratitude I earn; And if you too would love me true, Why! French then you must learn.

Refrain:-	Bon jour, monsieur,
	Pardonnez moi, mam'selle,
	Bon jour means good morning,
	You understand quite well;
	Pardonnez moi means pardon me,
	For any slight mistake,
	And in that land of courtesy,
	Mistakes you must not make.
(Chorus in unison):-	Repeat above
French soldiers:-	Allons enfants de la Patrie
	Le jour de gloire est arrivé:
	Contre nous de la tyrannie,
	L'étendard sanglant est levé
	Entendez vous dans les compagnes
	Mugir ces forces soldats.
	Ils viennent jusque dans vos bras
	Égorger vos fils vos compagnes.
	Aux armes citoyens!
	Formez des bataillons
	Marchons, Marchons
	Qu'un sang impur
	A breuvé nos sillons.[267]
Chorus:-	Oh! Come and join us in the fun,
	Our cups of joy have overrun,
	Upon this jolly Harvest Day,
	Oh! Let your troubles fly away;
	Let a lassie chose her lad,
	And merrily we'll say
	'Tis God alone has made us glad
	Upon this Harvest Day.
All:-	Repeat last 4 lines

=============

---

[266] Claude Joseph Roguet de Lisle's anthem dates from 1792!

Dialogue II

Gerald de Maur:-	"I thank you, my friends for the kind reception you have given me."
Squire Courtnay:	"Do not mention your Lordship, I am sure it is a pleasure to the villagers, is it not?"
Chorus:-	"Aye, aye, that it is."
G de Maur:- (aside)	"I am positively charmed by the looks of this beautiful maiden to the right of me ~~can be~~. I wonder who she can be. owever I will ~~con~~ enquire. (aloud) My dear Courtnay, who is this charming maiden here (pointing to Marie)
Squire Courtnay:-	"That is Marie Blanche, the unrivalled belle of the village. Come forward, Marie" (Marie comes forward)
G de M:-	"Hello, little girl. I was so charmed by your looks, that I had to enquire after you."
Marie:-	"Your Lordship flatters me."
G de M:-	"Not at all, I simply give you your due. But, I say, do you believe in love at first sight? (Chorus laugh)
Mdme G:- (aside)	"How very, romantic he is."
Marie:-	"Your Lordship perplexes me, but, I think I can answer that question."
G de M:-	"Well, what is your answer?"
Marie:-	"No, and nothing else. Your Lordship must understand that I have a lover, whom I love better than anything in the world."
G de M:-	"Pshaw, girl. 'Tis but a feeble excuse." (Jack comes foward) "Who is this impertinent knave?."
Squire Courtnay:-	"Your Lordship, he is my son."
Gerald de Maur:-	" Your son? Mon Dieu, he is er- rather of a bloodthirsty nature, is he not?"

227

Squire Courtnay:-	"Not as a rule, your Lordship. But if your lordship wishes it, I will punish him according to your desires"
G. de Maur:-	"No, no it doesn't matter now, but, I hope it will not occur again. Now then, what about retiring, for I am tired after a long journey. Shall we go?"
Squire C:-	"Certainly, your Lordship certainly."
G. de Maur:-	"Let us depart then au revoir."
Chorus:-	"Au river your Lordship, au river"

(Exit Lord Gerald de Maur, Squire Courtnay and followers.)

Papa O:	"Now then on to the wheatfields"
Chorus:-	"Hurrah, hurrah on to the wheatfields" (exit all except Marie and Jack)
Marie:-	" Dearie"
Jack:-	" Dearie"
(both):-	"I love you, and you love me"

No. 3   Duet and Dance (Marie and Jack)   "Dearie"

Jack:-	When a maiden woos a man,
	All she has to do:
	Is to stretch out her left hand,
	And say how I love you.
Marie:-	But that maiden may be shy,
Jack:-	Possibly like me:
Marie:-	What are they then both to do,
Jack:-	Just the same as we.
Refrain:-	
(Jack)	Dearie
(Marie)	Dearie
(Both)	I love you and you love me
(Jack)	Dearie
(Marie)	Dearie

(Both)   How happy we two could be
                  Faithful to one another.
                  We'd live and die;
                  Just dreaming and dreaming, not plotting and schemeing
                  Just you and I.   Dance

Dialogue III

(exit Marie and Jack dancing)(Chorus gradually enter on tip toes peeping
after Marie and Jack)

Mdme G:-   "Did you see them?"

Papa O:-   "What! trust me"

Madame G:-   "Oh! Of course, trust you. You know everything you do.
                 "But to return to the subject. It takes me back to my
                 younger days when I was woo'd, by a Lord of High
                 Degree –very much like the one, who is at present
                 staying here."

Chorus:-   "Tell us of your romance, Madame.

Madame G:-   "Ah! No, I cannot. My heart is too full to relate my past."

(Chorus nudge each other as if in sympathy.)

Papa O:-   "Oh! Do let us be brighter. Remember it is Harvest Day."

Nan O:-   "Yes. Well what about making a start Papa."

Papa O:-   "By all means, but, how shall I begin"

Madame G:-   "By giving us a song."

Papa O:-   "Ah a good idea. Shall I sing to you of when I was young."

No. 4   Song and Dance (Papa Oldham) "When I was Young"

Papa O:-   Listen while I tell you of my younger days,
                 The days when no-one had a hold on me;
                 I know 'tis hard to think,
                 That I've got no missing link,
                 But it's quite as true as true can be.

229

Now I'm old and shaken, but that does not alter,
What I now am going to say to you,
So sit and listen there,
For it isn't very fair,
For me to be so bright and you so blue.
Until I met the one.
And that's my wife that's dead and buried and is gone,
If she were here to-day I'd never sing this song,
When I was young I was so handsome and so gay,
Oh! Yes, when I was young.

Chorus:- (in unison)
When he was young, he was so handsome and so gay,
Oh! Yes when he was young.
He had a different sweetheart nearly ev'ry day,
Until he met the one.
And that's his wife that's dead and buried and is gone,
If she were here to-day he'd never sing this song,
When he was young he was so handsome and so gay,
Oh! Yes, when he was young.

Dialogue IV

Chorus:-   "Bravo Papa, bravo."

Mdme G:-   "Who would have thought, that an old man of your age, could dance and sing as you have done. You really have charmed me, and deserve good praise."

Papa O:-   "Do not mention it Madame. I endeavoured to brighten you up. I hope I have succeeded."

Mdme G:-   You have, and very well too. But, stay, who is this approaching? I do declare it is that French Lord, Gerald de Maur again."

Papa O:-   "But the Squire is not with him."

Mdme G:-   "No, a gypsy has taken his place. Now I wonder what he wants with a gypsy?"

Nan O:-   "Undoubtedly, he wants his fortune told"

Mdme G:-	"Of course. A wonder I did not think of that before. .
	Let us hide, and listen to what goes on between them."
Papa O:-	"No need to hide, for here they are.
Chorus:-	"Hurrah, hurrah, long live his Lordship."

(enter G de M with a Gypsy, behind them come G de M's followers.

24 No.5   Finale (Scene I)   "Tell me Gypsy"

G de M:-	Tell me Gypsy, tell me true;
	Whom I love the best tell me whom.
	Your life will forfeit be,
	If you cannot satisfy me.
Chorus:-	Tell him Gypsy, tell me true;
	Whom he loves the best tell him true.
	Your life your forfeiting,
	If you cannot satisfy him.
Gypsy:-	Tarry, tarry, Where is my fee?
G de M:-	Hurry, hurry, It shall double be
	Tell him Gypsy, tell me true;
	Whom he loves the best tell him true.
	Your life your forfeiting,
	If you cannot satisfy him.
Gypsy:-	"You say you love a maiden,
	You know not whom she is,
	Why should you ask a gypsy?
	(Her (His) knowledge thus to quiz.
	'Tis no use asking anyone,
	Your heart should direct you;
	And if that does not Well,
	What you going to do ?
G de M:-	"Today I met a maiden,
	With whom I fell in love;
	She seem'd just like an angel,
	Straight from the heaven above.

231

Gypsy:-	"Ah! That then is the maiden,
	Whom you love with all your heart;
	And having fallen in love with her
	You'll find it hard to part.
	Make love to this maiden,
	This fair pretty maiden,
	Reward shall be greater than kingdom or part;
	Be cautious in wooing,
	For death is pursuing,
	You as your making your way to her heart. (Twice)
	Chorus:-(in unison) Make love to this maiden etc
	Curtain end of Scene I

Scene II

No 6	Serenade (G de Maur and Marie)	"Moon, moon"

G de M:-	Moon, moon, moon,
	Bright in radiant splendour,
	Look down from your lofty seat,
	And bless her and defend her,
	The nightingale its song is ended,
	Night has cast her deadly pall
	Moon, moon, moon,
	Shine down and bless us all.

Marie (from window of house on right hand side where a candle is burning):-

	Sail, my boat of dreams
	Answer my prayer;
	Down the silv'ry streams,
	To my love.
(G de M and	Sail, my boat of dreams etc
Marie)	Shine you bright moonbeams,
	Shine your brightest gleams
	From above.

Father in heaven,

Answer my prayer;

Sail my boat of dreams.

(As the last bar is played, a shot is heard and G de M falls to the ground. Marie screams and rushes down from her room and bends over G de M.

Dialogue V (enter chorus carrying candles)

Mdme G:-   "What is the meaning of all this commotion at this time of --------? (screams and drops candle on seeing G de M's body) How is this? What has happened.?"

Marie;-   "I- I- I don't know."

Mdme G:-   "Come girl be reasonable, and tell us what has happened.?"

Marie;-   "I- I- I will tell you all I know, that is to say not much."

Papa O:-   "Well."

Marie:-   "It was like this. I was retiring for the night, when, I heard a voice singing beneath my window. I looked out and managed to discern a figure whom I recognised as Gerald de Maur I rushed from the room, in time to see a figure rush off; laughing to himself as he went. A second after that, Gerald de Maur gave his last breath, and died. "

Nan O:-   " How strange --------."

Mdme G:-   "It is not strange at all. Are you all blind?: Cannot you see? What did Jack Courtnay say this morning? What did that Gypsy prophesy? The real murderer is of course Jack Courtnay, and she (pointing to Marie) naturally is trying to shield him"

Nan O:-   "Oh! Madame how can you say so. I am quite sure that is not the case.

Mdme G;-   "Be silent. No one asked you to speak. Go back to your bed. You are only a nuisance and nothing else. Oh! Yes go on you. It would not be you, unless you went exactly opposite to (what) anyone said.

233

Papa O:-	"I would rather think you who does all that business." "But as I was saying it is Jack Courtnay is the murderer. Do you all agree?
Chorus :-	"Aye, aye ,we agree, we agree."
Mdme G:-	"Then all we have to do is to have him arrested and tried, and another thing, it is dangerous to have such a criminal at large. One does not know who is to be his next victim
Marie:-	"Madame how dare you say such things about my lover, who is as innocent as you yourself."

No 7   Prayer (Marie)

(Marie kneels down in the middle of the stage with her hands crossed)

Father in heaven,
Heed to my humble prayer;
Spare him oh! spare him,
He is to me so dear.
Father in heaven,
Heed to my humble prayer;
Keep him oh! keep him,
Keep him from danger there.

(soft voices are heard) repeat above 4 lines
Curtain end of Act I

Act II

Introductory Chorus "   Bring in the prisoner"

Chorus:-   Bring in the prisoner,
Bring in the prisoner,   Bring in the prisoner that's
guilty of crime,
Bring in the prisoner, Bring in the prisoner,
Bring in the prisoner he's wasting our time,
Bring in the prisoner,   Bring in the prisoner,
Bring in the prisoner, the jury and judge

	Bring in the prisoner, Bring in the prisoner,

Bring in the prisoner,   Bring in the prisoner,
Bring in the prisoner, we bear him no grudge

Jury:-   To-day we bring a prisoner,
Accused of murdering,
A rival whom he'd threatened,
A very wicked thing.
We are not very sure of course,
To prison he was sent;
Some of us think he's guilty,
And other innocent.

Marie:-   I swear he is,

Dame G.:-   I swear he's not

Both:-   I don't care what you say.

Marie:-   I swear he is,

Dame G.:-   I swear he's not

Both:-   Oh ! hush all your arguing

Judge B:-   I won't have this in my court,
For all your words they come to naught.
I don't care what you say.
You'll say not another thing.
This question is,
So difficult,

Chorus:-   This question is,
So difficult,
You don't know when your (you're) right or wrong,
This question is,
So difficult,
Oh! Come join us all in song.

All
{Marie:-   I swear he is,
{Judge B.:- I will not have
{Chorus:-   This question is,
{Marie:-   I swear he is,
{Dame G.:- I swear he's not

{Chorus:-	So difficult.
Chorus:-	Bring in the prisoner, Bring in the prisoner,
	Bring in the prisoner, the jury and judge,
	Bring in the prisoner, Bring in the prisoner
	Bring in the prisoner we bear him no grudge. (twice)

Dialogue VI

Janet:-	"I wonder where the prisoner is?"
Eliz:-	"Sh- do not say anything, but they think he has escaped"
Mdme G:-	"Escaped? Did I hear you hear you say escaped?"
Eliz:-	"Yes, you did"
Mdme G:-	"Impossible. I visited the prisoner this morning, and then he was guarded by four soldiers besides the Captain of the Guard."
Eliz:-	"Well; however, the rumour has it about that he has escaped."
Mdme G:-	"Fortunately, it is not true."
Charles:-	"Why fortunately Madame
Mdme G:-	"I have my own reasons, and I do not care to discuss them now."
Janet:-	"We are greatly surprised at you Madame. You have been employed by the Squire this twenty three years now, and you have said that he has been a good master to you, but yet you go against him in this matter, when he is most in need of a friend."
Madame G:-	"Hold you willing tongue child, the Judge is about to speak."
Judge Barton:-	"Silence in court. Bring in the prisoner. (enter Jack in a ruffled condition) Prisoner, what is your name?"
Jack:-	"Jack Courtnay, your worship."
Judge B:-	"Where do you reside?."

Jack:-	"At the Manor House Redlam. " [268].
Judge B:-	"Am I to understand that you are arrested on account of having murdered a man.".
Jack:-	"You are, your worship, tho' the charge be false."
Judge B:-	"Whether the charge be false or no will e left to be seen. Silence in court. Bring in the prisoner.
Jack:-	"Your worship. I crave a boon."
Judge B:-	"Providing it is a small one, it is granted."
Jack:-	"I crave to sing a song my mother taught me when I was young."
Judge B:-	"Your boon is granted."

No. 9   Ballad (Jack)   "The shades of night

Jack:-

The shades of night are falling,
The Curfew bell doth toll;
Its dark and solemn warning,
Its warning aye to all.
Aye thro' the evening pealing,
Those chimes so dear to all
Across the night air stealing
In answer to my call.
The night comes long and dreary,
With many anxious cares;
That make a heart so weary,
But day its wounds repairs.
How soon the night is over,
And dawn doth break again;
And in the sun the clover,
Doth raise its head again.
Repeat 8 lines of above 'The shades of night are falling' etc

---

[267] There is a Redlam as a district of Blackburn; here the name is surely fictional.

Dialogue VII

Judge B:-	"That old song has seen many years, but nevertheless it (is) none the worse for its agedness"
Jack:-	"No, your worship, it is as sweet to me as when I first learnt it."
Judge B:-	"I must not let my mind wander, or else we will never complete our business. Now, then, prisoner, what were you doing on the night of the murder?"
Jack:-	"I was at home, improving my knowledge."
Judge B:-	"What time was it when you were arrested?" .
Jack:-	"Twenty minutes past two o'clock in the morning."
Judge B:-	"Who discovered the crime?" .
Jack:-	"Madame Grenfell, your worship"
Judge B:-	"Let her be brought forward" .
Mdme G:-	"I will not brought forward at all. I will come forward of my own (will)"

(She comes forward and goes in witness stand)

Judge B:-	"Now then witness" .
Mme G:-	"Madame, if you please"
Judge B:-	"Well then, Madame. How did you discover the crime>" .

Madame G (indifferently):-

"Oh! Just a matter of course, that is all Only another. example of my wits. It has been said that I have the eyes of an eagle, meaning of course that nothing escapes them. Let me tell you my man its what you want and its wits I've got. I see that I keep them about me, my man."

No. 10   (Madame Grenfell)   "It is wits that you want"

It is wits you want and its wits I've got;
And I see that I keep them about me,
It is wits you want and its wits I've got;
Not a soul in the village will doubt me.

238

For Christmas time comes once a year,
And when it comes it brings good cheer;
It is wits you want and its wits I've got;
And I see that I keep them about me,
When Christmas is drawing nigh,
And around the fire we sit
I am the spark that sets the light;
With my little bit of wit.

Chorus:- It is wits you want and its wits I've got;
And I see that I keep them about me,
When Christmas is drawing nigh,
And around the fire we sit
 am the spark that sets the light;
With my little bit of wit.

Dialogue VIII

Judge B:- "You said you were the first to discover the crime. Did you?"

Mdme G:- "Yes, I did."

Judge B:- "How was it the that this opportunity for showing your wonderful wits came about?"

Mdme G:- " I will relate the whole story as I know it for the beginning to end (coughs and prepared herself as if for an ordeal) Yesterday, as you know, was Harvest Day, the most important day on the year. Well, however it happened that the Squire went to London last week, where he met a friend, whom he brought home with him. "

Judge B:- And, what pray, has that to do with his assassination?"

Mdme G:- "Have patience man, have patience. I am coming to the point. As I said, this friend was no other than the deceased, Lord Gerald de Maur.

Chorus:- "Bravo, Madame, bravo

Janet:-	"Pshaw, fancy saying bravo to that old duck, who at her best can only quack."
Mdme G:-	"Since you are so clever perhaps you do better?"
Judge B:-	"Silence in court. We must proceed with the trial, for delays are dangerous. Now then, Madame, perhaps you can inform us further upon this matter."
Mdme G:- (sarcastically)	

"Oh! Certainly, certainly anything to oblige. Have patience, man have patience. I am coming to the point. As I said, this friend was no other than the deceased. Lord Gerald de Maur. Naturally on going to the Squire's house, they had to pass through the Village, where we were all assembled. He was attracted by the beauty of Marie Blanche, the Belle of our village, and he asked if she believed in love at first sight. No sooner had he said that than Jack Courtnay and threatened him with his life, of he spoke to her again. That afternoon, however he consulted a Gypsy as to whom he loved and his answer was he loved Marie Blanche, but it was too dangerous for Him to make love to her. That night despite these warnings he made love to her and was shot. Now what more evidence do you want than that?"

Judge B:-	"None, I assure you, but , as there is another witness, we must give her a hearing , especially as she is the cause of the murder. Let her be brought forward. (Madame G comes out of the witness box and Marie takes her place.) Witness, am I to understand that you are the betrothed of the prisoner?
Marie:-	"You are , your worship."
Judge B:-	"Tell us then how the crime was com(m)itted?"
Marie:-	"It was like this. I was retiring for the night, when I heard a voice singing beneath my window. I looked out and managed to discern the figure of Gerald de Maur. Shortly afterwards a shot was heard and he fell wounded

	to the ground. I rushed from my room, in time to see a figure rush of(f); chuckling to himself, as he went. A second later, Gerald de Maur gave his last breath and died. They suspected Jack and arrested them."
Judge B:-	"And what do you say to that Prisoner?"
Jack:-	"Nothing, save that I am not guilty, and I am willing to swear that before a court of Ten Thousand Judges, or more if needs be"
Marie:-	"My beloved, I knew you were innocent. I am willing to bear you out."
Judge B:-	"It is now left to the jury to decide. Let them depart to their Consulting Room and be locked in until they can give us a satisfactory answer.(exit jury)
Marie:-	"Oh! That Gerald de Maur ever came to our village, all that he has brought with him is misery and pain. It is strange, but through all, love will find a way.

No 11   (Marie)   "Love finds a way"

In the springtime of the year
When the flowers begin to bloom
We are not shadowed by the thought,
Of winter and its gloom.
The Summer Sun shines brightly,
High high above the sky;
In the winter cold and drear,
Flowers fade and die.

Refrain:-

Love finds a way
To the brightness of the day.
From the darkness of the night,
To the morning, e'er so bright
Thro' the errors of this world,
Flies a banner unfurled,
For the brightness of the day,
Love will find a Way.

Dialogue IX

Janet:-   "What is the use of brooding over the result of the trial like this, it will only make things seem more terrible than they really are."

Marie:-   "You mean, that he will be found guilty and sentenced to death."

Janet:-   "Oh, no, my dear, you quite misunderstand me. I would not suggest such a thing for worlds. I expect that the result will be quite the contrary to what you think. We should be a bit merrier that is all. Do you all agree with me in this proposition?"

Chorus:-   "Aye, aye, we agree, we agree."

Janet:-   "Then let us proceed in our efforts, but wait a moment is there anyone who disagrees?"

Charles:-   "I do."

Janet:-   "And why pray will you not join in the fun?"

Charles:-   "I have a 'ransom'."

Janet:-   "Well, what is it? It shall be if it is within reason."

Charles:-   "I want a kiss from you."

Janet:-   "Your ransom shall be paid with a right good will."

No 12   Duet (Janet and Charles)   'I Want a Kiss from You'

Charles:-   Pretend you're a maid,
           Yes, a fair pretty maid
           And I'll be a brave toreador.
           I'll fight with a bull
           And I'll give him a pull
           Such that he won't fight any more.

Janet:-	No pretence. I'm a fair lady queen
	With much beauty unseen
	For a veil will I wear o'er my face
	And you'll be a king
	Such a brave hearty king
	And you'll bring me (?indesipherable) lace
Charles:-	I want a kiss from you.
Janet:-	I want a kiss from you.
Both:-	I want a kiss from you.
	Yes, on yes, I do.
Charles:-	And
Janet:-	And
Both:-	I want a kiss from you.
	Yes, I want a kiss from you.

Verse II

Charles:-	Pretend I'm a sailor,
	A very brave sailor,
	And far o'er the sea will I go.
	In a boat named Fortune,
	Yes for me and for you,
	And no-one need know any more.
Janet:-	No pretend. I'm a lady
	A very fine lady
	With jewels and dresses galore
	I'll go to a ball
	With a gentleman tall
	And I'll say as I've said before.
Charles:-	I want a kiss from you etc as before

No 12.   Song (Elizabeth)   'Early in the Morning'

243

Verse I	Sweet is the Song of Sunrise
	Sweet is the Song of Evening
	Sweet is the Song of Autumn
	But Winter for the song the cock doth sing.
Refrain:-	Early in the morning when the cock begins crowing,
	He wakes us from our slumber with his wonderful crowing,
	When we dream of pure gold
	Of knights and pretty damsels
	As in books of old
	We look down in the backyard
	And the day starts him crowing
	And chasing the sleep from our eyes.
Chorus:-	repeat refrain

Verse II

Elizabeth:-	Come, join with me in singing
	This song of paradise
	Where there is no interrupting
	And we may sleep and close our eyes.
	Repeat above refrain
Chorus in unison:-	repeat refrain

No.14   Intermezzo, and Chorus

Dialogue 11

Judge :-   "I think the jury has arrive at a conclusion." (Chorus whisper to each other)(to clerk) "Take the key and unlock the door of the consulting room, and let the jury be admitted." (exit clerk)

Janet:-	"I am all of a quiver, but then I don't see why I should be, for I am positively certain that he is innocent." (enter clerk)
Clerk:-	"Your worship, the jury." (enter jury and resume their seats)
Judge	"Have you reached a conclusion?"
1st Juryman:-	"We have, your worship."
Judge:-	"Let us hear it then."
2nd Juryman:-	"We have pondered over the words of both witnesses, and have at last decided in favour of the first which of course means that the prisoner is guilty." (Marie screams and goes to Jack, but the soldiers hold her back)
Judge:-	"Enough said, I will consult my books for they are true counsellors." (Clerk brings him book and turns the pages over as if in search of a certain paragraph) (Reads) "Murder is only punishable by death. The manner of execution should be after that which the murdered adopted in killing his victim." (to Jack) "Do you see, prisoner, evidence is against you. Let me pronounce the death sentence. I, Christopher Barton, do sentence you, Jack Courtenay, to be shot at the ringing of the Curfew tomorrow night. No souls, on this earth may alter what I have said. May God be with you, and forgive you."

No.15   Finale Act II

Marie:-   'Father in Heaven' as before

(Marie faints, Jack rushes forward to catch her falling. He lays her gently on the ground, and bends over her. She has her head on his knees. They remain like this until the curtain falls.)

Squire Courtenay:-

> Be careful what you say,
> He is my only son
> And if he dies, you shall repay
> The work that you have done.

Judge Barton:- I care not for your arguments,
> The rime lays on his head;
> And no-one in this whole wide world
> Will alter what I've said/

Chorus in
unison:-

> Ring, ring, Ring, ring,
> Ring, ring the Curfew bell
> Ring, ring, Ring, ring,
> Ring, ring the prisoner's knell.
> Whe day is turning into night,
> Leaving behind the day so bright
> Ring, ring, Ring, ring,
> Ring, ring the Curfew bell
> Curtain end of Act II

Act III

No. 16   Introduction and Duet (Marie & Jack) "Farewell"

(in a prison Jack is seen)

Jack;-_   The dreaded hour is drawing nigh
> In which from life I part

Marie:-   Say not. Oh! Well beloved,
> You know 't will break my heart.

Jack:-   For death no fears within me raise
> I know that you'll be with me;

Marie:-   Even to the bitter end,
> Ah! Yes I believe your
> Sweetheart I'll be with thee.

Refrain:-

Jack:-	Farewell,
Marie:-	Farewell,
Both:-	I'll meet you in Heav'n above;
Jack:-	Farewell,
Marie:-	Farewell,
Both:-	Farewell Oh! Farewell beloved
	Hopes I cherished do leave me
	And break my heart;
	Oh! Farewell beloved Oh! Farewell beloved
	We two must part.
Marie:_	Ah! No it cannot be,
	I will not part from thee;
	Whate'er befall (repeat)
	Repeat 1ˢᵗ section – where both sing

Dialogue XI

Marie:- "To think, that you go to your doom in half an hour. If only Cromwell would come before the Curfew rings we might appeal to his sense of Justice. Oh! I cannot bear it. If you die, I die also, for I cannot live without you. I will, once more, appeal, to the Bell Ringer, for here he comes." (enter Bell Ringer) do you know what love is?

Bell R.:- "Eh! What did you say, for I am deaf?"

Marie:- "I said, do you know what love is?"

Bell R.:- "Ay, ay, only too well."

Marie:- (aside) "Here is a chance." (aloud) "Well, then, prove your knowledge by answering this question. Will you prevent the bell from ringing, for the prisoner is my lover, and he dies to-night, if the Curfew rings?"

Bell R.:- "This twenty years I've rung that bell. And I'll ring it now, tho' tis his knell."

Marie;-	"What shall I do, what shall I do." (enter Squire C quietly behind Marie) "Ah! A plan has just struck me. I will enter the belfry, while there is no one about, climb the stairs and reach the Bell. The Bell Ringer who s deaf, will ring the Bell, and I will catch hold of it, thus preventing it from sounding."
Squire C:-	"How will that prevent the execution?"
Marie:- (aside)	"Is it possible that I am discovered, I am almost afraid to lokk around." (looks around) (aloud) "Ah! It is you. What a fright I had. I really thought that all my plans had been discovered. You said how will it prevent the execution? That is simple. You bribe Father Joseph[268] to give you his outfit, and address in it yourself. He wears a cowl, so you will, and no –one will know the difference. In the meanwhile, I will carry out my plan. You will tell the Captain of the Guard, that it is an order of the Judges that the bell does not ring, and they will take Jack, back to his cell. Cromwell will come, and I will appeal to his sense of Justice. It is, at least, an attempt to save Jack's life."
Squire C:-	"I will away, for there is no time to be lost. In the meantime, you remain here, and watch your chance." (exit)
Marie:-	"I knew, that through it all, Love would find a way."
No 17	Song (Marie) "Love finds a way"
	In the springtime of the year, etc and refrain as in Act II for verse I

---

[268] This part of the plotting does not ring true. The title Father is not used by 17th century Church of England clergy (Reverend Mister would be more likely). It is a more recent (!(th century)Catholic custom. Secondly, the use of a cowl relates to Roman Catholic pre-reformation monastic orders. Are Father Joseph, his priests and the church part of a local Catholic monastic enclave? Surely Cromwell would have reacted differently if they were?

Verse II	The King Cups and the Marguerites,
	Beside the flowing stream,
	Lift up their little hands to catch
	Each little bright sunbeam,
	And thro' the cornfields hand in hand,
	Two lovers pass their way;
	In their search for happiness
	And eternal day.
	Repeat refrain
	(exit Marie) (enter Soldiers)

No 18	Soldiers March Song	"March On"

Soldiers:-	March on, march on, March on then to victory
	March on, march on, March on then to freedom
	March on, march on, March on then to victory
	March on, march on, March on then to death
	March on, march on, March on then to victory
	March on, march on, March on then to freedom
	March on, march on, March on then to victory
	March on, march on, March on.
Captain:-	Attention, quick march; Attention, quick march;
	Obey my just commands, my just commands
	Attention, quick march; Attention, quick march;
	Left, right, left right, left, right, left,
	Attention, quick march.
Soldiers:-	March on repeated
	(enter priests)

No 19	Priests' Chorus	"Praise to the Lord"

Priests:-	Praise to the Lord
	The Lord, the God of all;
	All nations down before him fall.
	Praise to the Lord
	Who reigns enthron'd above;
	Praise to the Lord
	The God of Love (repeat)

Marie:- (sings from the tower of the church)

Father in heaven, etc (as in Act II)

Recit (Squire Courtenay) (Aside)

"Oh! Heavens, 'tis she,
We are undone.

(aloud) Who(m) is there?

Captain of the Guard
The tower must be searched.

(Squire Courtenay)

No time must be lost,
The Curfew must ring;
Delay u ntil afterwards,
Your search of the Tower.

No 21   March

Jack is brought to centre of stage, and soldiers fix their guns to shoot.)

No 22   Song (Jack)   "The Shades of Night "
                         Repeat as in Act II

Dialogue XII

Capt:-   "This is strange. The Curfew has not ring."

Squire C.:-	"No need of being alarmed Captain. I thought it would happen like this. It is undoubtedly, an order of the Judges that the execution is postponed."
Capt:-	"Ah! Yes, I believe you(')r(e) right. Well, anyway, the Curfew does not ring, and the prisoner does not die" (to soldiers) "Take him back to his cell, he is safer there."
Squire C.:-	"It is done. It is done. My son will be saved."

March No 23 (during which Jack is taken back to his cell.)

Dialogue XIII

(enter Cromwell) (enter Chorus one by one)

Chorus:-	"Cromwell, Cromwell, hurrah, hurrah
Crom:-	"My friends, how are you all assembled here?"
Capt.: -	"There was to be an execution at the ringing of the Curfew, but, as the Bell did not ring, the Prisoner did not die."
Crom.:-	"Very remarkable indeed. How was it, then that the Bell did not ring?"
Capt:-	"Father Joseph here says that it was an order of the Judges, and by the way, Father Joseph what became of that voice in the tower?"

(enter Marie from Church door, and bleeding)

Marie:-	"Cromwell, Cromwell, thank God you've come."
Crom:-	"Why? What's this?"
Marie:-	"Listen, listen, I have a tale to tell you. I am Marie Blanche, the beloved of the prisoner. Not very long ago, there came to this village a French Lord by the name of Gerald de Maur."
Crom:-	"Gerald de Maur. The very man."

Marie:-   "He brought with him nothing but misery and crime.
He took a liking to me, and serenaded me beneath my
window. He was shot, and Jack Courtenay as accused.
He was tried, and they found him guilty of the crime.
He was sentenced to death at the ringing of the curfew
this evening. I, and his father, conceived a plan between
us. We planned, that he should bribe Father Joseph for
his outfit and come here in his stead, so that he might
make excuses to the Captain for the Bell not ringing.
Then I entered the Belfry, and climbed the stairs, until
I came to Bell. The old Bellringer was deaf, so when
the Bell moved, I hung to the tongue and prevented it
from sounding. Now, I am here before you. I cast myself
upon your mercy. Spare him, and I will do anything for
you, even die or you."

Crom:-   "No, no my girl you should be restored to you lover,
even if he did commit the crime, but I happen to know
that he is innocent. Now, you should listen to my story.
A little while ago King Charles was executed, and on
the scaffold, he confessed that he was the murderer of
Gerald de Maur,[270] so that frees your lover from any
guilt, and to your bravery there shall be a monument,
for never I am sure was there ever braver woman in
English History."

Marie:-   "I do it for love, and nothing else."

Crom:-   "Let the prisoner be restored to his sweetheart." (Jack
is brought from his cell. He rushed to Marie and takes
her in his arms) "Young sir, you have no one to thank,
but this maiden, and your father for your prescence
(sic) here at this moment."(Jack rushes to his father,
and they both embrace) And now-----"

---

[269]   Again there are historical anomalies. The King was actually in custody as noted
in Act I. This part of the plot is not sufficiently thought through. Was some
Cavalier involved in G de M's earlier alleged treason as hinted in dramatis
personae and so did the deed rather than the King?

Mdme G:-	"Stay, I have a confession to make. A long while ago I married a Lord by the name of Gerald Felding. We lived, happily together, rearing one child. Then came a matter of treason. My husband was accused, but, as no evidence was brought up against him he was banished for ever from the country. He sought sanctuary, in the court of Louis, where he soon came into favour, adopting the name of Lord Gerald de Maur." (Chorus move back in horror) "He thought he would like to see me once again and risked his life in coming to England, where I was living, away from my daughter Marie Blanche ------------."
Marie:-	"Me, your daughter? Thank heaven I have found my mother."

(rushes to her and embraces her.)

Mdme G.:-	"As I said, he came to England with the purpose of seeing us. He serenaded Marie, with the purpose of finding out if she was true to her love as he had been, but, alas, he was shot," (to Cromwell) "As you say, by King Charles I.[271] I kept the secret from Marie, thinking perhaps it was best." (to Chorus) "Now perhaps you understand why I opposed the Squire in the trial."
Papa O.:-	"Yes, yes, We all understand, Popsy Wopsy, we all understand."
Eliz:-	"Popsy Wopsy? Why Popsy Wopsy?"
PapaO.:-	" Well, because we are going to get married."
Chorus:	"Married?"
Papa O. & Mdme G.:-	" Yes, married."
Charles:-	"I congratulate you, Papa."
Papa O.:-	"No need, I am sure, I mean, thank you very much."
Eliz.:-	"And I congratulate you, Madame."

---

[270] Not possible as Charles was a prisoner.

253

Mdme G.:-	"Oh! Thanks very much, and we're going to have a little cottage in the woods, aren't we dear?"
Papa O:-	"Oh! Yes, love. Two of them if you like." (aside) "Oh! Dash it (aloud) I mean on; will rose and jasmine and pinks--------."
Mdme G.:-	"And sows."
Papa O.:-	"I didn't say pigs, I said pinks."
Mdme G.:-	"Oh" never mind we'll have everything."
Chorus:-	"No."
Mdme G.:-	"We're going to call it our cottage of love."

No 24   (Mdme G & Papa Oldham)   "There'll be"

Verse I

Papa O:-	The scent of flowers round about you, Fill the air with perfume sweet;
Mdme G:-	The scent of flowers round about you, Nothing can their perfume beat.

Refrain (both)

There'll be a horse and a cow,
And a little bow-wow-wow,
In our cottage of love.
There'll be a pig and a sow,
Underneath the Chestnut Bough,
In our cottage of love.
In our cottage of love.
We'll have pretty rose growing round the door,
Pansies, stocks, ~~chrysto~~ chrysanthemums and pinks galore;
Here I'll be King, and you'll be queen, of the tardy forest green
In our cottage of love.

Chorus:-   repeat refrain

Verse II

Papa O.:-   I love you more than I can tell you
                And that's something true;
Mdme G.;-   I love you more than I can tell you
                And that's something too.
Refrain (both) (repeat refrain and then chorus)

Dialogue XIV

Crom.:-   "And now, all mysteries cleared away, the Curfew,
                shall ring for the marriage of Marie Blanche, and
                Jack Courtenay."

Chorus:-   "Hurrah, hurrah, long live the Curfew."

No 25 Finale

CHRONOLOGICAL LIST OF MUSICAL COMPOSITIONS

Abbreviations

ABPC = Associated British Picture Corportion

ATP = Associated Talking Pictures

Publishers:

CA = Cameo Publishing Co., 23 Denmark St. WC2

CH = Chappell Co. Ltd, 50 New Bond St. W1

EM = Empire Publishing Co Ltd, 319 Oxford St. WC2

FDH = Francis Day and Hunter & Co. Ltd, 138-140 Charing Cross Rd. WC2

ID = Irwin Dash Music CO. Ltd, 10 Denmark St. London WC2

KP = Keith Prowse & Co Ltd, 159 Bond St. W1

LW = Lawrence Wright Music Co. Ltd, Denmark St. WC2

PM = Peter Maurice, 21 Denmark St., WC2

ST = Sterling Music Co. Ltd, 52 Maddox St.

SU = Sun Music Publishing Co. Ltd, 23 Denmark St. WC2

VI = The Victoria Music Publishing Co. Ltd, 51 Maddox St, WC2

Date of release/ first performance	Name of item (lyricists other than or working with Harry)	Type/title/film director	Publisher	Musical Director / Arranger
early 1922	For Princess Royal's Wedding	Song		
c.1924-8	Cottage of Dreams Come True	Song		
c.1924-8	Drifting	Song		
c.1924-8	Harbour Lights	Song		
c.1924-8	Home (Judge Edward)	Song		
c.1924-8	Thro' skies that were blue	Song		
c.1924-8	*Mélodie*	Violin solo		
c.1924-8	*Legends*	Piano solo		
c.1924-8	*Le Rêve d'Amour*	Violin solo		
c.1924-8	*Nocturne*	Violin solo		
c. 1926	Foxtrot	Piano solo		
1927	**The Curfew** Overture **Act I** - Opening Chorus *Oh! Come all ye people* 2 - Scena *Hail to our Master"* 3 - Duet and dance *Dearie* 4 - Song and dance *When I was young* 5 - Finale (Scene I) *Tell me Gypsy* 6 –Baritone serenade, *Moon, Moon* 7 - Soprano solo with chorus, prayer *Father in Heaven*	School Operetta Harry's draft libretto, but no extant of score of 25 vocal pieces, overture and 2 act, 25 number and 12 pieces of dialogue at this stage planned (see Appendix 3)		

	Act II 8 - Chorus *Bring in the prisoner* 9 - Tenor solo *The Shades of Night* 10 -Mezzo solo *Its wits that you want* 11 -Soprano solo *Love finds a way* 12 Duet *I Don' t Want a Kiss from You* 13 Song *early in the Morning* 14 Intermezzo and chorus 15 Finale with reprise of Prayer **Act III** 16 Introduction and duet *Farewell* 17- Solo reprise *Love finds a way* 18 - Soldiers March *March on* 19 - Priests Chorus *Praise to the Lord* 20 - Prayer *Father in Heaven* 21 - Soldiers March 22 -Tenor solo reprise *The shades of night* 23 - Soldiers March 24 Duet *There'll b* 25 Finale			
c.1927	I'm Peter the Pup and I'm Twenty One To-day See also'Sing as We Go'	Song (for Julian Wylie)		
1927	Tesgar for (Tesgar Humphreys)	March (Organ)		
1928	Underneath the Moon in Old Shanghai	Song	EM	
1932 September	I Hate You	ATP Film - **Look on the Bright Side** Director Basil Dean	KP	Carol Gibbons
1933 27 July	A Melody at Dawn Happy Ending Mary Rose My Lucky Day When Cupid Calls (Harry and Gracie Fields)	Radio Picture Film – **This Week of Grace** Director Maurice Elvey	FDH	Thomas Percival Montague Mackey

259

1934 7 September	If All the World Were Mine Just a Catchy Little Tune Sing as We Go	ATP Film - **Sing as We Go** Director Basil Dean	FDH	Ernest Irving
	Croon to Me	Song		
	The Night You Sang 'O sole mio'	Song		
	Tree Top Lullaby	Song	KP	
	Blue Bird of Happiness	Song- Harry words only		
1935 4 August	Anna from Anacapresi Look Up and Laugh Love is Everywhere (Harry with Horatio Nicholls)	ATP Film - **Look Up and Laugh** Director Basil Dean	LW	Ernest Irving
28 October	Your Way is not My Way	ATP Film – **No Limit** Director Monty Banks		Ernest Irving
	Bring Back the Girl in the Old-fashioned Gown	Song		
	Carnival in Spain	Song		
	Erbert 'Enery 'Epplethwaite (Jeff Sullivan)	Song	FDH	
	Joe the Jolly Mariner (John P. Long)	Song	KP	
1936 27 January	On Top of the World	City Film Corporation **On Top of the World** Director Redd Davis	CH	Eric Spear
1 August	Binkie's Lullaby (Arthur Wilson)	ATP Film - **Keep Your Seats Please** Director Monty Banks		Ernest Irving

5 October	Do You Remember My First Love Song Why Did I have to Meet You (Clifford Grey)	ATP Film – **Queen of Hearts** Director Basil Dean	SU	Ernest Irving
	The Angel (Fairy) on the Christmas Tree (Roma Beaumont0	Song	SU	
1937 24 March	A Song in Your Heart My Love for You (both -Eddie Pola) Smile when You Say Good-bye The Show Goes On (Harry) We're All Good Pals Together (Will Haines and Jimmy Harper)	ATP Film - **The Show Goes On** Director Basil Dean	LW CA	Ernest Irving
	Let's Have an Old-fashioned Christmas	Harry		
1938 10 February	In My Little Snapshot Album (Will Haines and Jimmy Harper) Noughts and Crosses (Roma Campbell-Hunter)	ATP Film – **I See Ice** Director Anthony Kimmins	LW	Ernest Irving
3 July (USA)	The Sweetest Song in the World The Trek Song (from traditional South African melodies) Oh! You Naughty nNughty Man	20th Century Fox Film – **We are Going to be Rich** Director Monty Banks	FDH CH	Bretton Byrd
12 August	Giddy Up Swing Your Way to Happiness	20th Century Fox Film – **Keep Smiling** Director Monty Banks	FDH	Bretton Byrd
August	For the First Time in My Life I'm in Love Good Night Little Sweetheart	British National Production Film – **Lassie From Lancashire** Director John Paddy Carstairs	KP	Ronnie Munro

261

6 September	It's in the Air	ATP Film – **It's in the Air** Director Anthony Kimmins	KP	Ernest Irving
24 September	Learn How to Live a Love Song Stick Out Your Chin You Can't Have Your Cake and Eat It	ATP Film – **Penny Paradise** Director Carol Reed	KP	Ernest Irving and Gideon Fagan
	London is Saying Goodnight	Song	LW	
	Mother, Mother, Mother Mother	Song	LW	
	The Sweetest Girl in the World (with Horatio Nicholls and Roma Campbell-Hunter)	Song		
	The Sweetest Sweetheart of All (Joe Messini)	Song	ID	
1939 16 October	In Pernambuco Wish `Me Luck (Phil Park)	20th Century Fox Film –**Shipyard Sally** Director Monty Banks	CH	Louis Levy
14 November	Bubble, Bubble (Ralph Butler) Crash! Bang! I Want to Go Home (Ralph Butler) How Beautiful You are (Phil Park) Orchids in the Evening (Roma Campbell-Hunter) Three Shades of Blue (Harry)	George Black's Revue **Black Velvet** Producer Robert Nesbitt	CH	Debroy Somers
November 1939 Stockport1940 19 March Phoenix London	Come Out to Play Lucky Me, Lucky You Things are Going to be Different	George Black's Revue **Come Out to Play**	CH	Louis Levy

	As 'Round and 'Round We Go Ho-dle-ay Start the Day Right Stop! It's Wonderful Your Company's Requested	George Black's Revue **Haw -Haw**	ST	
	Love Never Grows Old	Song	CH	
	Little Swiss Yodelling Song The	Song	CH	
	Pretty Little Quaker Girl (Roma Campbell-Hunter)	Song	CH	
1940 23 March	Heaven Will be Heavenly (Barbara Gordon and Basil Thomas)	Gainsborough Film - **Band Waggon** Director Marcel Varnel		
7 August (closed after 4 days)	Alone With You Fount of Wisdom Love Stay in My Heart My Kind of Music My Wish We'll Go Smiling Along What Would You Do? Where the Blue Begins Why Worry Yet Another Day (Phil Park)	George Black's Revue **Top of the World**	CH	
	Here's To Her Majesty God Bless Her (Phil Park)	Song	CH	
	Lonely Serenade (Roma Campbell-Hunter)	Song - for Lew Stone	CH	
	My Capri Serenade(also arranged for Brass band)	Song	CH	
	September in Capri – An Italian Picture	Piano Solo		
4 December	So Deep in the Night *(Vocal arrangement of Chopin ballade for Zeigler and Booth)* Gangway My Paradise You Annoy Me So (Barbara Gordon and Basil Thomas)	George Black Revue - **Gangway**		

14 December	Sing a Happy-Go-Lucky Song (Phil Park)	Ealing Studios Film **Sailors Three** Director Walter Forde		Ernest Irving
1941	It Always Rains Before the Rainbow (Harry with Gordon Orbell)	Song	CH	
1942 P 18 February L 16 April	Be Refined (cut) Follow My Dancing Feet Full Swing Love is Love Everywhere Mamma Buy Me That Music Makes Me Mad Shopping, Eating and the Nine O'Clock News You Only Want It 'Cos You Haven't Got It (Barbara Gordon and Basil Thomas)	George Black Musical - **Full Swing**	CH	
8 May	Getting Rid of It (with Geoffrey Wright (musicand Herbert Farjeon lyrics) Hey-Ho the Merry-O The Lady in Grey - Wind 'Round My Heart Tin Pan Alley - Plugger's Lament When I Hear Music (Barbara Gordon and Basil Thomas)	Charles B Cochrane's Revue - **Big Top**	CH	
June	Every Night at Seven (Barbara Gordon and Basil Thomas)	Song in Associated British Picture Corporation, **Suspected Person**	CH	Charles Williams
L 16 September	Love Alone (Adrian Foley)	Insertion song – revival of musical **Belle of New York**	CH	
7 November	Best Bib and Tucker Gentlemen of Leisure (Barbara Gordon and Basil Thomas)	George Black's Revue **Best Bib and Tucker**		Debroy Somers

264

P 23 November L 7 June '43	Take the World Exactly As You Find It You are My Love Song (Phil Park)	Aldwych Film **Happidrome** Director Philip Brandon	CH	Bretton Byrd
1943 18 January	All the World Sings a Lullaby Barbara Gordon and Basil Thomas	Columbia British Film **We'll Meet Again** Director Philip Brandon	CH	Harry Bidgood
18 January	My Kind of Loving (Harold Purcell)	ABPC Film – **Women Aren't Angels** Director Lawrence Huntington		Charles Williams
P 31 May	Overture Carnival Song Follow on Behind the Drum For the First Time I've Fallen in Love Madame Louise Midnight Music Never Say Goodbye Pedro the Fisherman Serenade for Sale Someday we'll Meet Again Song of the Sunrise Ballet Music and Many Melos (Harold Purcell)	George Black's Musical – **The Lisbon Story**	CH	
1 July	If This is Love I Go on My Way Whistling I'm Telling Thee Kiss the Girls Mother Nature Tradition Well Done, Dean Whoopsy-Diddly-Dum-de Dumm You and the Moonlight Basil Thomas	George Black Musical –**The Knight was Bold**		Phil Green
1944 18 January	I'd Like to Share My Love with You (Harold Purcell)	British National Film **Candles at Nine** Director John Harlow	VI	Charles Williams

7 February	Bell Bottom George If I Had A Girl Like You Swim Little Fish (Phil Park)	Columbia British Film – **Bell Bottom** **George** Director Marcel Varnel		Harry Bidgood
20 April	We Shall Have To-day (Harold Purcell)	Play by Harold Purcell – **The** **Rest of Silence**	CH	
10 July	Arrangement for piano solo of *A Nightingale Sang in Berkeley* *Square*	for Lewes concert		
28 July	All Ashore, Valley of Dreams	ABPC Film - **It** **Happened One** **Sunday** Director Karel Lumac	CH	Charles Williams
P 12 September L 2 October	After All Annabella My Wish* Where the Blue Begins* Where the Rainbow Ends Why Worry* Yet Another Day* Overture and Ballet Music *St* *Ceiriol* (Harold Purcell)	George Black's Musical - **Jenny** **Jones**	CH *	
1945 11 September	Ending in Smoke Fine Feathers Make Fine Birds High Hat Time Sweet Virginia (Phil Park)	Robert Nesbitt Revue – **Fine** **Feathers**	CH	George Melachrino
(for provincial tour)	April in the Spring of Love Very Odd Fish (Harold Purcell)	George Black's Musical- **The** **Lisbon Story**	CH	Hans May
1946 2 February	Paris in My Heart (Harold Purcell)	Film - **The** **Lisbon Story** Director Paul L Stein	CH	
20 April	Down the Trail (Dick Hurran)	Val Parnell revue **High Time!**		

8 August	Song Harold Purcell)	BBC Home Programme music for radio play-*Dear Appointment*		
26 September	A Song and Story Bubbling Over Chanson de Paris – ballet Counting Sheep Disconcerto I Shall Always Remember It All Comes Back to Me Now Mary Must Have Music Passports for Two (Harold Purcell)	Firth Shephard's Revue -**The Shephard Show**	ST	
1947 16 January	Glen Echo	Song	CH	
31 December	The Years to Come (Douglas Furber)	Song	CH	
1948 31 March	Angela Mia (Harold Purcell)	Song		
	Annette	Song		
	Peter the Penguin (Harold Purcell)	Song	CH	
1949 P 19 April L 22 June	A Man about the House Diplomacy Sunday Morning in England (Harold Purcell) Incidental music m	Bernard Delfont Musical – **Her Excellency**	CH	
24 May	Maytime in Mayfair (Harold Purcell)	British Lion Film Corporation TV Film – **Maytime in Mayfair** Director Herbert Wilcox		Robert Farnon
30 May	Music (Harold Purcell)	BBC Home service Tom Ronald half hour feature **The House Next Door**		Ray Jenkins
4 September	A Gentleman in Love	Revue **Sauce Tartare Director Audrey Cameron**		

1950 P 31 July L 13 October	Overture A Certain Individual All's well Tonight Cowslip Wine I Can't Resist the Music I Leave My Heart in an English Garden Living A Dream Livvie's Had One of Her Turns March of the Redcoats Spring Will Sing a Song for You The Love of a Lass Wallflowers When Will You Marry Me and Carry Me Home Whisper While You Waltz Ballet Music and Melos (Christopher Hassall)	Musical – **Dear Miss Phoebe** Producer Charles Hickman	SU	Philip Martel
P 14 August L 13 October	A Little Bit on Account At Last It Happened A Year Ago To-day Blue for a Boy I Fancy My Chance Lying Awake and Dreaming You've Got Him Where You Want Him (Harold Purcell)	Emile Littler's Musical –**Blue for a Boy or what Shall we do with the Body**	SU	
1951 5 June	Any Friend of Yours Barbecue Day? Caribou Road? Cavaquinho I Can Always Get a Man I'm Not That Kind of Lady Indian Ceremony It's Spring Jump Through the Ring Mine All Mine? Mr Music Maker Opening chorus Our Melody? Overture and Ballet Music Precision Stakes Ranch in the Rockies Saturday Night Skip to Ma Lou 4 Speciality Numbers Square Dance The Musicians (a variety of authors)	Musical - **Ranch in The Rockies**		

Summer	(Harold Purcell)	**Vanity Fair** proposed		
1951 Summer	Lero Lero Lilibulero (Harold Purcell)	Song of the Festival Fires (Festival of Britain)	SU	
27 September	Love Calling me Home (Barabra Gordon)	Song	SU	
28 November	The Lady with the Mandoline (Jimmy Kennedy)	Song	CH	
1952 P November **1953** L 28 Februar	A Hop, a Skip and a Jigstep Bird Cage Walk Song of April The Glorious years The Song of England Up the Hill to Windsor Castle This last only song used in 1954 Everest Film version of show retitled **Lilacs in Spring** (Harold Purcell)	Tom Arnold Musical – **Glorious Years**	SU	
1955	(Christopher Hassall)	proposed musical - **Marry Me Margaret**		
	(Christopher Hassall)	**proposed** musical – **Caroline**		
	(Christopher Hassall)	proposed musical – untitled ˜˜˜˜˜ based on Ivor Novello play		
1956 21 February	Now and Forever (Christopher Hassall)	Film - **Now and Forever**	PM	

269

APPENDIX E

BIBLIOGRAPHY

Allsobrook, David Ian, 1992, *Music for Wales: Walford Davies and the National Council for Music 1918-1941*, University of Wales Press

Beckerleg, Edward - custodian of legacy of family archive material, owned by Toni Evans,i.e., photographs letters and press cuttings, and anecdotes from Harry's sister, the late 'Billie' David,

Deposited in Neath Library Archives

Breese, Charlotte, 1999, *Hutch*, Bloosbury

Bret, David, 1995, *The Real Gracie Fields*, J R Books Ltd

Bret, David, 1999, George Formby, Robson Books Ltd

Burgess, Muriel (with Tommy Keen), 1980, *Gracie Fields*, W H Allen,

Collen, Jean, 2006, *Sweethearts of Song, Anne Ziegler & Webster Booth*, Lulu

Coward, Noel p. vii in Raymond Mander and Joe Mitchenson, 1971, *Revue – a story in pictures*, Peter Davies

Crompton, Jenny, 2013, *Unbeleivable – the Bizarre World of Co-incidences*, Michael O'Mara

Evening Telegraph, Perth, 13 November 1950

Fields, Gracie, 1960, *Sing as We Go, The Autobiography of Gracie Fields*, Frederick Mulle

Fisher, John, 1975, *The Entertainers - George Formby*, Philip Oates

Ganzl, Kurt, 1986, *The British Musical Theatre* vol 2 Macmillan

www.billhanks.co.uk (no longer operational)

Hulbert, Jack, 1975, *The Little Woman's Always right*, WH Allen

Lassandro, Sebastiano, *Pride of Our Alley*, 2019, BearManor Media vol 1 & 2

Lawn, George R, 1995, *Music in State Clothing the Story of the Kettledrummers, Trumpeters and the Band of the Life Guards*, Lee Cooper

Louvish, Simon, 2009,Chaplin - The Tramp's Odyssey, Faber and Faber

Marshall, Michael, 1978, *Top Hat And Tails*, Elm Tree

Mitchinson, Joe & Mander, Raymond, 1969, *Musical Comedy*, P Davies

Moules, Joan, 1997, *Our Gracie, the Biography of Dame Gracie Fields*, Summersdale

Neagle Anna, 1974, *There will always be to-morrow*, W H Allen

The New Groves Dictionary of Music and Musicians, 2001, 2nd Edition, Oxford University Press

Plimmer, Martin & King, Brian, 2005, *Beyond Co-incidence*, Icon Books

Randall,Alan & Seaton, Ray, 1974 *George Fromby – a biography*, W H Allen

Self, Geoffrey, 1986, *In Town Tonight,- a centenary study of the life and music of Eric Coates*, Thames

Publishing

'Times' 1/11/1955 obituary

INDEX
(Real name in bold and brackets)

Campbell-Hunter, Roma, 1900-51, British lyricist, 26, 61, 75, 79

Carstairs, John Paddy (**John Nelson**), 1910-1970, English film producer, 80

Charlot, André Eugène Maurice, 1882-1956, French actor/impresario, 15

Coates, Eric, 1886 -1957, English composer of light music, 12, 22, 108, 174

Cochran, Charles Blake, 1872-1951, English actor/ impresario,15, 100, 122

Connery, Sean (**Thomas**) 1930 - , Scottish actor, 176

Courtneidge, Cicely, 1892-1980, Australian comedy actress, 120, 160-1, 163, 202

Cutts, Graham, 1885-1958, English director, 34

Daniels, Bebe, 1901-1971, American actress, 95-6, 101, 117

David, Geoffrey, 1901-1994, Harry's brother-in-law, 53, 170, 117

David, Marjorie ('Billie') (née Davies), 1911-2011, Harry's sister, 1, 14, 22, 53, 66, 159, 181, 182, 185, 204

Davies, David John, 1880-1951, Harry's father, 1, 2, 8, 14, 52-3, 66, 170, 184, 203

Davies, Glenys Kathleen , 1911-1974, Harry 's younger sister, 1, 14, 53, 66-7, 181, 182, 183, 185, 204

Davies, Henry Walford, 1869- 1941, British composer, 8, 11, 25, 98

Davies, Rosina (née Parr), 1883-1964, Harry's mother, 1, 2, 13, 33, 181, 184, 195

Dean, Basil, 1888-1978, British film director,14, 34. 47, 51, 61. 65, 81-2, 97

Desmond, Florence. 1905-1993, English actress, 51, 83

Drayton, Alfred, 1881-1949, British character actor, 53,

Driver, Betty, 1920-2011, British singing actress, 82-3

Dunleavy, Brian, 1899-1972, Ulster-born Hollywood actor, 76-7

Emney, Fred, 1900-1980, English comic actor, 122, 169

Elvey, Maurice, 1887- 1967, British film producer,14, 38

Farrar, David, 1908-1995, English actor, 176

Fields, Gracie, (**Grace Stansfield**), 1898-1979, English singer, comedienne and actress, vii, viii, xi, xiii, 1, 3, 13-9, 20, 21, 22, 24, 25, 27-79, 80, 82-4, 86, 87-9, 92, 94, 95, 97-8, 102, 103, 104-113, 114, 115, 116, 117, 118, 144, 151, 156, 159, 182, 184, 185, 187, 190, 191-7

Fields Tommy (**Stansfield**), c. 1908-1988, Gracie's brother, 16, 22, 33, 54, 55, 59,78

Finck, Herman (**van der Vinck**), 1872-1872-1939, British composer, 125

Flanagan, John, 1888-1976,Irish painter, 29, 43. 46, 52, 57

Flynn, Errol, 1909-59, Australian-born Hollywood star, 176

Formby, George junior (**George Hoy**), 1904-1961, English comedian, vii, viii, xi, 25, 55-6, 61, 64, 74,80-1, 82, 83, 97, 102, 119, 137-8, 193, 194, 195, 196

Frankel, Benjamin ,1906-1973, English composer, 94

Franklin, Gretchen, 1911-2005 , English character actress, 122

Furber, Douglas, 1885-1961, British lyricist, 159, 160

Gay, Noel, (**Reginald Armitage**), 1898-1954, English composer, 22, 101, 117, 160

German (**Jones**), Edward , 1862-1936,British composer, 12, 113, 22, 165

Gordon, Barbara, lyricist, 26, 87, 116, 120-1, 122, 130, 174

Graves, Lord Peter, 1911-1994, English aristocrat and actor,161, 164, 176

Gray, Eddie (**Edward Earl**), 1898-1963, British comedian, 78,157

Greenbaum, Hyam , 1901-1942, violinist and conductor, 70

Grey, Clifford, 1887-1941, British lyricist, 61, 62

Gwenn, Edmund, 1877-1959, Welsh film actor, 32

Hale, Sonnie (**John Robert Hale-Monro**), 1902-1959, English theatre and film actor and director, 93, 94

Hassall, Christopher, 1912-1963, English lyricist, 26, 158, 164-8, 169, 179, 181, 187, 188

Hayden, Walford, 1890-1982, British conductor, 79,

Hearne, Richard ,1919-1979, English comic actor, 157, 170

His Majesty's Life Guard's Band, (1941-6), 114,. 115, 116, 118, 121, 123, 124, 127, 138, 141-2, 143-9, 151, 152-3, 154, 2001

Holloway, Stanley, 1890-1982, English comic actor, 47, 57

Hulbert, Jack, 1892-1978, English character actor, viii, 120-1

Hutch, **Hutchinson Leslie)** 1892-1978, Grenada-born singer and pianist, viii, 33, 45, 120

Irving, Ernest, 1878-1953, English music director and arranger, 14, 25, 37, 47, 57, 61, 83, 142, 223, 226

Kirkwood, Pat, 1921-2007, English actress and singer, 87, 92, 100

Leigh, Vivien, 1913-1967, Indian born British actress, 53

Lemoine, Albert, , 1901-74, Lt-Colonel, HM Life Guards Band, 115, 124, 138, 147-8

Levy, Louis, 1893-1957, English film music director, 87, 224

Lieven, Albert, 1906-1971, English actor, 133

Lillie, Beatrice, 1894-1989, character actress, 122

Lipman, Annie Rachel, 1891-1954, singer, actress, conductor, ArchiePitt's mistress, later wife, 18, ,29, 43

Lister, Eve, 1913-1997, English actress, 170

Livesey, Jack, 1901-61, English actor, 78, 132

Loder, John, 1898-1988, English actor, 47, 61

Lynn, Vera Margaret, 1917-present, 88, 97, 117

Lynne, Carol **(Helen Violet Caroline Hayman)**, 1918-2008, actress,92, 139-40

Lyon, Ben ,1901-1979, American actor, 95-6, 101, 117

McGrath, Margaret, **(Maggie Rennie)** 1919-2017, English actress, 160

Mackey, Thomas Percival Montague, 1895-1950, British conductor, composer and music arranger, 38, 40

Maclean J. Charles FRCO, 1874-, ? organist, 8,

McLaglen, Victor ,1886-1959, English Hollywood film star, 76-7

Maltby, HF (**Henry Francis**) 1880-1963, South African actor and screenwriter, 61

Matthews, Jessie , 1907-1981, English actress, 93-4, 162

Melford, Austin, 1884-1971, English screen writer and actor, 169

Millar, Ronald ,(**Thomas Henry Sargent**), **94-5**1919-1998, English actor/writer, 140

Miller,Max, 1894-1963, British comedian, 94-5

Mitchell, Julian, 1888-1954, English actor, 81,

More, Kenneth, 1914-1982, English actor, 37, 53

Morris, Leonard John, 1913-67, Welsh conductor and music arranger, 175

Murdoch, Richard, 1907-90, British comedian, 86-7

Neagle, Anna (**Florence Marjorie Robinson**), 1904-1986, English actress, 104, 161, 176

Nesbitt, Robert, 1906-1995, British producer, 101, 153

Nicholls, Horatio (**Lawrence Wright**), 1888-1964, publisher and lyricist, 3-4, 7, 20-, 22, 51, 55, 63, 67-8, 79, 187, 219, 222, 224

O'Dea, Jimmy, 1899-1965, Irish actor, 83

O'Shea, Tessie 1913-1995, Welsh comedienne, 119, 156

Park, Phil ,1907-1987, British lyricist, 26, 88, 100, 102, 117, 141, 153

Pavlov, Muriel ,1921-2019 English actress, 37, 47

Perrott, Seymour FRCO, 1890-1974, Neath organist, 3, 8, 11-2, 25, 98, 170, 189

Pitt, Archie (**Archibald Selinger**), 1885-1940, Gracie's manager and 1st husband, 14, 15, 18, 29, 89

Pitt, Irene (née Bevin) Archie's daughter, actress, 15, 43

Pola, Eddie 1907-1995, British lyricist and composer, 26,66,92,94

Priestley, JB (**John Boynton**).1894-1984, British social writer 37, 46, 53

Posford, George, 1906-1976, English composer, 120

Purcell, Harold Vousden, 1907-1977, English lyricist and playwright, 26, 131-4, 138, 139-40, 143, 157, 158, 160, 163, 169, 172, 188

Raye, Carol, (**Kathleen Mary Corkney)** 1923-, Australian singing actress, 165,

Rawlings, Peggy (**Margaret),** 1906-1996, Japanese born British actress, 94

Reed, Carol, 1906-1976, English director, 82

Revnell, Ethel, 1896- 1978 singer dancer, 153

Roc, Patricia, (**Felicia Miriam Ursula Herold**) 1915-2003, English actress, 123

Sandler, Albert, 1905-1948, English popular violinist, 7,

Saunders, Mervyn, 1920=2000, british tenor and songwriter, 174-5

Somers, (**William**)Debroy, 1890-1952, Irish born music arranger and conductor,25, 92, 101, 117, 131, 140, 224, 226

Spear, Eric, 1906-1966, British composer, 55, 222

Stamp-Taylor, Enid, 1904-1969, English actress, 61, 125

Stansfield, Edith, 1901-1974, Gracie's sister, Duggie Wakefield's wife, 29

Tate, Harry, 1872-1940, Scottish actor, Maggie Teyte's brother

Tauber, Richard, 1891-1948, Austrian tenor, 155

Thomas, Basil, 1912 - c.1956, British lyricist, 26, 87, 116, 120-1, 122, 130

Todd, Ann , 1919-1993, British actress, 138

Trinder, Tommy, 1909-1989, English comedian, 100, 101, 102, 116, 125, 197, 199

Wakefield, 'Dougie' Douglas, 1899-1951, English acto, married to Edith Stansfield, 16, 20, 29, 33, 39, 54, 55, 83, 85, 153

Widdop, Walter, 1892-1949, British heldentenor, 45

Wilcox, Herbert 1892-1977, British film, 174

Williams, Charles (**Izaac Cozerbreit**), 1893-1978, composer-conductor, 25, 38, 137, 142, 226, 227, 228

Wilding, Michael (**Yarde**),1912-1979, English actor, 101, 161

Wilton, Robb, 1881-1957, English comedian, 42. 53

Wylie , Julian (**Julian Ulrich Mettenberg Samuelson**), 1878-1934, business impresario, 12, 16

Zeigler, Anne (**Irene Eastwood**), 1910- 2002, English soprano, 101, 117, 172

Lightning Source UK Ltd.
Milton Keynes UK
UKHW040656270220
359432UK00001B/54